ANALECTA BIBLICA

INVESTIGATIONES SCIENTIFICAE IN RES BIBLICAS

148

SANG-WON (AARON) SON

CORPORATE ELEMENTS IN PAULINE ANTHROPOLOGY

A study of selected terms, idioms, and concepts
in the light of Paul's usage and background

EDITRICE PONTIFICIO ISTITUTO BIBLICO - ROMA 2001

ISBN 88-7653-148-3

© E.P.I.B. – Roma – 2001

Iura editionis et versionis reservantur

EDITRICE PONTIFICIO ISTITUTO BIBLICO

Piazza della Pilotta, 35 - 00187 Roma, Italia

For
Hee Sook,
Daniel,
and
Joyce Son

PREFACE

One of the professors at my Ph.D. oral exam asked me what I, as a student from an Asian country, thought about modern western biblical scholarship. I instantly replied, "It is extremely analytical and individualistic." Although I am fully aware of the importance of the analytical study and the personal aspect of Christian faith, I think that one can easily miss the larger picture by being too analytical and too individualistic in the interpretation of the Bible. One of the prime examples of such a case may be the modern understanding of Paul's view of man that strongly emphasizes the individual aspect of his anthropology but ignores its corporate aspect. In the present study, therefore, I have investigated a number of elements (terms, idioms, and concepts) in Paul's letters that demonstrate his view of man as a corporate being. It is my desire that this study may be a corrective to some extent to the extreme individualistic understanding of Paul's view of man and consequently the rest of his theology.

My thanks goes first to Dr. E. Earle Ellis, who not only stimulated my interest in this subject but also offered invaluable comments and suggestions as I progressed in the study. I am also grateful to Dr. Bruce Corley whose seminar deepened my appreciation of Pauline theology. I am especially thankful to my parents who had to bear the unbearable pain of not seeing their beloved son so many years during my study. I am, however, most grateful to my wife, Hee Sook, and two children, Daniel and Joyce, for the joy and happiness they constantly add to my life. I also owe thanks to my good friend, Matthew Spann, for proofreading my work.

Sang-Won (Aaron) Son
Dallas Baptist University
2001

CONTENTS

LIST OF ABBREVIATIONS

Journals

AnBib	Analecta Biblica
Ang	Angelos
ATJ	Ashland Theological Journal
BBR	Bulletin for Biblical Research
BJRL	Bulletin of the John Rylands Library
BS	Bibliotheca Sacra
CBQ	Catholic Biblical Quarterly
CV	Communio Viatorium
EvQ	Evangelical Quarterly
Exp	Expositor
ExpTim	Expository Times
HR	History of Religions
Int	Interpretation
JAAR	Journal of the American Academy of Religion
JBL	Journal of Biblical Literature
JBR	Journal of Bible and Religion
JETS	Journal of the Evangelical Theological Society
JSNT	Journal for the Study of the New Testament
JTS	Journal of Theological Studies
NovT	Novum Testamentum
NTS	New Testament Studies
PRS	Perspective in Religious Studies
RB	Revue biblique
RR	Reformed Review
RSR	Recherches de Science Religieuse
RTR	Reformed Theological Review
SJT	Scottish Journal of Theology
TD	Theology Digest
Theo	Theology
TJ	Trinity Journal
TS	Theological Studies

TToday	Theology Today
VT	Vetus Testamentum
ZKG	Zeitschrift für Kirchengeschichte
ZNW	Zeitschrift für die neutestamentliche Wissenschaft

Apocrypha and Pseudepigrapha

Bar	Baruch
Apo. Mos.	Apocalypse of Moses
Jub	Jubilees
Sir	Sirach
Vit. Ad.	Vita Adam
Wis	Wisdom of Solomon

Philo

Cher.	De Cherubim
Conf.	De Confusione Linguarum
Ebr.	De Ebrietate
Immut.	Quod Deus Immutabilis Sit
Leg. All.	Legum Allegoriae
Migr.	De Migratione Abrahami
Opif.	De Opificio Mundi
Post.	De Posteritate Caini
Qu. Gen.	Quaestiones et Solutiones in Genesin
Quis Div.	Quis Rerum Divinarum Heres
Som.	De Somnis
Spec. Leg.	De Specialibus Legibus
Virt.	De Virtutibus
Vit. Con.	De Vita Contemplativa

Josephus

Ant.	Jewish Antiquities
Ap.	Against Apion
War.	The Jewish War

Rabbinic Literature

Abod.	Abodah Zarah
Ber.	Berakoth
Erub.	ʻErubin
Ket.	Kethuboth

Ḳidd.	Ḳiddushin
Meg.	Megillah
San.	Sanhedrin
Yeb.	Yebamoth
Nid.	Niddah
Gen R.	Genesis Rabbah (Midrash)
Pesiḳta R.	Pesiḳta Rabbati

(The prefixed *b* denotes Babylonian Talmud, *y* Jerusalem Talmud, *m* Mishnah, and *t* the tractates of the Tosefta)

Qumran Literature
QS	Temple Scroll
4QFlor.	4QFlorilegium

Classical Greek Literature
De Clem.	Seneca, *De Clementia*
Ep.	Seneca, *Epistulae Morales*
Marc.	Marcus Aurelius
Sym.	Plato, *Symposium*
Dis.	Epictetus, *Moral Discourses*

Others
TDNT	Kittel's *Theological Dictionary of the New Testament*
par	Parallel

INTRODUCTION

Anthropology has played a significant role in the studies of Pauline theology since the days of F. C. Baur. Closely related to the question of the origin of Paul's thought, it has been a fundamental underlying assumption for many scholars. For example, anthropology was one of the essential starting points for the existentialist interpretation of Paul. This is clearly evident in Bultmann's following statement:

> Every assertion about God is simultaneously an assertion about man and vice versa. For this reason and in this sense Paul's theology is, at the same time, anthropology . . . . Thus, every assertion about Christ is also an assertion about man and vice versa; and Paul's Christology is simultaneously soteriology. Therefore, Paul's theology can be best treated as his doctrine of man.[1]

If Bultmann's assessment is accurate, even in part, this means that how one understands Paul's view of man[2] greatly influences one's understanding of the rest of Paul's theology.

The discussion of Pauline anthropology basically deals with two key issues: (1) the nature of man—whether man is composed of three parts (trichotomy), two parts (dichotomy), or one (monism)—and (2) the individual and the corporate dimensions of Pauline anthropology. For many centuries a dualistic view of man, greatly influenced by Greek philosophy, has been widely accepted as Paul's view. During the twentieth century, however, this dualistic anthropology of man has been seriously challenged by a monistic

---

[1]Rudolf Bultmann, *Theology of the New Testament*, trans. Kendrick Grobel, vol. 1 (New York: Charles Scribner's Sons, 1951), 191.

[2]The generic use of the term "man," as it is employed in standard English, is important for a study of Pauline anthropology because no other term embraces both the individual and corporate dimensions of human personality.

view.[3]   Although the scholarly opinions are still widely divided between dualism and monism, the critical issues on both sides have been sufficiently exposed. Unfortunately, that is not the case for the issue of the individual and the corporate dimensions of Pauline anthropology. From the time of the Reformation until the beginning of the twentieth century when H. Wheeler Robinson called scholarly attention to the corporate aspect of biblical anthropology,[4] most scholars were concerned only with the individual person. Consequently, they did not pay due attention to the corporate aspect of Pauline anthropology or they understood it sacramentally.[5] This is still true for many modern western minds that are greatly influenced by extreme individualism.[6] While emphasizing the individual aspect, they often ignore or reject the corporate dimension in Pauline anthropology as non-essential or

---

[3]For the support of the view of the individual as a (complex) monism, see H. Wheeler Robinson, *The Christian Doctrine of Man*, 3rd ed. (Edinburgh: T. & T. Clark, 1947); Bultmann, *Theology*, 1:190-227; J. A. T. Robinson, *The Body: A Study in Pauline Theology* (Chicago: Henry Regnery, 1952), 11-33; W. David Stacey, *The Pauline View of Man: In Relation to Its Judaic and Hellenistic Background* (London: MacMillan, 1956), 121-241; M. E. Dahl, *The Resurrection of the Body: A Study of I Corinthians 15*, Studies in Biblical Theology, vol. 36 (London: SCM, 1962); D. R. G. Owen, *Body and Soul: A Study on the Christian View of Man* (Philadelphia: Westminster, 1956), 163-221; and E. Earle Ellis, "Sōma in First Corinthians," *Int* 44 (April 1990): 132-44=*Christ and the Future in New Testament History* (Leiden: E. J. Brill, 2000), 165-78. However, see Robert H. Gundry, *Sōma in Biblical Theology with Emphasis on Pauline Anthropology* (Cambridge: Cambridge University Press, 1976), who argues vigorously against Bultmann's monistic view, and John W. Cooper, *Body, Soul, and Life Everlasting: Biblical Anthropology and the Monism-Dualism Debate* (Grand Rapids: Eerdmans, 1989), who argues for a holistic-dualism from a more philosophical perspective.

[4]See H. Wheeler Robinson, *Corporate Personality in Ancient Israel*, rev. ed. (Edinburgh: T. & T. Clark, 1981), that contains the following two articles: "The Hebrew Conception of Corporate Personality" first published in 1935 and "The Group and the Individual in Israel" first published in 1936.

[5]For example, see R. Kabisch, *Die Eschatologie des Paulus* (Göttingen: Vandenhoeck & Ruprecht, 1893); Albert Schweitzer, *The Mysticism of Paul the Apostle*, trans. William Montgomery (London: A. & C. Black, 1931); and A. Wikenhauser, *Pauline Mysticism: Christ in the Mystical Teaching of St. Paul*, trans. Joseph Cunningham (New York: Herder and Herder, 1960).

[6]Eduard Schweizer, *The Church as the Body of Christ* (Richmond, VA: John Knox, 1964), 21, cites an interesting comment Martin Buber made on the difference between the Hebrew mindset and the Western mindset: "The Hebrew is used to seeing first the nation, the people, mankind, and only afterward the individual member of that nation, people, or mankind. . . . The Hebrew first sees the woods and only then single trees; whereas we in the Western world would see first the single tree, and only after a process of reflection do we call a thousand trees a wood. We Western people really miss the woods for the trees."

metaphorical. Since the initial works of H. Wheeler Robinson, a number of scholars have followed his steps and pointed out the texts in Paul's letters that suggest a Pauline understanding of man as a corporate being.[7] Unfortunately, many of their works are now out-dated or offer only a partial treatment of the evidence. This study, therefore, intends to investigate anew corporate elements in Pauline anthropology in the light of Paul's usage and background. The elements under investigation include (1) Paul's use of the ἐν Χριστῷ formula and related terms, (2) his comparison and contrast of Adam and Christ, (3) his concept of the church as the body of Christ, (4) his concept of the church as the temple, the house, and the building of God, and (5) his understanding of the nature of the "one flesh" union.

The investigation seeks to determine whether and in what respect Paul understood man as a corporate being. If it successfully demonstrates that Paul understands man not only as an individual but also as a corporate being, it will advance considerably the understanding of Paul's theology. As Bultmann's existentialist interpretation of Pauline individual anthropology affected the rest of Paul's theology, so also Pauline corporate anthropology, if successfully demonstrated, will affect other areas of Paul's thought, particularly his christology, ecclesiology, and eschatology. In addition, it will eventually contribute to a certain extent to the continuing discussion about the origin of Paul's thought and its relation to the teachings of Jesus.

A few remarks need to be made concerning the method of inquiry. First, in Paul's letters anthropology is closely interwoven with his other teachings. Consequently, it cannot be isolated and studied independently from the rest of his thought. In this study, therefore, it is treated in close relationship with other areas of his theology. Moreover, since anthropology is an underlying assumption rather than a specific Pauline theme, this study begins with more prominent themes in which Paul's assumption of corporate

---

[7]For example, see J. A. T. Robinson, *Body*; Ernest Best, *One Body in Christ: A Study in the Relationship of the Church to Christ in the Epistles of the Apostle Paul* (London: S. P. C. K., 1955); Russell Philip Shedd, *Man in Community: A Study of St. Paul's Application of Old Testament and Early Jewish Conceptions of Human Solidarity* (Grand Rapids: Eerdmans, 1964); Jean de Fraine, *Adam and the Family of Man*, trans. D. C. Raible (Staten Island, NY: Alba House, 1965); E. Earle Ellis, *Paul's Use of the Old Testament* (Edinburgh: T. & T. Clark, 1957; reprint, Grand Rapids: Baker, 1991), 60, 72-73, 95, 136-39; idem, *Pauline Theology: Ministry and Society* (Grand Rapids: Eerdmans, 1989; reprint, Lanham, MD: University Press of America, 1997), 8-17; and idem, *The Old Testament in Early Christianity: Canon and Interpretation in the Light of Modern Research*, 2nd ed. (Grand Rapids: Baker, 1992), 110-16.

anthropology is evident, that is, in his teaching about Christ and about the church. If the study demonstrates that Paul understands Christ as a corporate person in whom believers are included and that the church is the corporate solidarity inclusive of Christ and believers, it will confirm a broader Pauline assumption of the solidarity of believers in particular and of human beings in general. This approach represents, in a sense, a reversal of that of Bultmann, while it agrees with him on the importance of Pauline anthropology and its interrelation with other areas of his theology.

Second, the present inquiry is to be distinguished from those that begin with the more obvious corporate anthropology of the Old Testament and then argue that Paul as a "Hebrew of the Hebrews" must have retained this understanding of man as a corporate being. Such a deductive approach must establish first the corporate nature of Old Testament anthropology and the Hebraic origin of Paul's thought. Otherwise, any argument for a corporate Pauline anthropology will fail. Other studies of Pauline anthropology begin with modern presuppositions influenced by psychology, sociology, or philosophy. This approach risks assuming that one's own social or psychological reconstruction of reality is equivalent to that of ancient readers or participants.

The argument below, therefore, follows a more inductive approach. It (1) examines all the relevant Pauline texts in their grammatical, literary, and historical context; (2) making use of the different evaluations and interpretations of his thought in modern literature, draws theological implications from the analysis for Paul's view of man; and then (3), seeks to find possible backgrounds of his conception in Hellenism, in Judaism, in the Old Testament, and in the teachings of Jesus.

Third, due to the comprehensive nature of the study, it is quite impossible to discuss every exegetical issue pertaining to the interpretation of the scriptural passages under consideration and to catalog all the scholarly opinions. For example, passages such as Rom. 5:12-21, 1 Cor. 15:20-28, 42-49 are theologically very significant and involve much debated exegetical issues with regard to Paul's teachings on redemption and resurrection, but this study does not attempt to tackle all of these questions. This is also true of passages such as 1 Cor. 11:2-16, 1 Tim. 2:8-3:1a, Eph. 5:21-33, and Gal. 3:28, which have often been used in the debate about the relationship of man and woman and about the role of women in ministry. Although these issues may not be totally independent from Paul's anthropology, the study limits its discussion to the subject matter more directly related to the present topic, that is, the implications of the passages for the corporate aspect of Pauline anthropology.

Fourth, scholars often understand Pauline anthropology on the basis of the lexical meaning of certain anthropological terms. Robert Jewett has well pointed out the danger of a lexical method that abstracts the term from its context and, consequently, derives its meaning not in relation to the actual sentence where it is found or to the historical situation that it addresses but rather in relation to the framework provided by the researcher.[8] To avoid these dangers, the present inquiry seeks to examine the Pauline anthropological terms, idioms, and concepts in their proper literary and historical context.

Finally, this investigation includes all thirteen canonical letters of Paul for the following reasons: (1) The nineteenth-century Baur tradition that rejects Pauline authorship of a number of the letters (e.g., Ephesians, Colossians, 2 Thessalonians, and the Pastoral letters)[9] and dates them much later

---

[8]Robert Jewett, *Paul's Anthropological Terms: A Study of Their Use in Conflict Settings* (Leiden: E. J. Brill, 1971), 4.

[9] The Pauline authorship of Ephesians, Colossians, and the Pastoral letters has been most vigorously disputed: (1) The authenticity of Ephesians is affirmed by Heinrich Schlier, *Der Brief an die Epheser: Ein Kommentar* (Düsseldorf: Patmos-Verlag, 1962), 22-28; Donald Guthrie, *New Testament Introduction* (Downers Grove, IL: InterVarsity, 1970), 479-508; Alfred Wikenhauser, *New Testament Introduction*, trans. Joseph Cunningham (New York: Herder and Herder, 1958), 426-30; Markus Barth, *Ephesians: Introduction, Translation, and Commentary on Chapters 1-3*, Anchor Bible, vol. 34a (Garden City, NY: Doubleday, 1974), 36-50; and F. F. Bruce, *The Epistle to the Ephesians* (London: Fleming H. Revell, 1961), 11-12, but it is rejected by Edgar J. Goodspeed, *An Introduction to the New Testament* (Chicago: University of Chicago Press, 1937), 222-39; Joachim Gnilka, *Der Epheserbrief*, Herders Theologischer Kommentar zum Neuen Testament, vol. 10 (Freiburg: Herder and Herder, 1990), 1-48; C. L. Mitton, *Ephesians: Its Authorship, Origin, and Purpose* (Oxford: Clarendon, 1951); Werner Georg Kümmel, *Introduction to the New Testament*, rev. ed., trans. Howard Clark Kee (Nashville, TN: Abingdon, 1981), 357-63; and Ernest Best, *Ephesians*, International Critical Commentary (Edinburgh: T. & T. Clark, 1998), 6-36. (2) The Pauline authorship of Colossians is affirmed by Kümmel, *Introduction to NT*, 340-46; F. F. Bruce, *The Epistles to the Colossians, to Philemon, and to the Ephesians* (Grand Rapids: Eerdmans, 1984), 28-32; Peter T. O'Brien, *Colossians, Philemon*, Word Biblical Commentary, vol. 44 (Waco, TX: Word Books, 1982), xli-liv; Eduard Schweizer, *The Letter to the Colossians: A Commentary* (Minneapolis, MN: Augsburg, 1982), 15-24; Guthrie, *NT Introduction*, 551-58; and Markus Barth and Helmut Blanke, *Colossians: A New Translation with Introduction and Commentary*, Anchor Bible, vol. 34b (Garden City, NY: Doubleday, 1994), 114-26; but it is rejected by Eduard Lohse, *A Commentary on the Epistles to the Colossians and to Philemon*, trans. William R. Poehlmann and Robert J. Karris, Hermeneia (Philadelphia: Fortress, 1971), 177-83. (3) The authenticity of the

than Paul's death is open to serious question and appears to involve doubtful literary presuppositions.[10] This currently dominant tradition normally rests its argument on the vocabulary, style, and theological concepts. It often does not fully consider, however, changing circumstances or subject-matter, the use of non-authorial pre-formed traditions, and the role of the amanuensis in Paul's letters.[11] Moreover, the theological concepts that are claimed to be contradictory are often found to be complementary to those of Paul's letters undisputed in the Baur tradition. Evidence for this assertion will be given at appropriate points in the study. (2) Even if the Baur tradition is assumed to be true, the argument developed below will not be greatly affected because it is strongly supported from Pauline letters that the Baur tradition does not question.

Pastoral letters was questioned by J. E. C. Schmidt, F. Schleiermacher, J. G. Eichhorn, F. C. Baur, and H. J. Holtzmann and seriously challenged for stylistic and linguistic reasons by P. N. Harrison, K. Grayston and G. Herdan. See P. N. Harrison, *The Problem of the Pastoral Epistles* (London: Oxford University Press, 1921); idem, "The Authorship of the Pastoral Epistles," *ExpTim* 67 (December 1955): 77-81; and K. Grayston and G. Herdan, "The Authorship of the Pastorals in the Light of Statistical Linguistics," *NTS* 6 (October 1959): 1-15. For the critique of their argu-ments, see E. Earle Ellis, "The Authorship of the Pastorals," in *Paul and His Recent Inter-preters*, 5th ed. (Grand Rapids: Eerdmans, 1979), 49-57 and idem, "Pastoral Letters," in *Paul and His Letters*, ed. G. F. Hawthorne and Ralph P. Martin (Downers Grove, IL: Inter-Varsity, 1993), 658-66. Further, in support of Paul's authorship, J. N. D. Kelly, *A Commentary on the Pastoral Epistles: I Timothy, II Timothy, Titus*, Harper's New Testament Commentaries (New York: Harper, 1963), 1-34; J. Jeremias, *Die Briefe an Timotheus und Titus, der Brief an die Hebräer*, 12th ed. (Göttingen: Vandenhoeck & Ruprecht, 1981), 1-10; G. W. Knight, *The Pastoral Epistles: A Commentary on the Greek Text* (Grand Rapids: Eerdmans, 1992), 4-52; Gordon D. Fee, *1 and 2 Timothy, Titus* (Peabody, MA: Hendrickson, 1988), 23-26.

[10]Kümmel, *Introduction to NT*, 251, makes a similar remark of more radical criticism, although he by no means accepts all thirteen letters. Cf. F. C. Baur, *Paul the Apostle of Jesus Christ, His Life and Work, His Epistles and His Doctrine: A Contribution to a Critical History of Primitive Christianity*, rev. ed., ed. and trans. Eduard Zeller and A. Menzies, 2 vols. (London: Williams and Norgate, 1876). For a critique of the Baur tradition, see Theodor Zahn, *Introduction to the New Testament*, trans. John Moore Trout and others (Edinburgh: T. & T. Clark, 1909), 1:152-64, 491-514, 2:85-122 and more recently, E. Earle Ellis, *The Making of the New Testament Documents* (Leiden: E. J. Brill, 1999), 320-29; idem, "Toward a History of Early Christianity," in *Christ and the Future*, 212-41.

[11]Concerning the role of the amanuensis, see Otto Roller, *Das Formular der paulinischen Briefe* (Stuttgart: W. Kohlhammer, 1933) and E. Randolph Richards, *The Secretary in the Letters of Paul*, WUNT diss. series 42 (Tübingen: J. C. B. Mohr, 1991). On preformed traditions, see Barth, *Ephesians*, 6-10; G. E. Cannon, *The Use of Traditional Materials in Colossians* (Macon, GA: Mercer University Press, 1983); and Ellis, *New Testament Documents*, 49-117, 406-25.

CHAPTER 1

THE ἐν Χριστῷ FORMULA AND RELATED TERMS

The ἐν Χριστῷ formula has been an important subject in Pauline studies since Adolf Deissmann.[1]   Albert Schweitzer claims that it is "the prime enigma of the Pauline teaching: once grasped it gives the clue to the whole."[2] Despite its importance, however, surprisingly little work has been done on the subject since Neugebauer and Bouttier.[3]

The study of the formula basically deals with two issues, the origin of the formula and its meaning.   Concerning the origin of the formula most scholars now agree with Deissmann's conclusion that Paul is "the originator of the formula, not in a sense that he used for the first time the preposition 'ἐv' with the personal pronoun in a singular form, but in a sense that he created a great new technical term by utilizing the language that already existed."[4]   The opinions about the precise meaning of the formula, however,

---

[1]Adolf Deissmann, *Die neutestamentliche Formel "in Christo Jesu"* (Marburg-Lahn: N. C. Elwert Verlag, 1892); idem, *Paul: A Study in Social and Religious History*, 2nd ed., trans. William E. Wilson (New York: Harper & Brothers, 1957).   For a history of the study of the ἐν Χριστῷ formula, see Fritz Neugebauer, *In Christus* (Göttingen: Vandenhoeck & Ruprecht, 1961), 18-33; Michel Bouttier, *En Christ: Etude d'Exegese et de Theologie Pauliniennes* (Paris: Presses Universitaires de France, 1962), 5-22; Wikenhauser, *Pauline Mysticism*, 95-103; and Best, *One Body*, 8-19.

[2]Schweitzer, *Mysticism*, 3.

[3]For recent insightful discussions of the subject, see Josef Georg Ziegler, ed., *In Christus* (Ottilien: EOS Verlag, 1987), which contains a number of articles concerning ethical implications of the formula; C. F. D. Moule, *The Origin of Christology* (Cambridge: Cambridge University Press, 1977), 54-69; A. J. M. Wedderburn, "Some Observations on Paul's Use of the Phrases 'in Christ' and 'with Christ'," *JSNT* 25 (October 1985): 83-97; Brenda B. Colijn, "Paul's Use of the 'in Christ' Formula," *ATJ* 23 (1991): 9-26; and also J. A. Ziesler, *Pauline Christianity*, rev. ed. (Oxford: Oxford University Press, 1990), 47-63.

[4]Deissmann, *In Christo*, 70.   See Wikenhauser, *Pauline Mysticism*, 61-62 and A. Oepke, "ἐv," in *Theological Dictionary of the New Testament*, ed. Gerhard Kittel, trans. Geoffrey W. Bromiley, 2:541 (henceforth *TDNT*).   A question has been raised whether and to what degree the Septuagint influenced Paul's use of ἐν Χριστῷ.   Although the preposition ἐν with a personal dative occurs in the Septuagint, the great majority of these are either literal translations of

vary greatly from mystical to metaphorical.   Whether mystical or metaphorical, scholars agree at least that the formula has a special bearing on
Paul's understanding of the relationship between the exalted Christ and
believers.   This relationship has implications not only for Paul's view of
Christ and of the church but also for his view of man because these themes are
all closely interrelated.[5] The following study, therefore, carefully investigates
Paul's use of the ἐν Χριστῷ formula to determine whether and to what extent
the formula has implications for Paul's view of man, especially for his
understanding of man as a corporate being.

Although the ἐν Χριστῷ formula is definitely one of the most
significant and most frequently recurring phrases in Paul's letters, it is not the
only phrase that Paul uses to describe the relationship between Christ and
believers. He employs other related and similar phrases such as Χριστὸς ἐν
ὑμῖν, ἐν πνεύματι, σὺν Χριστῷ, and εἰς Χριστόν. To comprehend the full
significance of the ἐν Χριστῷ formula, therefore, this study examines Paul's
use of these phrases as well.

Analysis of Paul's Usage

ἐν Χριστῷ

Occurrences

The ἐν Χριστῷ formula occurs 165 times in Paul's letters.[6] This is a
ratio of 1.9 times per chapter. The occurrence is not only frequent but also,
with the exception of Titus, consistent throughout the entire corpus of Paul's

---

the Hebrew ב or cases where ἐν is used psychologically. See Best, *One Body*, 32-33 and
Oepke, "ἐν," 541.

[5]Cf. Bultmann, *Theology*, 1:191; E. Käsemann, *Leib und Leib Christi* (Tübingen: J. C.
B. Mohr, 1933), 183-84; and Udo Schnelle, *Neutestamentliche Anthropologie: Jesus-Paulus-
Johannes* (Neukirchen-Vluyn: Neukirchen Verlag, 1991), 6-7.

[6]This number includes 2 Thess. 1:12, but not Col. 2:15 because αὐτῷ in 2 Thess. 1:12
probably refers to the Lord, but αὐτῷ in Col. 2:15 to the cross rather than to Christ. Gal. 6:15 is
included in Deissmann's list but not here due to weak textual support. While ἐν γὰρ Χριστῷ
Ἰησοῦ οὔτε is supported by A C D F G 𝔐 lat sy[h**] sa[mss] bo, the reading without the formula is
supported by 𝔓[46] Ψ 33. 1175. 1739[*] r (sy[p]) sa[mss]. For the total number of occurrences, disper-
sion, and variations of the form, see Appendix ("Occurrences of the ἐν Χριστῷ formula in
Paul's Letters").

letters. It appears in various forms. In addition to ἐν Χριστῷ, there occur ἐν Χριστῷ Ἰησοῦ, ἐν Χριστῷ Ἰησοῦ τῷ κυρίῳ ἡμῶν,[7] ἐν κυρίῳ, ἐν κυρίῳ Ἰησοῦ, ἐν Ἰησοῦ, and other variants such as ἐν αὐτῷ, ἐν ᾧ, ἐν τῷ ἠγαπημένῳ, and ἐν τῷ ἐνδυναμοῦντι. Three most frequent forms are, however, ἐν Χριστῷ (32 times), ἐν Χριστῷ Ἰησοῦ (44 times), and ἐν κυρίῳ (43 times).[8]

A number of scholars have attributed special significance to the variations of the form.[9] Neugebauer, for example, claims that Paul uses ἐν Χριστῷ in the context of verbs in the indicative mood and ἐν κυρίῳ in the imperative mood.[10] According to him, ἐν Χριστῷ, as determined by the context, expresses the view that the eschatological salvation has happened, is happening, and will happen. It reaches back to the events of the cross and resurrection and looks forward to the final consummation. Ἐν κυρίῳ, however, calls for preserving in this world what has been received ἐν Χριστῷ.[11] In other words, for Paul the expressions associate Χριστός with God's salvation history and κύριος with its implementation and working out in human conduct. Bouttier succinctly describes this relationship when he says, "Become in the Lord what you are already in Christ."[12]

This classification seems, however, too restrictive.[13] Such tendencies appear in Paul's use of the formula, but they are only tendencies. They are not uniform or consistent rules.[14] For example, there is essentially no difference between 1 Cor. 15:19, ἐν Χριστῷ ἠλπικότες (also, Eph. 1:12) and Phil. 2:19, ἐλπίζω ἐν κυρίῳ; between Eph. 4:1, ὁ δέσμιος ἐν κυρίῳ and Philem. 23, ὁ συναιχμάλωτός ἐν Χριστῷ Ἰησοῦ; and between 1 Thess. 4:1,

---

[7]This form appears in a reversed order without ἡμῶν in 1 Thess. 1:1 and 2 Thess. 1:1.

[8]See Appendix ("Occurences of the ἐν Χριστῷ formula").

[9]See Werner Schmauch, *In Christus: Eine Untersuchung zur Sprache und Theologie des Paulus* (Gütersloh: Bertelsmann, 1935); Friedrich Büchsel, "'In Christus' bei Paulus," *ZNW* 42 (1949): 141-58; Bouttier, *En Christ*, 54-55; Neugebauer, *In Christus*; idem, "Das paulinische 'in Christo'," *NTS* 4 (January 1958): 124-38; Werner Kramer, *Christ, Lord, Son of God*, trans. Brian Hardy (Naperville, IL: Alec R. Allenson, 1966).

[10]Neugebauer, *In Christus*, 149. Similarly, Bouttier, *En Christ*, 60-61.

[11]Neugebauer, *In Christus*, 148.

[12]Bouttier, *En Christ*, 60.

[13]See Best, *One Body*, 30-31 and Moule, *Origin*, 59-60. Cf. Bouttier, *En Christ*, 58, 60, who basically agrees with Neugebauer, but recognizes the danger of a too rigid classification between ἐν Χριστῷ and ἐν κυρίῳ.

[14]See Moule, *Origin*, 58; Hans Conzelmann, *An Outline of the Theology of the New Testament*, trans. John Bowden (New York: Harper & Row, 1969), 211; Best, *One Body*, 31; and Ziesler, *Pauline Christianity*, 48.

παρακαλοῦμεν ἐν κυρίῳ Ἰησοῦ and 2 Thess. 3:12, παρακαλοῦμεν ἐν κυρίῳ Ἰησοῦ Χριστῷ.[15] On several occasions, Paul uses ἐν Χριστῷ where ἐν κυρίῳ might be more appropriate or vice versa.[16] Moreover, six times he employs the form ἐν Χριστῷ Ἰησοῦ κυρίῳ in which Christ, Jesus, and Lord are all combined in a single form.[17] In Romans 16, Paul uses ἐν κυρίῳ seven times and ἐν Χριστῷ four times. It is extremely difficult to explain why they are distributed as they are, unless it may be for purely stylistic reasons and to relieve monotony[18] or perhaps from a purely mental association of a particular word with a particular form of the formula.[19]

It is interesting and may be significant to observe the distribution and the incidence of the formula among Paul's letters.[20] A few observations are as follows: (1) The three main forms are quite evenly dispersed in Romans, 1 Corinthians, Ephesians, and 1 Thessalonians. (2) The form ἐν Χριστῷ Ἰησοῦ is absent from 2 Corinthians and 1 Thessalonians while it is the only form appearing in 1 and 2 Timothy. (3) The variants such as ἐν αὐτῷ and ἐν ᾧ are mostly found in Ephesians and Colossians, and ἐν τῷ Ἰησοῦ is used only once in Eph. 4:21b.[21] (4) Only in the Thessalonian letters is ἐν Χριστῷ combined

---

[15]For more examples, see Rom. 16:3, τοὺς συνεργούς μου ἐν Χριστῷ Ἰησοῦ with 19:9, τὸν συνεργὸν ἡμῶν ἐν Χριστῷ and Col. 1:2, πιστοῖς ἀδελφοῖς ἐν Χριστῷ with Philem. 16, ἀδελφὸν ἀγαπητόν . . . ἐν κυρίῳ.

[16]For example, see 2 Tim. 3:12, Rom. 9:1, 2 Cor. 2:17, 12:19, Phil. 4:21, and Philem. 20b.

[17]Rom. 6:23, 8:39, 1 Cor. 15:31, Eph. 3:11, 1 Thess. 1:1, 2 Thess. 1:1.

[18]So, Moule, *Origin*, 59.

[19]So, Best, *One Body*, 31. For example, πείθεσθαι is usually associated with ἐν τῷ κυρίῳ (2 Thess. 3:4, Gal. 5:10, Rom. 14:14, Phil. 1:14, 2:24).

[20]See Appendice ("Occurrences of the ἐν Χριστῷ Formula" and "Classification of the ἐν Χριστῷ Formula").

[21]John A. Allan, "The 'In Christ' Formula in Ephesians," *NTS* 5 (October 1958): 54-62, examines Paul's use of the formula in Ephesians and concludes that the formula in Ephesians is used predominantly, if not exclusively, in the instrumental sense and completely lacks the Pauline idea of incorporation into Christ that is found in the genuine Pauline letters. However, Andrew T. Lincoln, *Ephesians*, Word Biblical Commentary, ed. David A. Hubbard and Glenn W. Barker, vol. 42 (Dallas: Word Books, 1990), 22, argues that although the formula in Ephesians has a predominantly instrumental force, it is hard to avoid the more intensive incorporative connotation in 2:6 where believers are said to have been raised and seated in the heavenly realms together with Christ "in Christ Jesus" and likewise in 1:3 where believers are said to experience the blessings of the heavenly realms not only through Christ's agency but also because they are incorporated into the exalted Christ as their representative, who is himself in the heavenly realms. Also see R. G. Hamerton-Kelly, *Pre-existence, Wisdom, and the Son of Man: A Study of the Idea of Pre-Existence in the New Testament* (Cambridge: Cambridge University

with ἐν θεῷ (1 Thess. 1:1, 2 Thess. 1:1). Finally, (5) in 1 and 2 Timothy, the formula is nearly always used to describe the *locus* of something impersonal.[22]

Classification

The classification of the formula is important for establishing an objective basis for interpretation, but it is not always easy. First, it poses a difficulty in the determination of the case of the third inflected form Χριστῷ. By the time of the New Testament, dative, locative, and instrumental blended into one form. As a result, it became difficult to draw a line of distinction, especially between locative and instrumental.[23] Second, the preposition ἐν, which is most frequently used in the New Testament (2698 times), also poses a difficulty. The relation between words was expressed at first by the case alone, but as the language developed, the burden on the cases grew heavier. To clarify the meaning of the cases in a given context, therefore, prepositions were introduced.[24] The Greek prepositions at the time of the New Testament were, however, very versatile. Even though their ground meaning always remained the same, their applied meaning was often determined by the case.[25] For example, the ground meaning of the preposition ἐν is always "in," but depending on the case, it can mean "in," "into," "at," "among," "by," "through," "with," "in the manner of," or "with reference to."[26] The series of

---

Press, 1973), 180-82, who argues that Eph. 1:3 is an example of either representation (the race being identified with the ancestor) or incorporation.

[22]See Moule, *Origin*, 55. Cf. J. A. Allan, "The 'In Christ' Formula in the Pastoral Epistles," *NTS* 10 (October 1963): 115-21.

[23]See A. T. Robertson, *Grammar of Greek New Testament in the Light of Historical Research* (Nashville, TN: Broadmann, 1934), 526 and Nigel Turner, *A Grammar of New Testament Greek*, vol. 3, *Syntax* (Edinburgh: T. & T. Clark, 1963), 236.

[24]See Robertson, *Grammar*, 554; James Brooks and Carlton L. Winbery, *Syntax of New Testament Greek* (New York: University Press of America, 1979), 3; and H. E. Dana and Julius R. Mantey, *A Manual Grammar for the Greek New Testament* (New York: MacMillan, 1955), 96-98.

[25]Robertson, *Grammar*, 554, insists: "The notion, therefore, that prepositions 'govern' cases must be discarded definitely. . . . It is the *case* which indicates the meaning of the *preposition*, and not the preposition which gives the meaning to the *case*."

[26]For a grammatical explanation of the use of the preposition ἐν and the Greek case, see Robertson, *Grammar*, 584-91; James H. Moulton and Wilbert F. Howard, *A Grammar of New*

ἐν and διά that Paul uses in 2 Cor. 6:4-7 well demonstrates the versatility of the Greek prepositions. In this respect, Wedderburn's comment is noteworthy:

> Such grammatical categories as place, manner, etc., are the result of a modern analysis and they should not be regarded as watertight compartments; these are distinctions of which the writers and readers of ancient texts may have been largely unconscious as they freely wandered to and fro across the frontiers that modern grammarians have detected.[27]

In Paul's use of the ἐν Χριστῷ formula there are a considerable number of instances where it is extremely difficult to determine whether ἐν is used as locative, instrumental, or simply dative of reference. To solve the problem, scholars often appeal to the context. In many cases, however, the context itself is uncertain. For this reason, as Bouttier rightly points out, the determination of the case and thus the classification of the formula have been often influenced by one's overall interpretation of Paul's theology.[28]

Having acknowledged the difficulties involved in the classification of the formula on the basis of the grammatical analysis of the case, this study intends to pay more attention to the syntactical relationship of ἐν Χριστῷ to the other parts of the sentence. The determining factor in a syntactical analysis is often the verb. Since the reason for the classification of the formula in this study is to identify instances, if there are any, in which the formula is clearly used in a locative sense, this study does not intend to determine the case of every instance in which ἐν Χριστῷ occurs. It is neither necessary nor possible.

To accomplish the stated objective, the instances in which the ἐν Χριστῷ formula occurs are first classified by the subject involved, whether it is (A) personal (someone) or (B) non-personal (something). Since the concern of this study is to investigate the relationship of the formula to Paul's understanding of man, the primary interest is in the instances where a person is clearly involved.[29] These instances are, then, classified by the verb, explicit

---

Testament Greek, vol. 2, *Accidence and Word-Formation* (Edinburgh: T. & T. Clark, 1908), 260-65; and Brooks and Winbery, *Syntax*, 2-64.

[27]Wedderburn, "Some Observations," 86.

[28]Bouttier, *In Christus*, 29. See also Wedderburn, "Some Observations," 87.

[29]It is true that a person is often implied where a non-personal subject is present, but to reduce the complexity and to avoid any premature theological interpretation, this study limits its classification to a grammatical sense.

or implied: Does it denote (a) a being ("A is in Christ"), (b) a state or status ("someone is x in Christ"), or (c) an activity ("A does x [to B] in Christ").[30] Of particular interest are the instances where the verb denotes a being because in such cases, a locative sense clearly dominates and the preposition ἐν fully retains its locative meaning. Instances where a copulative verb is explicit or implied usually denote a status or state of a person in Christ. In this case, the formula often becomes equivalent to the word "Christian." When replaced by "Christian," however, the formula loses a sense of personal connection with the historical Christ which the phrase ἐν Χριστῷ retains.[31] In instances where the verb denotes a status or state of a person, an instrumental sense is rarely present, although not impossible, and the sense is more likely locative or simply dative of reference. If an action verb is explicit or implied, thus denoting an activity of a person, it often becomes difficult to determine whether the formula is used in a locative or instrumental sense. It is more so when God is stated or implied as the subject of an activity or when an action verb is used in a passive voice without a specified subject. In addition, when an action verb is used in a passive voice, it seems to imply not only an activity but also a state of the person which is produced by that activity.[32]

A. Personal

First, there are instances in which the verb, stated or implied, denotes a being in Christ. For example, Paul describes as existing in Christ "the church" or "churches,"[33] "the saints," "a man," obviously referring to Paul himself, "brethren," "the dead," "you all,"[34] and believers in general.[35] Since the verbs γέγοναν in Rom. 16:7 and εὑρεθῶ in Phil. 3:9 strongly denote a

---

[30]Cf. Best, *One Body*, 1-7 and Oepke, "ἐν," in *TDNT*, 2:541.

[31]See Best, *One Body*, 4 and Moule, *Origin*, 54.

[32]For example, see 1 Cor. 1:2, 5, Eph. 2:10, Col. 2:7, Col. 2:10, and 2:11, 12.

[33]1 Thess. 1:1, 2 Thess. 1:1, 2:14, Gal. 1:22. Cf. Ernest Best, *A Commentary on the First and Second Epistles to the Thessalonians* (New York: Harper & Row, 1972), 62, who insists that since it is uncharacteristic of Paul to speak of the church as existing in God the Father, the preposition ἐν in 1 Thess. 1:1 and 2 Thess. 1:1 has a strong instrumental force: "the Christian community brought into being by God the Father and our Lord Jesus Christ."

[34]Phil. 1:1, Eph. 1:1, 2 Cor. 12:2, Col. 1:2, 1 Thess. 4:16, 1 Cor. 1:30.

[35]Referred by various pronouns such as οἵ (Rom. 8:1, 16:11), τις (2 Cor. 5:17), and πάντες (1 Cor. 15:22). Since Paul nowhere speaks of the salvation of all people, but only of believers who are in Christ, πάντες in 1 Cor. 15:22 must be limited by ἐν Χριστῷ.

place or a sphere in Christ, these instances should be also included in this category.[36]

Second, there are instances in which the verb, explicit or implied, denotes a "status" or "state" of a person in Christ. For example, Paul uses ἐν Χριστῷ to describe the status of all believers as "sons of God," Prisca and Aquila as "my fellow workers," the Corinthian believers as "babies," "my workmanship," and as "the seal of my apostleship," and Timothy as "my beloved and faithful child."[37] He uses the same idiom to describe the status of the Gentile believers as "fellow heirs, members of the same body, and partakers of the promise" and believers altogether as "one body" in Christ and "the righteousness of God." He also describes his own status in Christ as a "father" and a "prisoner."[38] He represents the state of believers "in Christ" in several ways. For example, they are "alive to God," "beloved," "approved," "eminent," "joined together," and "filled."[39]

Third, there are instances in which the verb denotes an action "in Christ." (1) Paul refers to an activity in Christ without an object. For example, he describes his own activities: "to convince," "to hope," "to become weak," "to rejoice," and "to benefit."[40] He also speaks similarly of the activities of others: "to work," "to grow," "to boast," "to fall asleep," "to become strong," "to be confident," "to stand firm," "to rejoice," and "to live," all qualified by the phrase "in Christ."[41] (2) Paul denotes an activity in Christ with a stated or implied object. For example, he describes his own activities

---

[36]Best, *One Body*, 1, includes in this catagory Phil. 4:21, Philem. 16, Rom. 6:11, Gal. 3:26, and 2 Tim. 3:12. In Phil. 4:21, however, ἐν Χριστῷ Ἰησοῦ is probably related to ἀσπά-σασθε, thus denoting an activity. Otherwise, all the instances in Romans 16 must be understood as denoting a being. Philem. 16, Rom. 6:11, and Gal. 3:26 may be better classified as instances denoting a state or status. In 2 Tim. 3:12, what is in Christ is probably εὐσεβῶς ζῆν, thus a non-personal subject.

[37]Gal. 3:26, Rom. 16:3 (cf. 16:9), 1 Cor. 3:1, 9:1, 2, 4:17a. Also, Eph. 5:8 (the Ephesian believers as "light"), Eph. 6:21 and Col. 4:7 (Tychicus as "the beloved brother and faithful minister"), Philem. 16 (Onesimus as "beloved brother") and Philem. 23 (Epaphras as "my fellow prisoner").

[38]Eph. 3:6, Rom. 12:5, 2 Cor. 5:21, 1 Cor. 4:15b, Eph. 4:1.

[39]Rom. 6:11, 16:8, 10, 13, Eph. 2:21a, and Col. 2:10. Also, 1 Cor. 4:10 ("wise"), 11:11 ("not independent"), Gal. 3:28 ("one"), Col. 1:28 ("mature"), and Gal. 5:6 ("In Christ neither circumcision nor uncircumcision is of avail").

[40]Rom. 14:14, Gal. 5:10, Phil. 2:24, 2 Thess. 3:4 (cf. Phil. 1:14), 1 Cor. 15:19, Phil. 2:19 (cf. Eph. 1:12), 2 Cor. 13:4, Phil. 4:10, Philem. 20a.

[41]Rom. 16:12, Eph. 2:21b, 1 Cor. 1:31, 2 Cor. 10:17, Phil. 3:3, 1 Cor. 15:18, Eph. 6:10, Phil. 1:14, 3:1, 4:1, 4, 1 Thess. 3:8, Col. 2:6.

in Christ with a non-personal object: "to speak the truth," "to hear the word of the truth," "to do all things," "to have boldness," and "to refresh my heart." He also describes activities in Christ with a personal object, sometimes stated and other times simply understood: "to have guides," "to receive," "to greet," "to obey," "to marry," "to speak," "to witness," "to agree," "to exhort," and "to govern."[42]   (3) When the verb is used in a passive voice, it indicates an activity done in Christ upon a person. It often represents God as the one who initiates the action. Although in this case the verb denotes an activity in Christ, there is also a strong sense of the state of a person which is produced by that activity. For example, believers are described in Christ as being "called," "justified," "sanctified," "joined together," "glorified," and so forth.[43]   Finally, (4) God is sometimes directly stated as the subject of activities in Christ: God "leads us into triumph," "reconciles the world to Himself," "blesses us," "chooses us," "bestows His grace upon us freely," "unites all things," "works," "raises us up and makes us sit with Him,"[44] "shows His grace toward us," "creates in Himself one new man," "brings the hostility to an end," "forgives," "supplies all the needs," and "gives us grace."[45]

B. Non-Personal

There are instances in which the subject, stated or implied, is non-personal. First, something is in Christ: "redemption," "faith," "love," "freedom," "truth," "salvation" and so forth.[46]   Second, something is "x" in

---

[42]Rom. 9:1, Eph. 1:13a, 3:12, Phil. 4:13, Philem. 8, 20b, 1 Cor. 4:15a, Rom. 16:2, Phil. 2:29, Rom. 16: 22, 1 Cor. 16:19, Phil. 4:21, Eph. 6:1, 1 Cor. 7:39, 2 Cor. 2:17, 12:19, Eph. 4:17, Phil. 4:2, 1 Thess. 4:1, 2 Thess. 3:12, 1 Thess. 5:12.

[43]1 Cor. 7:22, Eph. 1:11, Gal. 2:17, 1 Cor. 1:2, 6:11, Eph. 2:21, and 2 Thess. 1:12. Also, 1 Cor. 1:5 ("enriched"), Eph. 1:13b ("sealed"), 2:10 ("created"), 2:13 ("brought near"), 2:22 ("built together"), 4:21a ("taught"), Col. 2:7 ("rooted and built"), 2:11 ("circumcised"), 2:12 ("raised together"). Within the litrary context, ἐν αὐτῷ in 2 Thess. 1:12, probably refers to his name.

[44]2 Cor. 2:14, 5:19, Eph. 1:3, 4, 6, 10, 11, 20, 2:6, Col. 2:12. Ἐν ᾧ in Col. 2:12, however, seems to refer to baptism rather than Christ.

[45]Eph. 2:7, 15, 16, 4:32, Phil. 4:19, 2 Tim. 1:9. Technically speaking, 2 Cor. 1:20 also belongs here.

[46]Rom. 3:24, Eph. 1:7 (cf. Col. 1:14), Rom. 8:39, Gal. 3:26, Eph. 1:15, Col. 1:4, 1 Tim. 1:14, 3:13, 2 Tim. 1:13, 3:15 (cf. 1 Cor. 16:24), and 2 Tim. 2:10. Also, Rom. 15:17 and 1 Cor. 15:31 ("boast"), 2 Tim. 2:1 ("grace"), Gal. 2:4 ("freedom"), Eph. 1:9 ("pleasure"), 3:11 ("eter-

Christ: "The gift of God is eternal life"; "Your labor is not in vain"; "The whole fullness of deity dwells"; "It (to be subject to the husband) is fitting"; "It (to obey the parents) is acceptable"; and "It (to give thanks in all circumstances) is the will of God."[47] Third, something does "x" in Christ: "The law of the Spirit of life has set me free"; "A door was opened for me"; "The blessing of Abraham might come upon the Gentiles"; "Your boast may increase"; and "the peace of God will keep your hearts and your minds."[48] Fourth, something is done in Christ: "The grace of God which was given to you"; "It (the veil) is taken away"; and "All things were created."[49]

Several preliminary results emerge from this analysis. (1) There are instances in which Paul clearly uses the formula in a locative sense.[50] (2) It is not only an individual believer who exists and does certain things in Christ, but believers as a whole also exist and do certain things in Christ.[51] (3) Throughout all the instances, whether the verb denotes a status/state or an activity in Christ, a locative sense still remains. Even in the instances where an instrumental sense dominates, one cannot completely eliminate a locative sense. (4) The formula in Paul's usage is very comprehensive. It qualifies not only the believers' being and status/state in Christ but also their activities. Moreover, it embraces, like an umbrella, Paul's other fundamental ideas. (5) The formula has implications not only for the relationship of believers to Christ, but also their relationship to one another.[52] Because of this

---

nal purpose"), 3:21 ("glory"), 4:21b ("truth"), Phil. 1:13 ("imprisonment"), 2:1 ("encourage-ment"), 2:5 ("mind"), 1 Cor. 4:17b ("my ways"), Col. 2:3 ("treasures of wisdom and knowl-edge"), 4:17 ("ministry"), Phil. 3:14 ("prize"), 2 Tim. 1:1 ("promise of the life"), and 3:12 ("a godly life"). In some instances (Rom. 15:17, 1 Cor. 1:4, 15:31, Gal. 2:4, Eph. 1:7, 9, 3:11, Col. 1:14, 4:17), the subject is personal in a grammatical sense and an action verb is present, but the basic idea is non-personal, basically stating that something is in Christ. These   instances are classified as non-personal.

[47]Rom. 6:23, 1 Cor. 15:58, Col. 2:9 (cf. 1:19), 3:18, 20, 1 Thess. 5:18. Technically speaking, 2 Cor. 1:19 also belongs here.

[48]Rom. 8:2, 2 Cor. 2:12, Gal. 3:14, Phil. 1:26, 4:7.

[49]1 Cor. 1:4, 2 Cor. 3:14, Col. 1:16.

[50]Such instances include 1 Thess. 1:1, 2 Thess. 1:1, 2:14, Gal. 1:22, Phil. 1:1, Eph. 1:1, 2 Cor. 12:2, Col. 1:2, 1 Thess. 4:16, 1 Cor. 1:30, Rom. 8:1, 16:11, 2 Cor. 5:17, 1 Cor. 15:22, Rom. 16:7, and Phil. 3:9.

[51]The references to an individual existence include Rom. 8:1, 16:7, 11, 1 Cor. 1:30, 15:22, 2 Cor. 5:17, 12:2, Col. 1:2, 1 Thess. 4:16, and Phil. 3:9, while the references to a cor-porate existence of believers include Gal. 1:22, 1 Thess. 1:1, 2:14, and 2 Thess. 1:1 (cf. Phil. 1:1, Eph. 1:1).

[52]See Rom. 12:5, 16:3 (cf. Rom. 16:9), 1 Cor. 3:1, 4:15b, 17a, 9:1, 2, 11:11, Gal. 3:28, 5:6, Eph. 2:21, 3:6, 4:1, 6:21 (cf. Col. 4:7), Philem. 16 and 23.

relationship, believers are expected to act in a certain way toward one another in Christ.[53]

Χριστὸς ἐν ὑμῖν

Since Deissmann first introduced the idea of reciprocity between "believers in Christ" and "Christ in believers,"[54] many scholars have assumed that a complete reciprocity also exists in Paul's letters, as it does in John's writings.[55] This assumption is, however, questionable for the following reasons. (1) If Paul assumed such reciprocity, it is strange that he refers to Christ's indwelling in believers only six times[56] while referring to ἐν Χριστῷ 165 times. (2) In all the instances except one (Gal. 2:20), he uses the expression in a plural form and thus it can mean "Christ among believers." Christ's indwelling among believers is not the same as Christ's personal indwelling in each believer.[57] (3) In Gal. 4:19 the progressive idea of the formation of Christ in believers strongly indicates the growth of a Christian character in believers rather than the indwelling of Christ himself.[58] (4) Interestingly, in half of the instances, the phrase "Christ in us" is closely associated with the concept of faith and the Spirit.[59] Moreover, whereas Paul seldom speaks of Christ's indwelling, he frequently speaks of the indwelling of the Spirit.[60]

---

[53]See 1 Cor. 4:15a, Eph. 6:1, Rom. 16:2 (cf. Phil. 2:29), 16:22 (cf. 1 Cor. 16:19, Phil. 4:21), 1 Cor. 7:39, Eph. 4:17, Phil. 4:2, 1 Thess. 4:1 (cf. 2 Thess. 3:12), and 5:12.

[54]Deissmann, *In Christo*, 91-92; idem, *Paul*, 140. Cf. Best, *One Body*, 9-10, who well argues against Deissmann's attempt to associate "believers in Christ" with "Christ in believers." He argues that since the "in Christ" formula is linked with other formulas such as "dying and rising with Christ" (Rom. 6:1-11, Col. 2:10-12), "of Christ" (Gal. 3:26-29), and "Christ for us" (2 Cor. 5:14-17), it is arbitrary to select one formula to associate with the "in Christ" formula and to ignore the other formulas which are also associated with it.

[55]In John's writings, the formula is wholly reciprocal and there are also frequent references to "being in God," which is rare in Paul. For example, see John 14:10, 11, 15:5, 7, 17:21, 22, 23, 1 John 2:5, 6, 24, 27, 3:6, 24, 4:4, 12, 13, 15, and 5:20.

[56]Χριστὸς ἐν ὑμῖν (Rom. 8:10, 2 Cor. 13:5, Col. 1:27), μορφωθῇ Χριστὸς ἐν ὑμῖν (Gal. 4:19), κατοικῆσαι τὸν Χριστὸν ἐν ταῖς καρδίαις ὑμῶν (Eph. 3:17), and ζῇ ἐν ἐμοὶ Χριστός (Gal. 2:20).

[57]Cf. Moule, *Origin*, 56-57 and Bouttier, *En Christ*, 80-81.

[58]Cf. Moule, *Origin*, 57.

[59]2 Cor. 13:5, Gal. 2:20, Eph. 3:17. Conzelmann, *Theology*, 211, claims that where Paul reverses the phrase so that it becomes "Christ in me," the concept of faith appears.

[60]It is noteworthy that in Rom. 8:9-11 Paul indicates the indwelling of the Spirit four times, but Christ's indwelling only once.

This brief analysis, therefore, indicates (1) that there is not sufficient evidence upon which to found a notion of complete reciprocity between "Christ in believers" and "believers in Christ." (2) It is probably the Spirit rather than Christ who dwells in believers. (3) Christ's indwelling in believers probably has something to do with Paul's conception of faith and the work of the Spirit.

ἐν πνεύματι

In Paul's letters, ἐν πνεύματι occurs twenty-one times in nineteen verses.[61] The phrase appears in various forms: ἐν (τῷ) ἑνὶ πνεύματι, ἐν πνεύματι ἁγιῳ, ἐν τῷ πνεύματι τοῦ θεοῦ (ἡμῶν), ἐν πνεύματι, ἐν τῷ αὐτῷ πνεύματι, and ἐν ᾧ referring to the Holy Spirit of God.[62] The phrase ἐν πνεύματι appears so closely related to Paul's use of ἐν Χριστῷ that many scholars consider the two phrases as identical and attempt to interpret ἐν Χριστῷ in the sense of ἐν πνεύματι.[63] Deissmann is again the pioneer in this attempt. Beginning with the passages where Paul describes the exalted Christ as the Spirit,[64] he provides parallels between the use of ἐν Χριστῷ and the fifteen instances in which ἐν πνεύματι occurs.[65] Through this process, he

---

[61]Rom. 2:29, 8:9, 9:1, 14:17, 15:16, 1 Cor. 6:11, 12:3a, 3b, 9a, 9b, 13, 2 Cor. 6:6, Eph. 2:22, 3:5, 4:30, 5:18, 6:18, Phil. 1:27, Col. 1:8, 1 Thess. 1:5, 1 Tim. 3:16. 2 Cor. 6:6 is often omitted from the count, but included here. Ἐν πνεύματι in Gal. 6:1 and ἐν ἑνὶ πνεύματι in Eph. 2:18 are not included in the list because they probably refer to a human spirit. Phil. 1:27, though included here, is somewhat questionable because it also likely refers to a human spirit.

[62]1 Cor. 12:9b, 12:13, Phil. 1:27, Rom. 9:1, 14:17, 15:16, 1 Cor. 12:3b, 2 Cor. 6:6, 1 Thess. 1:5, 1 Cor. 6:11, 12:31, Rom. 2:29, 8:9, Eph. 2:22, 3:5, 5:18, 6:18, Col. 1:8, 1 Tim. 3:16, 1 Cor. 12:9a, Eph. 4:30.

[63]For example, see Deissmann, *In Christo*, 84-98; Johannes Weiss, *The History of Primitive Christianity*, vol. 2, trans. and ed. Frederick C. Grant (New York: Wilson-Erickson, 1937), 463-71; and Ziesler, *Pauline Christianity*, 60-62. However, cf. Wikenhauser, *Pauline Mysticism*, 49-108 and Best, *One Body*, 11-12, who make a great effort to distinguish between ἐν Χριστῷ and ἐν πνεύματι.

[64]2 Cor. 3:17, 1 Cor. 6:17, 15:45.

[65]Deissmann, *In Christo*, 85-6: πίστις (1 Cor. 12:9a with Gal. 3:26; cf. Gal. 5:6, Eph. 1:15, 3:12, Col. 1:4, 1 Tim. 3:13, 2 Tim. 3:15), δικαιοσύνη (Rom. 14:17 with 2 Cor. 5:21; cf. Phil. 3:9), δικαιοῦσθαι (1 Cor. 6:11 with Gal. 2:17), εἶναι (Rom. 8:9 with 1 Cor. 1:30; cf. 2 Cor. 5:17, Rom. 8:1, 16:11), στήκειν (Phil. 1:27 with Phil. 4:1; cf. 1 Thess. 3:8), χαίρειν and χαρά (Rom. 14:17 with Phil. 3:1; cf. Phil. 4:4, 10), χάρισμα (1 Cor. 12:9b with Rom. 6:23; cf. Eph. 4:32), ἀγάπη (Col. 1:8 with Rom. 8:39; cf. Gal. 5:6, 1 Cor. 16:24, 1 Tim. 1:14, 2 Tim. 1:13), εἰρήνη (Rom. 14:17 with Phil. 4:7), ἡγιασμένος (Rom. 15:16 and 1 Cor. 6:11 with 1

basically argues for the identification of the exalted Christ with the Spirit, and thus the identification of ἐν Χριστῷ with ἐν πνεύματι. As a result, for him "being in Christ" simply means "being in the Spirit."

Although there are apparent similarities between ἐν Χριστῷ and ἐν πνεύματι, it is questionable whether from these similarities one can draw a perfect equation between the two. As Best rightly points out, Deissmann's comparisons are often based on verbal similarities and not on real parallelism in thought.[66] In other words, his parallels are often a comparison of apples with oranges. For example, while πίστις ἐν τῷ αὐτῷ πνεύματι in 1 Cor. 12:9 refers to "faith" as a spiritual gift, πίστις ἐν Χριστῷ in Gal. 3:26 refers to justifying faith. Moreover, in this passage ἐν Χριστῷ Ἰησοῦ probably needs to be connected with υἱοὶ θεοῦ ἐστε and not with διὰ τῆς πίστεως. Another similar example is his comparison of χάρισμα . . . ἐν τῷ ἑνὶ πνεύματι in 1 Cor. 12:9 with χάρισμα . . . ἐν Χριστῷ in Rom. 6:23. While the former is given to the members of the church as a spiritual gift to use for the benefit of the church, the latter is a personal endowment and not a spiritual gift. Furthermore, ἐν Χριστῷ Ἰησοῦ τῷ κυρίῳ ἡμῶν probably needs to be related to ζωὴ αἰώνιος rather than to τὸ χάρισμα. Deissmann's comparison of ἀγάπη ἐν πνεύματι in Col. 1:8 with ἀγάπη . . . ἐν Χριστῷ in Rom. 8:39 is another such example because while the former speaks of a human love, the latter speaks of God's love which is in Christ. His comparison of Phil. 1:27, στήκετε ἐν ἑνὶ πνεύματι, μιᾷ ψυχῇ συναθλοῦντες, with Phil. 4:1, στήκετε ἐν κυρίῳ, is also inappropriate because πνεῦμα in Phil. 1:27 probably does not refer to the Holy Spirit, but simply means "totally," as the synonymy of ψυχή proves. While there is considerable similarity in the usage of the two phrases, one cannot say that they cover exactly the same ground. The two expressions certainly overlap in places, but each has an area peculiar to itself.[67]

Cor. 1:2), σφραγίζεσθαι (Eph. 4:30 with Eph. 1:13; cf. 1 Cor. 9:2), περιτέμνεσθαι and περι-τομή (Rom. 2:29 with Col. 2:11), μαρτύρεσθαι and συμμαρτυρεῖν (Rom. 9:1 with Eph. 4:17), λαλεῖν (1 Cor. 12:3 with 2 Cor. 2:17; cf. 2 Cor. 12:19, Rom. 8:15, 9:1), πληροῦσθαι (Eph. 5:18 with Col. 2:10), ἕν σῶμα (1 Cor. 12:13 with Rom. 12:5), and κατοικητήριον (Eph. 2:22) with ναὸν ἅγιον (Eph. 2:21). Deissmann, however, does not give parallels to Eph. 3:5, 6:18, 1 Thess. 1:5, and 1 Tim. 3:16.

[66]Best, *One Body*, 11. For more detailed criticism of Deissmann's comparison, see Ferdinand Prat, *The Theology of Saint Paul*, vol. 2, trans. John L. Stoddard (London: Burns, Oates and Washbourne, 1945), 394-95 and Wikenhauser, *Pauline Mysticism*, 80-91.

[67]See Best, *One Body*, 12 and D. E. H. Whiteley, *The Theology of St. Paul*, 2nd ed. (Philadelphia: Fortress, 1964), 129.

An analysis of Paul's use of ἐν πνεύματι, which is based on the same criteria as those applied to the analysis of his ἐν Χριστῷ formula, reveals another significant distinction. Unlike his use of the ἐν Χριστῷ formula, Paul rarely speaks of the believer's indwelling or state/status in the Spirit. Only in Rom. 8:9 does he possibly refer to a personal indwelling in the Spirit.[68] He frequently refers, however, to the Spirit's indwelling in believers.[69] In most instances in which ἐν πνεύματι occurs, Paul employs an action verb, thus denoting some kind of activity in the Spirit. It is also interesting to notice that when Paul refers to an objective act of redemption, he usually employs a passive voice in which the preposition ἐν has a more instrumental than locative sense.[70]

σὺν Χριστῷ

Although the phrase σὺν Χριστῷ occurs much less frequently than ἐν Χριστῷ in Paul's letters, it also has a special implication for Paul's understanding of the relationship between Christ and the believer. Two Greek prepositions in the New Testament signify "with." They are μετά and σύν.[71] Paul uses both prepositions, probably without a clear distinction in meaning.[72] Interestingly, however, he uses only σύν with Christ. He employs the phrase σὺν Χριστῷ twelve times[73] and also utilizes numerous σύν compound words to describe a similar idea.[74]

---

[68]The only instance in which Paul denotes a non-personal state in the Spirit is Rom. 14:17.

[69]Rom. 8:9, 11, 1 Cor. 3:16, 6:19, 2 Tim. 1:14.

[70]For example, ἀπελούσασθε, ἡγιάσθητε, and ἐδικαιώθητε (1 Cor. 6:11, cf. Rom. 15:15), ἐβαπτίσθημεν (1 Cor. 12:13), ἐσφραγίσθητε (Eph. 4:30), ἐδικαιώθη (1 Tim. 3:16), and ἐγνωρίσθη (Eph. 3:5).

[71]Μετά means "in the midst," "between," or "among," while σύν means "together" and expresses "togetherness" or "coming together." In the New Testament, both prepositions are used. Μετά is used 364 times, mostly found in the historical books, and σύν is used 127 times, more commonly in Luke and Paul. For the discussion of the use of μετά and σύν, see Walter Grundmann, "σύν-μετά," in *TDNT*, 7:766-97 and Robertson, *Grammar*, 609-12, 626-28.

[72]Cf. σύν in 1 Cor. 15:10 with μετά in Rom. 16:20, 2 Cor. 13:14, 2 Thess. 3:18.

[73]Rom. 6:8, 8:32, 2 Cor. 4:14, 13:4, Phil. 1:23, Col. 2:13, 20, 3:3, 4, 1 Thess. 4:14, 17, 5:10.

[74]Paul uses the following compound word to describe a sharing in Christ's death and life: συμμορφίζομαι (Phil. 3:10), σύμμορφος (Rom. 8:29, Phil. 3:21), σύμφυτος (Rom. 6:5), συναποθνήσκω (2 Tim. 2:11), συμβασιλεύω (2 Tim. 2:12), συνδοξάζομαι (Rom. 8:17),

Occurrences of σὺν Χριστῷ reveal a couple of interesting characteristics. (1) The phrase σὺν Χριστῷ usually appears in either apocalyptic or baptismal contexts.[75] (2) Although σὺν Χριστῷ usually denotes the Christian hope of eternal being with Christ,[76] it is closely related to Paul's idea of dying and rising, either of Christ or of the believer.[77] While Paul places Christ's death and resurrection definitely in the past,[78] he tends to describe the believer's dying with Christ as a past event[79] and rising with him as a future event.[80] This is, however, only a tendency because he also refers to the believer's past rising up with Christ, his present dying (or suffering) with Christ, and his present life with Christ, which is yet hidden.[81]

συνεγείρω (Eph. 2:6, Col. 2:12, 3:1), συζάω (Rom. 6:8, 2 Tim. 2:11), συζωοποιέω (Eph. 2:5, Col. 2:13), συνθάπτομαι (Rom. 6:4, Col. 2:12), συγκαθίζω (Eph. 2:6), συνκληρονόμος (Rom. 8:17), συμπάσχω (Rom. 8:17), and συσταυρόομαι (Rom. 6:6, Gal. 2:19).

He also employs other σύν compound words to describe the common state, experience, privilege, and task of believers. These words include: συναγωνίζομαι (Rom. 15:30), συναθλέω (Phil. 1:27, 4:3), συναιχμάλωτος (Rom. 16:7, Col. 4:10, Philem. 23), συνανπαύσωμαι (Rom. 15:32), συναποθνήσκω (2 Cor. 7:3), συμβασιλεύω (1 Cor. 4:8; cf. 2 Tim. 2:12), συμβιβάζω (Eph. 4:16, Col. 2:2, 19), συνδέσμος (Eph. 4:3, Col. 2:19, 3:14), σύνδουλος (Col. 1:7, 4:7), συνεργέω (1 Cor. 16:16, 2 Cor. 6:1), συνεργός (Rom. 16:3, 9, 21, 1 Cor. 3:9, 2 Cor. 1:24, 8:23, Phil. 2:25, 4:3, Col. 4:11, 1 Thess. 3:2, Philem. 1, 24), συζάω (2 Cor. 7:3), σύζυγος (Phil. 4:3), συγκληρονόμος (Eph. 3:6; cf. Rom. 8:17), συγκοινωνέω (Eph. 5:11, Phil. 4:14), συγκοινωνός (Rom. 11:17, 1 Cor. 9:23, Phil. 1:7), συμμιμητής (Phil. 3:17), συνοικοδομέω (Eph. 2:22), συμπαρακαλέομαι (Rom. 1:12), συμπάσχω (1 Cor. 12:26; cf. Rom. 8:17), συμπολίτης (Eph. 2:19), συστενάζω (Rom. 8:22), συστρατιώτης (Phil. 2:25, Philem. 2), συνυπουργέω (2 Cor. 1:11), συγχαίρω (1 Cor. 12:26, 13:6, Phil. 2:17-18), σύμψυχος (Phil. 2:2), and συνωδίνω (Rom. 8:22).

[75]The most obvious apocalyptic passages are 1 Thess. 4:14, 17, and 5:10 while the most obvious baptismal passages are Rom. 6:8, Col. 2:13, 20, and 3:3. Eduard Schweizer, "Dying and Rising with Christ," in *New Testament Issues*, ed. Richard Batey (New York: Harper & Row, 1970), 174-76, argues that the contexts for 2 Cor. 4:14, 13:4, Phil. 1:23, and Rom. 8:32 are also apocalyptic.

[76]1 Thess. 4:14, 17, 5:10, Phil. 1:23, 2 Cor. 4:14, Rom. 8:32, Col. 3:4.

[77]Rom. 6:8, 8:32, 2 Cor. 4:14, 13:4, Col. 2:13, 2:20, 3:3. 1 Thess. 4:14, 5:10.

[78]1 Thess. 4:14, 5:10, 2 Cor. 4:14, 13:4, Rom. 8:32.

[79]Rom. 6:8, Col. 2:13, 20, 3:3 (cf. 2 Tim. 2:11, Rom. 6:4, 5, 6, 8, Gal. 2:19, Eph. 2:6, Phil. 3:10, Col. 2:12).

[80]1 Thess. 4:14, 17, 5:10, Phil. 1:23, 2 Cor. 4:14, 13:4, Rom. 6:8, Col. 3:4 (cf. 2 Tim. 2:11, 12, Rom. 6:8, 8:17). Cf. Schweizer, "Dying and Rising," 180.

[81]Rom. 6:8-11, Col. 2:13; Rom. 6:4, Gal. 2:19-20, Eph. 2:5, 6, Col. 2:12, 13, 3:1; Rom. 8:17; 1 Cor. 15:31, 2 Cor. 4:10-12, Phil. 3:10; Col. 3:3 (cf. Gal. 2:20).

εἰς Χριστόν

In Paul's letters, the phrase εἰς Χριστόν occurs fifteen times,[82] but most of these instances are normal uses of the preposition εἰς[83] and do not suggest a corporate relationship between Christ and the believer. For example, εἰς in Gal. 3:24 has a temporal sense, "until," while that in Eph. 5:32 has a sense of reference, "with regard to" or "concerning." Εἰς in Rom. 16:5, 2 Cor. 11:3, and Phil. 1:6 means "unto" while that in 1 Cor. 8:12 denotes "against." The expression in Col. 1:17 is not much different from those in 1 Cor. 8:6 and Rom. 11:36. Πιστεύειν εἰς Χριστὸν is probably a general New Testament formula replacing the more classical πιστεύειν with the simple dative.[84] It is interesting, however, to notice that while Paul connects the verb πιστεύειν with εἰς Χριστόν, he connects the noun πίστις with ἐν Χριστῷ.[85] The only exception to this is Col. 2:5 where πίστις is connected with εἰς Χριστόν. Εἰς also can, like ἐν, convey a locative sense. The difference is, however, that unlike ἐν there is a sense of movement when governed by the accusative case with a verb of motion.[86] For example, βαπτίζειν εἰς Χριστόν, βεβαιοῦν εἰς Χριστόν, and αὐξάνειν εἰς Χριστόν certainly convey a sense of movement into a place.[87]

There are two instances in which Paul relates εἰς Χριστόν to baptism (Rom. 6:3, Gal. 3:27). Significantly, he connects βαπτίζειν with εἰς Χριστόν and not with ἐν Χριστῷ. While in Rom. 6:3 "to be baptized into Christ" is "to be baptized into Christ's death," in Gal. 3:27 it is identified as "putting on Christ." Similar expressions occur elsewhere in Paul's letters. In 1 Cor. 10:2 the phrase is "to be baptized into Moses" and in 1 Cor. 12:13, "to be baptized into one body."[88] The expression "putting on the Lord Jesus Christ" in Rom.

---

[82]εἰς Χριστόν (Rom. 6:3, 16:5, 1 Cor. 8:12, 2 Cor. 1:21, 11:3, Gal. 2:16, 3:24, 3:27, Eph. 4:15, 5:32, Phil. 1:6, Col. 2:5), εἰς ὅν (Rom. 10:14), εἰς αὐτόν (Eph. 4:15, Phil. 1:29, Col. 1:16).

[83]For the use of the preposition εἰς, see Moulton and Howard, *Accidence*, 304; Turner, *Syntax*, 66-67; Oepke, "εἰς," in *TDNT*, 2:420-34.

[84]Rom. 10:14, Gal. 2:16, Phil. 1:29. Πιστεύειν εἰς in relation to Christ is found twice in the Synoptics (Mark 9:42, Matt. 18:6), three times in Acts (10:43, 14:23, 19:4), over thirty times in the Gospel of John between 2:11 and 17:20, and only once in the letter of John (1 John 5:10).

[85]Gal. 3:26, 1 Tim. 1:14, 2 Tim. 3;15, Eph. 1:15, Col. 1:4, 1 Tim. 3:13.

[86]See Robertson, *Grammar*, 591-94 and Bouttier, *En Christ*, 35.

[87]Rom. 6:3, Gal. 3:27, 2 Cor. 1:21, Eph. 4:15. Cf. Oepke, "ἐν," 433 and Bouttier, *En Christ*, 38.

[88]βαπτίζειν εἰς τὸ ὄνομα appears in 1 Cor. 1:13 and 15.

13:14 is apparently equivalent to "putting on the new man" in Eph. 4:22, 24 and Col. 3:9-10 where the "new man" Jesus Christ is contrasted with the "old man" Adam.[89] These two instances, therefore, have special significance for Paul's understanding of the relationship between Christ and believers.

Implications

The analysis of Paul's use of ἐν Χριστῷ has revealed that at least in a number of instances, Paul uses the phrase in a genuinely locative sense.[90] One may still argue in some instances for a meaning other than locative, but it will be extremely difficult to dismiss them all together as non-locative.[91] If Paul uses ἐν Χριστῷ in a locative sense, even in a limited number of instances, it is christologically and anthropologically significant, for it indicates, as Moule writes, "a more than individualistic conception of the person of Christ"[92] and of man as well.

The Meaning of Being in Christ

How can a believer be in Christ? This has been a puzzling question for many people.[93] Several explanations have been offered. First, there are

---

[89]1 Cor. 15:45, Rom. 6:6. See Ellis, *Pauline Theology*, 12-13.

[90]See pp. 13-15 above. Such instances include Rom. 8:1, 16:7, 16:11, 1 Cor. 1:30, 15:22, 2 Cor. 5:17, 12:2, Gal. 3:26, Col. 1:2, Phil. 3:9, 1 Thess. 4:16, Gal. 1:22, 1 Thess. 1:1, 2 Thess. 1:1, 2:14, Phil. 1:1, and Eph. 1:1. Cf. Moule, *Origin*, 55-56, who recognizes as locative: Rom. 8:1, 16:7, 1 Cor. 15:22, 2 Cor. 5:17, Phil. 3:8-9, Gal. 1:22, Phil. 1:1, 1 Thess. 1:1, 2:14, and 2 Thess. 1:1; Lincoln, *Ephesians*, 21: Rom. 8:1, 2 Cor. 5:17, and Phil. 3:9; Margaret E. Thrall, *A Critical and Exegetical Commentary on the Second Epistle to the Corinthians*, International Critical Commentary, ed. J. A. Emerton, C. E. B. Cranfield, and G. N. Stanton, vol. 1 (Edinburgh: T. & T. Clark, 1994), 425, n. 1638: Rom. 8:1, 12:5, 16:7, 1 Cor. 1:30, 2 Cor. 12:2, Gal. 1:22, 3:28, 5:6, Phil. 1:1, and 1 Thess. 2:14; Best, *One Body*, 1: Rom. 8:1, 16:7, 11, 1 Cor. 1:30, 2 Cor. 5:17, 12:2, Gal. 3:26, Eph. 1:1, Phil. 1:1, 14, 3:9, 4:21, Col. 1:2, 2 Tim. 3:12, and Philem. 16; and Richard N. Longenecker, *Galatians*, Word Biblical Commentary, ed. David A. Hubbard and Glenn W. Barker, vol. 41 (Dallas: Word Books, 1990), 41: Gal. 1:22, 1 Thess. 1:1, 2:14, 2 Thess. 1:1, and Phil. 1:1.

[91]See Moule, *Origin*, 62 and James D. G. Dunn, *The Theology of Paul the Apostle* (Grand Rapids: Eerdmans, 1998), 400.

[92]Moule, *Origin*, 62.

[93]For example, Moule, *Origin*, 51, after having expressed other scholars' puzzlement over this question, expresses his own puzzlement: "Thus, Lady Oppenheimer, Professor

scholars who argue that being in Christ means being in the Spirit. Deissmann
initiated this interpretation. Beginning from the locative meaning of the
preposition ἐν, he establishes his argument on the basis of two assumptions,
namely, (1) identification of ἐν Χριστῷ and ἐν πνεύματι and (2) association
of "Christ in believers" and "believers in Christ." Based on these assumptions, he asserts that believers are physically in Christ, that is, the "pneumatic
Christ." He then explains the intimate reciprocal relationship between Christ
and believers by using the analogy of air: As people live in the air and the air
is in them, so believers are in Christ and Christ is in believers.[94] Although
Deissmann never states that this "pneumatic Christ" is impersonal, the use of
air indicates his understanding of Christ in this way. Johannes Weiss reaches
somewhat similar conclusion to that of Deissmann, but goes further and
explicitly states that Christ is impersonal. He claims that "this manner of
thought is possible only upon the supposition that—at least at the moment
when the formula was first conceived and expressed—the fixed outlines of the
personality (i.e., of Christ) had been softened and dissolved, and replaced by
the idea of a formless, impersonal, all-penetrating being."[95] More recently,
Ziesler has offered a view not much different from that of Deissmann and
Weiss in that he also interprets ἐν Χριστῷ in the sense of ἐν πνεύματι.[96]
According to him, however, being in Christ means being "in Christ's sphere
of power."[97] He, therefore, states:

Cunliffe-Jones, and Dr. Arthur Peacocke express puzzlement. . . . I am not going to attempt to
reply to the puzzlement: I am among the puzzled myself."

[94]Deissmann, *In Christo*, 77-98. Although Deissmann's unitary interpretation of ἐν as
locative and his use of the analogy of air received immediate criticism, many scholars have
adopted his "mystical" interpretation of the formula. For example, Schweitzer, *Mysticism*,
accepts the mystical understanding of the formula, but interprets it from an eschatological point
of view. James S. Stewart, *A Man in Christ: The Vital Elements of St. Paul's Religion* (New
York: Harper and Brothers, 1935) and Wikenhauser, *Pauline Mysticism*, take "mysticism" as
the center of the Pauline theology. Also, see C. A. A. Scott, *Christianity according to St. Paul*
(Cambridge: Cambridge University Press, 1966); and Elias Andrews, *The Meaning of Christ
for Paul* (New York: Abingdon-Cokesbury, 1946).

[95]Weiss, *Primitive Christianity*, 2:465.

[96]Ziesler, *Pauline Christianity*, 58-63.

[97]Ibid., 60, 63. Interestingly, Eduard Schweizer, *Jesus*, trans. David E. Green (Richmond, VA: John Knox, 1971), 107, suggests that the power of Jesus is love and thus the phrase
denotes living in an atmosphere informed by this love. James D. G. Dunn, *Jesus and the Spirit:
A Study of the Religious and Charismatic Experience of Jesus and the First Christians as Reflected in the New Testament* (Philadelphia: Westminster, 1975), 324, on the other hand, claims
that the phrase denotes "religious experience as experience of Christ—deriving from Christ as
to both its source and its character and that it expresses not merely a rational conviction, but

To be in Christ now is to be in the Spirit, i.e. within the sphere of his power.
That is to say, the equivalence of the two expressions indicates that Christ
as exalted is now a centre of power, so that to be in him means, not to be in
his person, but to be in his sphere of power.[98]

There are a couple of problems with this explanation: (1) As already
pointed out above,[99] although ἐν Χριστῷ and ἐν πνεύματι are closely related
and overlap in places, they do not cover the same ground. Being in Christ is,
therefore, not the same as being in the Spirit. (2) A non-personal understanding of the exalted Christ is not acceptable because Paul never conceives
Christ as non-personal.[100] He regards the exalted Christ as the same one who
died on the cross, rose again on the third day, ascended into the heaven, and
who will return in glory. He never softens or dissolves Christ's personality
into something impersonal. His comparison of Christ with Adam is only
possible when both Christ and Adam are understood as persons. Paul claims
that those who have been baptized into Christ have put on (ἐνδύειν) Christ.
In Eph. 4:24 and Col. 3:9-10 he employs the same expression "putting on
(ἐνδύειν) the new man." The "new man" in these verses probably refers to
Christ. Paul's description of Christ as the body which consists of many
members is a further evidence that Paul understands the exalted Christ as a
person.[101]

Second, there are other scholars who regard being in Christ as
practically equivalent to being in the church, that is, the body of Christ.[102]
According to them, to be baptized into Christ is baptism into the one body
that is in some sense identified with Christ. To belong to the church is,
therefore, to be in Christ or in the Lord.[103] These scholars usually do not
reject the fundamental truth of Deissmann's view of personal mysticism, but
point out a communal or social aspect of the formula. Interestingly, Bultmann

---

something more—a sense that Christ is thoroughly involved in the situation or action in question—a *consciousness of Christ*."

[98]Ziesler, *Pauline Christianity*, 63.

[99]See p. 19 above.

[100]See Moule, *Origin*, 60.

[101]See 1 Cor. 15:3-8, Col. 3:1, 4, Rom. 5:12-21, 1 Cor. 15:21-22, 45-49, Gal. 3:27 (cf.
Rom. 13:14), 2 Cor. 5:3, and 1 Cor. 12:12.

[102]So, Käsemann, *Leib und Leib Christi*, 156-59, 183-4; R. N. Flew, *Jesus and His
Church*, 2nd ed. (London: Epworth, 1943), 153-54. Cf. Best, *One Body*, 1-30.

[103]Cf. 1 Cor. 1:30, 12:12-13, 27; Rom. 16:7, 11.

who regards ἐν Χριστῷ as purely metaphorical[104] and rejects any mystical interpretation also asserts that being in Christ primarily refers to "the state of having been articulated into the 'body of Christ' by baptism."[105] A major problem with this explanation is that although ἐν Χριστῷ and the body of Christ are closely related, they are not completely identical because Paul always maintains the distinction between Christ and his body, that is, the church.[106] Moreover, those who accept this interpretation often assume that Paul derived the ἐν Χριστῷ formula from his "body of Christ" concept.[107] There is, however, no conclusive, direct evidence for this assumption.[108]

Third, there are still others who insist that ἐν Χριστῷ basically refers to the objective events of salvation history.[109] To them ἐν Χριστῷ is simply a metaphorical expression, predominantly used in an instrumental sense, of what God has done through Christ. The phrase, they argue, does not have any mystical sense, either individual or communal. It simply denotes that Christ is the instrument of God for salvation and that he is the source, cause, and power of the believer's life.[110] It is true that in some instances the instrumental force dominates and the formula strongly denotes the saving events of Christ but, as already pointed out above,[111] it is extremely difficult to dismiss all the instances as non-locative. Moreover, Paul's use of the formula is often too realistic to be regarded as purely metaphorical.[112]

---

[104]Bultmann, *Theology*, 1:329, states that the phrase ἐν Χριστῷ simply fills "the place of an adjective or adverb which the linguistic process had not yet developed: 'Christian,' 'as a Christian,' or 'in a Christian manner.'"

[105]Ibid. 311.

[106]Eph. 4:12, 15, 5:23, Col. 1:18, 2:19. See p. 109 (ch. 3) below.

[107]It was A. Schweitzer who pioneered in this attempt. See Schweitzer, *Mysticism*, 122-23.

[108]See Best, *One Body*, 15. Cf. Ernst Percy, *Der Leib Christi (soma Christou) in den paulinischen Homologumena und Antilegomena*, Lunds Universities Arsskrift (Lund: Gleerup/Leipzig, 1942), 43-45, who argues for the exactly opposite, that is, to explain the "body of Christ" from the "being in Christ."

[109]So, Conzelmann, *Theology*, 208-12; Neugebauer, *In Christus*, 147-49, 171-74; Kramer, *Christ, Lord, Son of God*, 141-46; Günther Bornkamn, *Paul*, trans. D. M. G. Stalker (New York: Harper & Row, 1971), 154-56; and also Bultmann, *Theology*, 1:311, 327-29.

[110]Conzelmann, *Theology*, 210, states: "The evidence of the text points us to the objective saving work. . . . 'In Christ' thus means that here, in him and not in me, salvation has taken place." Also, see Neugebauer, *In Christus*, 112.

[111]See pp. 13-16 above. Cf. Moule, *Origin*, 62 and Dunn, *Theology*, 400.

[112]Schweitzer, *Mysticism*, 13, 15, states: "One thing which surprises us in the Pauline Christ-mysticism is its extraordinary realistic character. The being-in-Christ is not conceived as a static partaking in the spiritual being of Christ, but as a real co-experiencing of His dying

Finally, a number of scholars claim that ἐν Χριστῷ denotes the believer's existence in the "corporate Christ."[113] According to them, Paul conceives Christ as a "corporate personality," a conception that is rooted in the Old Testament conception of man.[114] They argue that Paul's Adam-Christ typology, particularly in 1 Cor. 15:22 where "in Christ" is contrasted with "in Adam," casts a clear light on the interpretation of ἐν Χριστῷ.[115] In this passage, Adam and Christ stand over against each other in the history of redemption as the two great representative figures of two ages, two societies, or two humanities, Adam representing the old and Christ the new.[116] They are corporate persons who include their respective followers. The believer's being in Christ means, therefore, being in this corporate Christ. Some scholars question whether "corporate personality" is a valid Old Testament concept and if so, whether it is an appropriate term to describe it. They also question whether Paul's conception of the corporate Christ was directly influenced by this Old Testament conception.[117] This explanation, however, seems to do more justice to Paul than other explanations at least for two reasons: (1) It recognizes the locative use of the formula and (2) it conceives of Christ as a person.

Paul speaks of existence in Christ not only of individual believers but also of all believers as a whole. He refers (1) to the churches of Judea and of the Thessalonians, (2) to all the saints, and (3) even to the dead, as being in

---

and rising again (13) . . . . Dying and rising with Christ is for him not something merely metaphorical, which could at need be expressed also in a different metaphor, but a simple reality (15)."

[113]So, Moule, *Origin*, 47-96; Best, *One Body*, 20-23; Herman Ridderbos, *Paul: An Outline of His Theology*, trans. John Richard de Witt (Grand Rapids: Eerdmans, 1975), 58-62; Ellis, *Pauline Theology*, 10-13; idem, *Old Testament*, 110-12; idem, *Paul and His Recent Interpreters* (Grand Rapids: Eerdmans, 1961), 31-33; idem, "Sōma," 138-40; C. K. Barrett, *From First Adam to Last: A Study in Pauline Theology* (New York: Charles Scribner's Sons, 1962), 73, 77-78 and passim; Richard Longenecker, *Paul: Apostle of Liberty* (New York: Harper & Row, 1964), 160-70; Gerald F. Hawthorne, *Philippians*, Word Biblical Commentary, ed. David A. Hubbard and Glenn W. Barker, vol. 43 (Waco, TX: Word Books, 1983), 6-7; and Oepke, "ἐν," in *TDNT*, 2:542.

[114]The term "corporate personality" is first used by H. Wheeler Robinson. Moule, *Origin*, 95, however, calls it an "inclusive personality" while Oepke, "ἐν," in *TDNT*, 2:542, calls it a "universal personality."

[115]Cf. Rom. 5:12-21 and 1 Cor. 15:45-49.

[116]See Ridderbos, *Paul*, 60-61; Oepke, "ἐν," in *TDNT*, 2:542; Ellis, *Pauline Theology*, 10-13; idem, *Old Testament*, 112; idem, "Sōma," 138-39; and Ethelbert Stauffer, "εἰς," in *TDNT*, 2:436-38.

[117]For a summary and an evaluation of the concept, see pp. 75-79 (ch. 2) below.

Christ.[118] When Paul places not only the living, but also the dead in Christ, he says, in effect, that believers who die do not pass out of Christ but still remain in him. The expression "saints" also refers to a unity rather than to individuals. According to J. V. Bartlet, a righteous man in both the Old Testament and the New Testament is rarely called individually a saint or the saint. "A man's standing in relation to God is not regarded as one of isolated consecration or holiness, but as something attaching to him as a member of a larger whole."[119] In the Old Testament Israel was the larger whole, but in the New Testament it is the church. Following Bartlet's argument, then, the "saints" for Paul are really a unit, and it is this unit that is said to be also in Christ.[120] The ἐν Χριστῷ formula, therefore, denotes a relationship of many believers with one Christ.

If believers are in Christ, how can Christ be in believers at the same time? Does Paul really speak of mutual indwelling of Christ and believers? It has been already pointed out that Paul speaks of Christ's indwelling in believers only six times, most of which can be understood differently, and that Paul seldom speaks of the believer's existence in the Spirit but often of the indwelling of the Spirit in believers.[121] From these facts, one may safely conclude either (1) that it is the Spirit rather than Christ himself who dwells in believers[122] or (2) that Christ's indwelling takes place through the Spirit.[123]

---

[118]Gal. 1:22, 1 Thess. 1:1, 2:14, 2 Thess. 1:1, Eph. 1:1, Phil. 1:1 (cf. Rom. 1:7, 16:15, 1 Cor. 1:2, 2 Cor. 1:1, 13:12, Phil. 4:21, 22, Col. 1:2), 1 Thess. 4:16.

[119]J. V. Bartlet, "Saints," in *Dictionary of the Bible*, ed. J. Hastings (Edinburgh: T. & T. Clark, 1963), 4:352.

[120]See Ridderbos, *Paul*, 330-33; W. D. Davies, *Paul and Rabbinic Judaism: Some Rabbinic Elements in Pauline Theology* (New York: Harper & Row, 1967), 100-01.

[121]See pp. 18-20 above.

[122]Andrews, *Meaning of Christ*, 149; George E. Ladd, *A Theology of the New Testament* (Grand Rapids: Eerdmans, 1974), 490.

[123]The relation between Christ and the Spirit is beyond the scope of this study. However, the statement "Christ is the spirit" (2 Cor. 3:17, 1; cf. 1 Cor. 6:17 and 15:45) seems to indicate that Christ exists in the mode of the Spirit. The fact that Paul's use of ἐν πνεύματι is usually related to the believer's activities may also indicate that the Spirit is the operative power or agent in Christ and that the Spirit is Christ himself present in his church. See Eduard Schweizer, "πνεῦμα, πνευματικός," in *TDNT*, 6:433-34; D. Hill, *Greek Words and Hebrew Meaning: Studies in the Semantics of Soteriological Terms* (London: Cambridge University Press, 1967), 278-81; N. Q. Hamilton, *The Holy Spirit and Eschatology in Paul* (Edinburgh: Oliver and Boyd, 1957), 12-15; Andrews, *Meaning of Christ*, 145-50; C. H. Dodd, *The Meaning of Paul for Today* (New York: George H. Doran, 1922), 127; and Ladd, *Theology*, 488-94.

The Means of Incorporation into Christ

By what process then do believers come into the state of being in Christ? Paul asserts that they were brought into Christ through baptism.[124] In Rom. 6:3-6, he states that believers were "baptized into Christ," that is, "baptized into his death" (6:3, 4), that they were united (σύμφυτοι) with Christ in the likeness of his death and will be with him in the likeness of his resurrection (6:5), and that consequently, they are freed from sin (6:7) and death no longer has dominion over them (6:9). Believers are dead to sin and alive to God in Christ Jesus (6:11). It is interesting to observe that in this passage Paul starts with εἰς Χριστόν (6:3, 4), continues with σὺν Χριστῷ (6:8), and ends up with ἐν Χριστῷ (6:11).[125] Also in Gal. 3:27-28, Paul implies that believers are baptized εἰς Χριστόν (3:27) and as a result they became all one (εἷς) ἐν Χριστῷ (3:28). Being in Christ must be, therefore, the state resulting from baptism into Christ, that is, the believer's participation in the death and the resurrection of Christ.

Paul's expressions such as "baptism into Christ," "dying and rising with Christ," and "being in Christ" seem to imply not only the believer's participation in and incorporation into, but also a solidarity with Christ. Paul claims that as believers were united to the Lord, they have become "one spirit" (ἓν πνεῦμα) with him. They have put on Christ. They have put off the old man and put on the new man. They have become members of the body of Christ, and Christ is present in every part of the body.[126] Each member of the body of Christ should, therefore, express the character of Christ. It is probably in this sense that Paul exhorts the Philippian believers to have the mind of Christ and proclaims in Galatians: "I have been crucified with Christ; it is no longer I who live, but Christ who lives in me."[127] Believers have

---

[124]The relationship between faith and baptism and the question whether one should understand baptism as baptism into the Holy Spirit (Ellis) or as water baptism (Schweitzer) and if the latter, whether sacramentally or symbolically are matters beyond this study. It may be well to point out, however, that Schweitzer's view that believers are literally brought into Christ through water baptism without faith on the part of the believer seems too extreme (see Schweitzer, *Mysticism*, 117). Paul's teaching on baptism must always be viewed in the closest conjunction with his teaching on faith in Christ. See Whiteley, *Theology*, 172 and Shedd, *Man in Community*, 177-89. For baptism into Christ as baptism "in (ἐν) the Spirit," see 1 Cor. 6:11, 12:13 and Tit. 3:5-6; cf. Ellis, *Pauline Theology*, 30-33, 45.

[125]Best, *One Body*, 69, also makes this observation.

[126]1 Cor. 6:17, Gal. 3:27, Col. 3:10, 1 Cor. 12:12, Eph. 4:16, Col. 2:19.

[127]Phil. 2:5, Gal. 2:19-20.

participated in Christ's death and resurrection. Through their participation, they were brought into Christ. Brought into Christ, they have become members of the body of Christ, thus creating a solidarity with him. In a sense, it is more than a solidarity. Paul seems to imply that believers together form a personality with Christ.

Does incorporation into Christ mean the loss of individuality of believers? The passage which comes nearest indicating the loss of all personal identity is again Paul's confession in Gal. 2:19-20a: "I have been crucified with Christ; It is no longer I who lives, but Christ who lives in me." This phrase is, however, immediately followed by his other confession, "the life which I now live in the flesh I live by faith in the Son of God" (Gal. 2:20b). It is the life of Christ that Paul has, but it is still Paul who lives that life.[128] Paul nowhere indicates that believers lose their individualities when incorporated into Christ. They certainly form a corporate solidarity with Christ, but it is not at the expense of losing their individuality. As one in Christ, they should reflect the character of Christ in every possible way, but their personalities are not fused with Christ's.[129]

Before going into the next section, it is necessary to reiterate briefly what has been said thus far for Paul's conceptions of Christ and of man as well: (1) The analysis of Paul's use of the ἐν Χριστῷ formula has demonstrated that at least in some instances Paul uses the formula in a clearly locative sense. (2) The locative meaning of the formula may imply that Paul understands Christ as a corporate person in whom believers are included. (3) If Paul truly conceives believers as existing together in Christ, forming a corporate body with Christ and with one another but without losing their individualities, it certainly implies his understanding of Christ as well as of man as a corporate being. Finally, (4) Paul's use of εἰς Χριστόν and σὺν Χριστῷ in a close relation to the ἐν Χριστῷ formula indicates the believer's "participation in" Christ's death and resurrection which results in "incorporation into" and "existence in" the corporate Christ.

---

[128]Weiss, *Primitive Christianity*, 470, points out that by adding this phrase Paul deliberately guards against the possible pantheistic interpretation by reasserting the religious attitude where "Thou" and "I" stand over against each other. See also Steward, *Man in Christ*, 167 and Davies, *Paul and Rabbinic Judaism*, 91.

[129]Best, *One Body*, 23; Wikenhauser, *Mysticism*, 184-86.

Possible Backgrounds

Paul's expressions such as "being in Christ," "baptism into Christ," and "dying and rising with Christ" are unique in the sense that they rarely, if ever, occur in New Testament witnesses earlier than Paul's letters.[130] This fact has led many scholars to wonder about the origin of these expressions. Three possible backgrounds have been extensively argued: (1) Hellenistic mystery religions, (2) Jewish apocalyptic writings, and (3) the Old Testament as interpreted and mediated through the teachings of Jesus.

Hellenistic Mystery Religions

Although now largely discredited, a number of scholars claimed that they had found the origin of Paul's expressions, especially "dying and rising with Christ," in the hellenistic mystery religions. Reitzenstein pioneered this attempt and his work was further carried on by A. Loisy and W. Bousset.[131] These scholars heavily rely on the sources such as the Hermetic writings and the Magical Papyri for their argument.[132]

---

[130]The expression "ἐν Χριστῷ" occurs, besides the letters of Paul and John, only in 1 Peter 3:16, 5:10, 14, Rev. 1:9, and Acts 4:2.

[131]Richard Reitzenstein, *Hellenistic Mystery-Religions: Their Basic Ideas and Significance*, 3rd ed., trans. John E. Steely (Pittsburgh, PA: Pickwick, 1978); Wilhelm Bousset, *Kyrios Christos*, 5th ed., trans. John Steely (Nashville, TN: Abingdon, 1970), 153-210. Reitzenstein's view was vigorously and effectively criticized by H. A. A. Kennedy, *St. Paul and the Mystery-Religions* (London: Hodder and Stoughton, 1913); J. Gresham Machen, *The Origin of Paul's Religion* (New York: Macmillan, 1921; reprint, Grand Rapids: Eerdmans, 1975), 211-90; Albert Schweitzer, *Geschichte der paulinischen Forschung von der Reformation bis auf die Gegenwart* (Tübingen: J. C. B. Mohr, 1911), 141-84; idem, *Mysticism*, 26-40, and by Prat, *Theology*, 2:40-42, 383-90.

[132]The Hermetic writings received their name from Hermes Trismegistos, the Egyptian god of revelation. The Hermetic Corpus consists of eighteen tracts and a work called "Asclepius" which survives in Latin. A considerable number of fragments are preserved by Johannes Stobaeus, a writer of the fifth century A.D. See Arthus Darby Nock, ed., *Corpus Hermeticum*, Société d'édition "Les Belles Lettres," 4 vols (Paris: n. p., 1945); Walter Scott, ed. and trans., *Hermetica: the Ancient Greek and Latin Writings Which Contain Religious or Philosophic Teachings Ascribed to Hermes Trismegistus*, 3 vols (Oxford: Clarendon, 1924). Richard Reitzenstein, *Poimandres: Studien zur griechisch-ägyptischen und frühchristlichen Literatur* (Leipzig: Druck und Verlag, 1904), also contains some of the tracts of the Hermetic writings. The most important part of the Magical Papyri is called "Liturgy of Mithras." See H.

There are certain resemblances between Paul and the mystery religions. For example, (1) like Christ who died and rose again, in the hellenistic mystery religions there is often the figure of a god (e.g., Attis, Osiris, or Dionysus) who died and rose again. (2) As Paul desires to achieve union with Christ, so the initiates of the mystery religions desire to achieve union with their god. (3) Paul's expression of dying and rising with Christ through baptism often appears to be like the ritual acts of the mystery religions by which the union with the god is achieved.[133] From these resemblances between the two Reitzenstein draws a conclusion that Paul's language, images, and concepts are all borrowed from the hellenistic mystery religions.[134] To support this conclusion he claims that Paul, after his first instruction by a hellenistic Christian, went into the Arabian territory without further investigation of the life of Jesus, joined a hellenistic community of a mystery religion there, and was greatly influenced by their language and cultus.[135]

Reitzenstein's conclusion is very presumptuous for a number of reasons: (1) There are no reliable sources for Paul's life in the Arabian desert. It is impossible to know for certain what Paul did there or whether he stayed there for those two years. (2) It is most unlikely that Paul, after becoming a Christian, joined a community of a hellenistic mystery religion. (3) The similarities of language between the two are somewhat superficial and do not necessarily mean an influence of one upon the other.[136] As Kennedy rightly points out, many of the mystery conceptions and terms in which they are set forth spring directly from the common strain of mysticism which seems to be

---

D. Betz, *The Greek Magical Papyri* (Chicago: University Press, 1986) and Marvin W. Meyer, ed. and trans., *The "Mithras Liturgy"* (Missoula, MT: Scholars, 1976).

Good secondary sources on the mystery religions include Kennedy, *Mystery-Religions*; Machen, *Origin*; Wikenhauser, *Pauline Mysticism*, especially 163-242; M. J. Vermaseren, *Mithras: the Secret God*, trans. Therese and Vincent Megaw (New York: Barnes & Noble, 1963); Friedrich Solmsen, *Isis among the Greeks and Romans* (Cambridge, MA: Harvard University Press, 1979); Sarolta A. Takács, *Isis and Sarapis in the Roman World* (Leiden: E. J. Brill, 1995); Sharon Kelly Heyob, *The Cult of Isis among Women in the Graeco-Roman World* (Leiden: E. J. Brill, 1975); Walter Burkert, *Ancient Mystery Cults* (Cambridge, MA: Harvard University Press, 1987).

[133]See Weiss, *Primitive Christianity*, 2:520 and Bousset, *Kyrios Christos*, 188-200. Cf. Kennedy, *Paul and Mystery-Religions*, 90-92 and Machen, *Origin*, 234-36, 280-90.

[134]Reitzenstein, *Mystery-Religions*, 536.

[135]Ibid. However, see Machen, *Origin*, 73, 256-61.

[136]See Machen, *Origin*, 262-73,

everywhere latent in humanity.[137]   Moreover, for one religious form to influence another, it is necessary that the first should be earlier or at least contemporaneous with the second.   Most literary sources of the mystery religions, however, are later products than Paul's letters, although it is not impossible that they contain some earlier traditions.[138]   It is, therefore, a questionable hypothesis to ascribe to Paul any direct literary acquaintance with mystery ideas.[139]   (4) If Paul adopted the language and the concepts of the hellenistic mystery religions, it is strange that neither the primitive Jerusalem Christianity nor the immediately following generations rejected Paul's teaching as foreign to it.[140]   Finally, (5) various passages in Paul's letters strongly indicate that Paul is not the kind of person who would syncretize Christianity with pagan mystery religions.[141]

Despite the similarities in expressions, there are profound conceptional differences between Paul and the mystery religions: (1) The pantheistic conception of god that is often found in the mystery religions is foreign to Paul.[142]   Moreover, while the gods of the mystery religions were originally

---

[137]Kennedy, *Paul and Mystery-Religions*, 120. Also, see Prat, *Theology*, 2:386.

[138]See Machen, *Origin*, 237-43. See also Prat, *Theology*, 2:387, who argues that Mithras acquired a place in the Roman pantheon under Commodus and attained his highest prominence in the third century. In A.D. 248, Origen (*Contra Celsum*, 4.23) treats Mithraism as an obscure sect and a negligible quantity. Organized in little autonomous groups of at most a hundred adherents, it never aimed at universality. Therefore, it cannot be claimed with any degree of probability that Paul borrowed anything from it. The Magical Papyri are not earlier than the third or fourth century, although they probably contain more ancient documents. As for the Hermetic Books, they are also, in their present form, of the fourth century, or, at the earliest, of the third.

[139]See Kennedy, *Paul and Mystery-Religions*, 118; Whiteley, *Theology*, 2; Davies, *Paul and Rabbinic Judaism*, 89-90; and Wikenhauser, *Mysticism*, 169-70.

[140]According to Scott, *Christianity*, 125, the only exceptions are the Didache, Ignatius, and Justin Martyr, and they are not weighty. See Schweitzer, *Mysticism*, 39 and Davies, *Paul and Rabbinic Judaism*, 90.

[141]See Gal. 1:6-12, Phil. 3:5, Col. 2:8, 1 Cor. 10:21-22, and 2 Cor. 6:14-16.

[142]Cf. Arthur Darby Nock, *Early Gentile Christianity and Its Hellenistic Background* (New York: Harper, 1964), 55-65, 109-22; idem, "Hellenistic Mysteries and Christian Sacraments," in *Essays on Religion and the Ancient World*, vol. 2 (Oxford: Clarendon, 1972), 791-820; Schweitzer, *Mysticism*, 15-16. For example, a pantheistic idea is clearly present in the following statement of Tat, a mystic (see Scott, Libellus XIII, *Hermetica*, 247): "Father, God has made me a new being, and I perceive things now, not with bodily eyesight, but by the working of mind . . . . I see myself to be the All. I am in heaven and in earth, in water and in air; I am in beasts and plants; I am a babe in the womb, and one that is not yet conceived, and one that has been born; I am present everywhere."

"mythological personifications of the processes of vegetation,"[143] Paul's Christ is firmly rooted in history. Christ is the same Jesus who actually lived, died, and rose again.[144]   (2) Deification through union with the god, the ultimate goal of the mystery religions, is absolutely unthinkable for Paul. (3) While union with the god in the mystery religions is strictly individualistic, Paul's conception of "being in Christ" has a corporate aspect.[145]   (4) While in the mystery religions the initiates repeat the experience of the god through rites, Paul does not regard baptism as an imitative representation. Finally, (5) unlike that of the mystery religions, Paul's conception of dying and rising with Christ has eschatological and ethical connotations.[146]

The question is not whether Paul was acquainted with the hellenistic mystery religions or not, but whether and how far he was influenced by them. Since Paul lived and taught his gospel in a world where the mystery religions were present, he might have had a good knowledge of the mysteries of Eleusis, Isis, Osiris, Cybele and Attis, and even the cult of Mithras, if they existed at the time of Paul. He might have even used terms and expressions which were also used by the mystery religions. For the reasons detailed above, however, it is very improbable that Paul intentionally and deliberately borrowed the expressions and concepts of pagan mystery religions.[147]

Jewish Apocalyptic Writings

Vigorously rejecting Reitzenstein's claim, A. Schweitzer argues that Paul's understanding of the believer's being in Christ originated in the concept of the solidarity of the Elect with the Messiah and with one another often found in Jewish apocalyptic writings.[148] According to Schweizer, both Jesus and Paul shared this concept, and from it Paul developed the mystical "body of Christ" and taught that believers became a part of this corporate

---

[143]See Kennedy, *Mystery-Religions*, 213 and Machen, *Origin*, 235.

[144]See 1 Cor. 15:3-8 and Col. 3:1, 4.

[145]See Schweitzer, *Mysticism*, 23; Davies, *Paul and Rabbinic Judaism*, 87, 90; and Best, *One Body*, 25-30.

[146]See Robert C. Tannehill, *Dying and Rising with Christ: A Study in Pauline Theology* (Berlin: Verlag Alfred Töpelmann, 1966), who rightly points out the eschatological connotation of "dying and rising with Christ."

[147]See Prat, *Theology*, 2:388-89 and Davies, *Paul and Rabbinic Judaism*, 98.

[148]A few evidences that Schweitzer cites for the Messianic community include Dan. 7:27, *1 Enoch* 38:1-5, 62:7-8, 14-15, and *4 Ezra* 9:38-10:57.

body by means of water baptism in a literal sacramentalist sense.[149] He then argues that the "body of Christ" as the common denominator prompted all other Pauline expressions such as "in Christ," "with Christ," "into Christ," and "to put on Christ."[150] The expression "being-in-Christ" is, therefore, according to Schweitzer, "merely a brachyology for being partakers in the Mystical Body of Christ."[151] Concerning the most frequent occurrences of "being-in-Christ" in Paul's letters, Schweitzer comments:

> Being-in-Christ" is therefore the commonest, but not the most appropriate expression for union with Christ. It becomes the most usual, not only because of its shortness but because of the facility which it offers for forming antitheses with the analogous expressions "in the body," "in the flesh," "in sin," and "in the spirit," and thus providing the mystical theory with a series of neat equations.[152]

Schweitzer's attempt to find a common conception behind variously related expressions in Paul is definitely an advance beyond Reitzenstein, for it is usually a conception that prompts an expression rather than the reverse. His view, however, poses several problems: (1) It seems to force everything into a predefined eschatological framework that is built upon a still debatable concept of the solidarity of the Elect with the Messiah.[153] (2) Although the "body of Christ" may well express the concept of solidarity, perhaps even the solidarity of the predestined Elect with the Messiah and with one another, his attempt to explain the "body of Christ" from this conception and, further, the "being in Christ" from the "body of Christ" involves too many assumptions.[154] (3) His sacramentalist view of solidarity of the Elect with Christ is

---

[149]Schweitzer, *Mysticism*, 117.

[150]Ibid., 122.

[151]Ibid., 122-23.

[152]Ibid., 123.

[153]It is still debatable whether the solidarity of the Elect with the Messiah in the apocalyptic writings denotes a corporate conception of the Messiah or simply a racial solidarity among them. In order to produce a corporate conception of the Messiah from the apocalyptic writings and to explain Paul's underlying conception of Christ, one must necessarily identify the "one like unto a son of man" (Dan. 7:13), who is also the "Saints of the Most High" (Dan. 7:18, 22, 27), with the "Son of Man" in *1 Enoch* (38:1-5, 62:7, 8, 14, 15) and in the Synoptics (Matt. 9:6, 26:64). Cf. T. W. Manson, *The Teaching of Jesus*, 2nd ed. (Cambridge: Cambridge University Press, 1935), 171-236, who argues in this way.

[154]See Percy, *Leib Christi*, 43-45, who explains the "body of Christ" from the "being in Christ."

too realistic and too physical.[155]   Finally, (4) apart from parts of 1 Enoch, which were found at Qumran, it is probable that most, if not all, extant Jewish apocalyptic pseudepigrapha that Schweitzer cites are post-Pauline.[156]

The Old Testament and the Teachings of Jesus

Others such as J. G. Machen, W. D. Davies, and E. E. Ellis find the background of Paul's concept in the Old Testament as it was interpreted and mediated through the teachings of Jesus and through the apostolic traditions.[157]   Ellis, for example, argues that the ἐν Χριστῷ and the "body of Christ" concepts are closely related both to the Adam-Christ typology and to the "stone-temple" imagery that are ultimately rooted in the teachings of Jesus.[158]   He, however, admits: "Which type is more basic is a moot point. The inter-relation of these expressions probably points to their development as one comprehensive idea."[159]   He thinks that the underlying idea is the corporate dimension of human existence, a concept that both Jesus and the other New Testament writers share and of which the primary background is found in the Old Testament concept of man both as an individual and as a corporate person.[160]   Paul's expression ἐν Χριστῷ denotes his understanding of Christ as a corporate person in whom believers exist.   In Christ they form a corporate body, made up of individual believers who have become part of the resurrection reality.   This body is also called a new creation.   To express this corporate dimension of the new creation, Ellis argues, Paul employs expressions such as being in Christ or in the Spirit, and he designates the church as the body of Christ.[161]

Paul describes the church not only as the body of Christ but also as the true Israel or the remnant, a concept that again is not Paul's own invention but

---

[155]See Schweitzer, *Mysticism*, 117, 127-29.

[156]See E. Earle Ellis, "New Testament Teaching on Hell," in *The Reader Must Understand: Eschatology in Bible and Theology*, ed. K. E. Brower and M. W. Elliott (Leicester, UK: Apollos, 1997), 205-06.

[157]See Machen, *Origin*; Davies, *Paul and Rabbinic Judaism*; Ellis, *Paul's Use*, 85-113; idem, "Jesus' Use of the Old Testament and the Genesis of New Testament Theology," *BBR* 3 (1993): 59-75; idem, *Old Testament*, 110-16; and also Shedd, *Man in Community*.

[158]Ellis, *Paul's Use of the OT*, 89-98.

[159]Ibid., 95, n. 7.

[160]Ellis, *Pauline Theology*, 8-10.

[161]Ibid., 8.

is rooted in the teaching of Jesus.[162] At this point, Davies claims that as the community of Israel is a unity of past, present, and future, so the new (or true) Israel is a unity of all believers, past, present, and future.[163] He then explains Paul's concept of the dying and rising with Christ by using the analogy of the Passover: As participation in the Passover signified the entry into the Old Israel, so the dying and rising with Christ marks the entry into the new (or true) Israel.[164] To support this argument Davies quotes a few passages from the Haggadah and the Old Testament in which all subsequent generations are regarded as having participated in the Passover in Egypt, having stood at the foot of Sinai, and having experienced the events of the Exodus and of the Sinai covenant.[165] From such passages Davies deduces: "The external facts of [past] history have to become living, present realities: the realization of one's own personal participation, as it were, in these external acts of history *ipso facto* makes one a member of the nation."[166] Now, by pointing to the underlying Exodus motif in Paul's letters,[167] Davies concludes that the concept of participation in the Passover serves as the underlying assumption for Paul's expression "dying and rising with Christ." He states:

> Paul's conception of the dying and rising with Christ by which the Christian individual re-enacts in his own experience the life of Christ as it were, is probably derived from the same world of thought as is indicated for us in the liturgy of the Passover, where the historical event calls for personal appropriation by the individual Israelite, i.e. just as the true Jew is he who has made the history of his nation his own history, so the Christian is he who has made the history of Christ his own.[168]

Although this study intends to analyze their claims in a greater detail in subsequent chapters, their explanation deserves a couple of preliminary comments: (1) It strives to demonstrate a continuity from the Old Testament through the teachings of Jesus and through the apostolic traditions to Paul.

---

[162]Ibid., 87, 94-95, 136-39; Davies, *Paul and Rabbinic Judaism*, 100-01; Shedd, *Man in Community*, 127-36.

[163]Davies, *Paul and Rabbinic Judaism*, 108.

[164]Ibid., 102.

[165]*Pesaḥ.* 10:6, in *The Mishnah*, trans. Herbert Danby (Oxford: Oxford University Press, 1933), 151. Cf. Joshua 24, Deut. 26:5-6, Gen. 17:14, Deut. 31:16, 20, Jer. 11:10, and 31:33. A. A. Green, trans. and ed., *The Revised Hagada* (New York: Bloch, 1897), 27, 29, 31, 51.

[166]Davies, *Paul and Rabbinic Judaism*, 104.

[167]For example, see 1 Cor. 5:6-8, 10:1-5, 15:20, and 2 Cor. 3:1-11.

[168]Davies, *Paul and Rabbinic Judaism*, 107.

This is an important step forward for understanding Paul's theology from a proper perspective because Paul obviously shares some common conceptions with other New Testament writers, refers to the teachings of Jesus, and directly quotes or alludes to Old Testament passages. (2) It also endeavors to find a common idea which might have prompted Paul's various expressions, a conception that is, according to them, the corporate dimension of human existence.

The explanation of possible backgrounds of Paul's expressions such as "being in Christ (ἐν Χριστῷ)," "baptism into Christ (εἰς Χριστόν)," and "dying and rising with Christ (σὺν Χριστῷ)" invites some tentative conclusions at this point: (1) Although Paul and the mystery religion texts have some common expressions, it is most unlikely that Paul is dependent on their language, images, and concepts. (2) Paul and the apocalyptic writings may share some common concepts, but it is improbable that Paul was directly influenced by the apocalyptic writings. (3) Paul seems to share some common expressions and concepts with Jesus and other New Testament writers. Finally, (4) there seems to be a more basic conception that might have prompted Paul's various expressions. Whether this basic conception is the corporate dimension of human existence as Ellis argues will be further investigated.

CHAPTER 2

ADAM AND CHRIST

Paul's Adam christology has been the subject of much scholarly debate.[1] The debate basically deals with three issues: (1) the occurrence of Adam in Paul's letters, (2) the role of Adam in Paul's theology, and (3) the sources from which Paul possibly derived his idea. Although explicit reference to Adam and Christ occurs only in 1 Cor. 15:20-28, 42-49, and Rom. 5:12-21, implicit references occur in several other passages.[2] Paul clearly states in Rom. 5:14 that Adam is a "type (τύπος) of the one to come" and in 1 Cor. 15:45 that Christ is "the last (ἔσχατος) Adam." In what sense is Adam a type of the one to come and Christ the last Adam? What part does Adam play in these passages and in Paul's theology as whole? The scholarly opinion varies from treating Paul's Adam as something peripheral to insisting on its absolute centrality. The opinions about the origin of Paul's Adam christology are also diverse. The following study examines some of these issues. The primary interest of the study is, however, in investigating whether Paul's Adam christology has any implication for his understanding of man as a corporate being. Scroggs has convincingly argued that Paul's Adam christology is "primarily directed toward illuminating and assuring the

---

[1]A few significant works on the subject include Davies, *Paul and Rabbinic Judaism*; Jacob Jervell, *Imago Dei: Gen. 1.26f. im Spätjudentum, in der Gnosis und in den paulinischen Briefen* (Göttingen: Vandenhoeck & Ruprecht, 1960); Barrett, *First Adam to Last*; Egon Brandenburger, *Adam und Christus: Exegetisch-religionsgeschichtliche Untersuchung zu Röm. 5.12-21 (1 Kor. 15)*, Wissenschaftliche Monographien zum Alten und Neuen Testament 7 (Neukirchen: Neukirchener, 1962); Robin Scroggs, *The Last Adam: A Study in Pauline Anthropology* (Philadelphia: Fortress, 1966); and A. J. M. Wedderburn, "Adam and Christ: An Investigation into the Background of 1 Corinthians xv and Romans v 12-21" (Ph.D. diss., University of Cambridge, 1970).

[2]Such passages include Phil. 2:5-11, Col. 1:15-20, 3:9-10, Rom. 1:18-32, and Eph. 4:22-24.

Christian's hope of eschatological humanity." In this respect, he argues, Paul is basically concerned with anthropology when he speaks of the first and the last Adam.[3] If so, the study of Paul's Adam christology will reveal his understanding not only of Christ but also of man generally. Since Paul's Adam christology presupposes the Adam-Christ typology, the following study discusses his typology first.

Paul's Adam-Christ Typology

Typology served as an important exegetical principle not only for Paul but also for other New Testament writers.[4] They employed typology with a conviction that in God's salvation history His acts in the Old Testament corresponded to those in the New Testament.[5] Accordingly, they viewed certain Old Testament persons, institutions, and events as shadows, types, or promises for the New Testament realities. The New Testament typology

---

[3]Scroggs, *Last Adam*, 59, 111. See also Seyoon Kim, *The Origin of Paul's Gospel*, 2nd ed. (Tübingen: J. C. B. Mohr, 1984), 266 and Ziesler, *Pauline Christianity*, 50-51.

[4]Leonhard Goppelt, *Typos: The Typological Interpretation of the Old Testament in the New*, trans. Donald H. Madvig (Grand Rapids: Eerdmans, 1982), 237, claims: "The typological approach is most important for us as a central theological interpretation of the present salvation in Paul's writings and in the rest of the NT." Ellis, *Old Testament*, 105, also says: "Typological interpretation . . . became, in early Christianity, a basic key by which the Scriptures were understood."

For discussions of the New Testament typology, see Goppelt, *Typos*; idem, "τύπος," in TDNT, 8:246-59; Ellis, *Old Testament*, 105-09; idem, *Paul's Use*, 126-35; idem, *Prophecy and Hermeneutic in Early Christianity: New Testament Essays* (Tübingen: J. C. B. Mohr, 1978), 165-69; David L. Baker, *Two Testaments, One Bible: A Study of Some Modern Solutions to the Theological Problem of the Relationship between the Old and New Testaments*, rev. ed. (Downers Grove, IL: InterVarsity, 1977), 183-99, 240-61; Richard T. France, *Jesus and the Old Testament* (London: Tyndale, 1971), 38-80; Walter Eichrodt, "Is Typological Exegesis an Appropriate Method?" in *Essays on Old Testament Hermeneutics*, ed. C. Westermann (Richmond, VA: John Knox, 1963), 224-45; and Richard M. Davidson, *Typology in Scripture: A Study of Hermeneutical ΤΥΠΟΣ Structures* (Berrien Springs, MI: Andrews University Press, 1981), 15-93, where he provides a comprehensive survey of literature on the subject.

[5]Ellis, *Paul's Use*, 127-28.

reveals certain characteristics:[6] (1) Unlike allegory, it is firmly grounded in history.[7] The "type" always has its own historical value, although its real significance is typologically revealed in the "anti-type" or fulfillment.[8] (2) It is derived mostly from the creation or from the covenant with Israel.[9] For example, the creation is clearly in view when Adam is presented as "a type of the one to come" and the age to come is described in terms of Paradise or of a new creation.[10] The covenant is, however, in the background when the persons, events, and institutions of the Exodus are compared to or contrasted with the New Testament realities.[11] Ellis points out, however, that since the "new covenant" associated with Jesus' death is closely related to the new

---

[6]For what follows, see Goppelt, *Typos*, 16-17, 199-202, 218-23, 237; Ellis, *Paul's Use*, 127-28; idem, *Prophecy and Hermeneutic*, 165-69; idem, *Old Testament*, 105-09; idem, "Biblical Interpretation in the New Testament Church," in *Mikra: Text, Translation, Reading and Interpretation of the Hebrew Bible in Ancient Judaism and Early Christianity*, ed. Martin Jan Mulder (Philadelphia: Fortress, 1988), 713-16; Baker, *Two Testaments*, 185-99; Eichrodt, "Typological Exegesis," 225-31; Francis Foulkes, *Acts of God: A Study of the Basis of Typology in the Old Testament* (London: Tyndale, 1958), 34-40; Davidson, *Typology*, 397-408; and David Alan Sapp, "An Introduction to Adam Christology in Paul: A History of Interpretation, the Jewish Background, and an Exegesis of Romans 5:12-21" (Ph.D. diss., Southwestern Baptist Theological Seminary, 1990), 176-82.

[7]For the significance of the historicity of Adam for Paul's typology, see J. P. Versteeg, *Is Adam a "Teaching Model" in the New Testament?: An Examination of One of the Central Points in the Views of H. M. Kuitert and Others*, trans. Richard B. Gaffin (Nutley, NJ: Presbyterian and Reformed, 1977), 1-67.

[8]See Ellis, *Paul's Use*, 128; Richard C. Oudersluys, "Paul's Use of the Adam Typology," *RR* 13 (May 1960): 8; G. R. Osborne, "Type," in *International Standard Bible Encyclopedia* 4 (1988), 930-32; and Versteeg, *Adam*, 10-12. But see Gerhard von Rad, *Old Testament Theology*, vol. 2, *The Theology of Israel's Prophetic Traditions*, trans. D. M. G. Stalker (New York: Harper & Row, 1965), 357-87 (esp. 364-66) and Walther Eichrodt, *Theology of the Old Testament*, vol. 1, trans. J. A. Baker (Philadelphia: Westminster, 1961), 28-33.

[9]Ellis, *Old Testament*, 106-08; idem, *Paul's Use*, 129-35.

[10]Rom. 5:14, Luke 3:22, 38, Rev. 2:7, 22:2; cf. Luke 23:43, 1 Cor. 15:21-22, 45-46.

[11]Paul specifically writes that the Exodus events were intended as "types" (τύποι) for us and "were written down for our admonition, upon whom the end of the ages has come" (1·Cor. 10:6). Ellis, *Paul's Use*, 130, claims that for Paul the Exodus covenant is built upon the idea of two covenants, Abrahamic and Sinaitic, which Paul draws from the Sarah-Hagar 'allegory' (cf. Gal. 4:22-31).

creation associated with his resurrection, these "two typologies may be closely interwined."[12] (3) An Old Testament type stands not only in positive correspondence but also in contrast to the New Testament reality. For example, Adam stands in correspondence to Christ in both being the "son of God" and the head of the race. In contrast, however, Adam brings sin and death to all men while Christ brings righteousness and eternal life.[13] Likewise, while the Abrahamic covenant stands in continuity with the "new covenant," the "old covenant" of Sinai stands in contrast. Thus, the ritual laws from Sinai were only "a shadow of what was to come (σκιὰ τῶν μελλόντων)."[14] The Exodus "Passover lamb" was a type of Jesus who in his sacrificial death brought the "old covenant" of Sinai to its end (or fulfillment) and established a new covenant.[15] (4) The antitype does not merely repeat or restore the type, but often intensifies and escalates its meaning. For the New Testament writers, therefore, Christ is not simply a new prophet, priest, or king, but one greater than Jonah, the temple, and Solomon.[16]

Paul's Adam-Christ typology shares these characteristics:[17] (1) It is firmly grounded in history. (2) When Paul speaks of Adam, he explicitly refers to the creation accounts in Genesis. In this respect, the Adam-Christ typology is a typical example of the creation typology. (3) Adam and Christ stand both in correspondence and in contrast. Various introductory formulas that Paul employs in Rom. 5:12-21 and 1 Cor. 15:22, and a series of contrasts

---

[12]Ellis, *Old Testament*, 107-08.

[13]Rom. 5:12-21, 1 Cor. 15:20-28, 45-49; cf. Luke 3:22, 38.

[14]Col. 2:16-17, Heb. 8:5, 10:1.

[15]John 1:19, 1 Pet. 1:19, Heb. 9:12, Gal. 3:24-25, 4:2, 2 Cor. 3:1-18. Ellis, *Paul's Use*, 131, points out more examples of the covenant typology: "As those redeemed by Moses were baptized εἰς τὸν Μωϋσῆν in the cloud and sea, so those redeemed in Christ's death and resurrection are baptized εἰς Χριστὸν (1 Cor. 10:3; cf. Rom. 6:3, 1 Cor. 1:30, Gal. 3:27, Eph. 1:14, 4:30). The Old Covenant like the New had a food and drink in which Christ was (typically) present (1 Cor. 10:4; cf. John 6:31f). As the Old Covenant had a Law written in stone, so the New Covenant had a Torah, an ἐπιστολὴ Χριστοῦ, written on men's hearts (2 Cor. 3:3). Under the Old Covenant there was a tabernacle—and later a temple--in which the 'Presence' or She-kinah of God dwelt and where sacrifices for sin were offered; in the New Covenant Christ and His Church are the temple and Christ's Cross the altar of sacrifice."

[16]Mark 14:58, Matt. 12:6, 41-42, John 2:19-21.

[17]For discussion of the characteristics of Pauline typology, see Goppelt, *Typos*, 218-23 and Ellis, *Paul's Use*, 129-34.

between Adam and Christ in 1 Cor. 15:45-49 demonstrate this well. Finally, (4) as clearly seen in Romans 5, the antitype (Christ) surpasses the type (Adam).[18] With these characteristics in mind, a number of passages in which Paul explicitly or implicitly refers to Adam and Christ are analyzed below.

Analysis of Paul's Usage

Explicit Passages

1 Cor. 15:20-28

1 Corinthians 15 is a "self-contained treatise on the resurrection of the dead."[19] It is Paul's response to some Corinthians who say, "there is no resurrection of the dead" (v. 12).[20] In order to correct their misunderstanding, Paul first reminds them of the Gospel he preached (vv. 1-2). The Gospel that he preached to them was indeed about the death, burial, and resurrection of

---

[18]Rom. 5:15b, 20b.

[19]So, Hans Conzelmann, *A Commentary on the First Epistle to the Corinthians*, ed. George W. MacRae, trans. James W. Leitch (Philadelphia: Fortress, 1975), 249 and Martinus C. de Boer, *The Defeat of Death: Apocalyptic Eschatology in 1 Corinthians 15 and Romans 5*, Journal for the Study of the New Testament Supplement Series 22 (Sheffield: Sheffield Academic, 1988), 93.

[20]The identification of the Corinthian deniers and the nature of their belief have been much debated. The opinions can be grouped under the following headings: (1) Some Corinthians did not believe in resurrection at all. (2) They believed that only those alive at the Parousia would participate in resurrection, but not those who died prior to the Parousia. (3) They denied the notion of a bodily resurrection (cf. 6:12-20; 15:35-44). (4) They, like the false teachers of 2 Tim. 2:18, were spiritual enthusiasts with a gnostic anthropology who believed that the resurrection of the dead had already taken place. Although it is difficult to know the exact nature of their belief, it is unlikely that they rejected any resurrection of the dead because the Corinthians obviously accepted the resurrection of Christ. To identify the Corinthian deniers with the false teachers in 2 Tim. 2:18 is also not warranted. Since Paul focuses on the bodily resurrection of the dead at the Parousia, it is probable that they rejected the future (bodily) resurrection of the dead. For helpful summaries of the opinions, see J. H. Wilson, "The Corinthians Who Say There Is No Resurrection of the Dead," *ZNW* 59 (1968): 90-107; K. A. Plank, "Resurrection Theology: The Corinthian Controversy Re-examined," *PRS* 8 (Spring 1981), 41-54; and de Boer, *Defeat of Death*, 96-7.

Christ (vv. 3-11). Paul confirms the reality of the resurrection of Christ by mentioning the numerous resurrection appearances of Christ (vv. 5-8). He also reminds them of the terrible consequences that the denial of the resurrection of the dead will bring upon their faith (vv. 12-19). As he approaches the passage under consideration in which the Adam-Christ typology explicitly occurs (vv. 20-28), he emphatically proclaims that "Christ has indeed been raised from the dead as the first fruits (ἀπαρχή) of those who have fallen asleep" (v. 20). In a sense, this propositional statement, with the introduction of the word ἀπαρχή, provides an outline for the succeeding verses through verse 28. The resurrection of Christ not only confirms the reality of the resurrection of the dead but also points to the reality of the resurrection of believers, just as ἀπαρχή signifies the impending full harvest.[21] The resurrection of Christ is, therefore, only the beginning of what is yet to come in full, that is, the future resurrection of believers. In other words, the resurrection of the believer is "implicated in, dependent upon, and derivative from the resurrection of Christ."[22]

To amplify further and explain this unity between the resurrection of Christ and that of believers Paul employs the Adam-Christ typology (15:21-22):

v. 21 ἐπειδὴ γὰρ δι ἀνθρώπου θάνατος,
        καὶ δι ἀνθρώπου ἀνάστασις νεκρῶν.

v. 22 ὥσπερ γὰρ ἐν τῷ Ἀδὰμ πάντες ἀποθνήσκουσιν,
        οὕτως καὶ ἐν τῷ Χριστῷ πάντες ζῳοποιηθήσονται.

As seen in the layout of the Greek texts above, the Adam-Christ typology is set forth in a double parallelism, obviously the second one clarifying the first:[23] (1) The ἄνθρωποι of verse 21 are now identified as Adam and Christ.

---

[21]The term ἀπαρχή is undoubtedly derived from the Old Testament where it denotes the first portion of the crop (of flock) which is offered in thanksgiving to God (cf. Lev. 23:10-14). For discussion of the term ἀπαρχή, see G. Delling, "ἀπαρχή," in *TDNT*, 1:485; Robert Murray, "New Wine in Old Wineskins XII First Fruits," *ExpT* 86 (March 1975): 164-68; Conzelmann, *1 Corinthians*, 268; C. K. Barrett, *A Commentary on the First Epistle to the Corinthians*, Harper's New Testament Commentaries (New York: Harper & Row, 1968), 350-51; and de Boer, *Defeat of Death*, 109.

[22]Ellis, *Pauline Theology*, 33.

[23]See Gordon Fee, *The First Epistle to the Corinthians*, New International Commentary on the New Testament, ed. F. F. Bruce (Grand Rapids: Eerdmans,

(2) Verse 22 replaces the preposition διά with ἐν. In doing so, the ἐν Χριστῷ formula and the Adam-Christ typology are formally linked together. Since the preposition ἐν is clearly used here in a locative sense, πάντες must be understood as being in either ἐν Ἀδάμ or ἐν Χριστῷ.[24] (3) The term ἀποθνήσκουσιν corresponds to θάνατος and ζῳοποιηθήσονται to ἀνάστασις νεκρῶν. Finally, (4) the added factor in verse 22 is an indication of the relationship between "one man" and "all men": "For as in [one man] Adam all [men] die, so in [one man] Christ all [men] shall be made alive." The relationship between the resurrection of Christ and that of believers must be understood within this framework. Verses 21a and 22a, although chronologically earlier than Romans, theologically presuppose what is discussed in Romans 5:12-21, that is, Adam's sin and its consequence. Even though Paul does not specifically speak of Adam's sin in this passage, he is certainly dependent, as in Romans 5, on the Genesis accounts for his depiction of Adam.

1987), 749; Swee-Hwa Quek, "Adam and Christ according to Paul," in *Pauline Studies: Essays Presented to Professor F. F. Bruce on His 70th Birthday*, ed. Donald A. Hagner and Murray J. Harris (Grand Rapids: Eerdmans, 1980), 68; and Larry Kreitzer, "Christ and Second Adam in Paul," *CV* 32 (Spring-Summer 1989), 70.

[24]Although the first πάντες probably refers to the whole humanity, the second πάντες denotes only those who belong to Christ. The reasons are as follows: (1) Verse 23b specifies a particular group who will be raised at the parousia as οἱ τοῦ Χριστοῦ. (2) The universal salvation is contrary to the overall teaching of Paul. (3) The present position of πάντες after ἐν Ἀδάμ and ἐν Χριστῷ is probably for the purpose of creating a parallelism with verse 21. Therefore, as Ellis insists, the more accurate understanding of verse 22 would be: "As all who are in Adam die, so all who are in Christ will be made alive." See Ellis, *Pauline Theology*, 10. For a similar understanding, see Barrett, *1 Corinthians*, 352; Brandenburger, *Adam and Christus*, 72; W. V. Crockett, "Ultimate Restoration of All Mankind: 1 Corinthians 15:22," in *Studia Biblica 1978 III. Papers on Paul and Other New Testament Authors*, ed. E. A. Livingston (Sheffield: JSOT, 1980), 83-87; A. T. Robertson and Alfred Plummer, *A Critical and Exegetical Commentary on the First Epistle on St. Paul to the Corinthians*, International Critical Commentary, ed. Charles Augustus Briggs, Samuel Rolles Driver, and Alfred Plummer (Edinburgh: T. & T. Clark, 1914), 353; Raymond B. Brown, *Acts-1 Corinthians*, Broadman Bible Commentary (Nashville, TN: Broadman, 1970), 388; C. E. Hill, "Paul's Understanding of Christ's Kingdom in I Corinthians 15:20-28." *NovT* 30 (October 1988): 307; Fee, *1 Corinthians*, 750; and Scroggs, *Last Adam*, 83. Otherwise, see de Boer, *Defeat of Death*, 112-14.

Verse 23 simply states that there is an order (τάγμα) in the resurrection process:[25] ἀπαρχὴ Χριστός, ἔπειτα οἱ τοῦ Χριστοῦ ἐν τῇ παρουσίᾳ αὐτοῦ. The re-introduction of the word ἀπαρχή along with the temporal adverb ἔπειτα strongly indicates that there is a temporal gap between the resurrection of Christ and that of believers.[26]   Although the resurrection process has already begun with the resurrection of Christ, the resurrection of believers still awaits at the Parousia of the Lord. For Paul the Parousia of the Lord signifies the end (τὸ τέλος),[27] that is, the time when the Son hands over the kingdom to the Father and when the Son submits even himself to the Father in order that God may be πάντα ἐν πᾶσιν (v. 28). All the cosmic and soteriological events

---

[25]The word τάγμα can designate an orderly division, standing, or rank. See G. Delling, "τάγμα," in *TDNT*, 8:31-32 and Barrett, *From First Adam to Last*, 354.

[26]Because ἀπαρχή and ἔπειτα are immediately followed by another temporal adverb εἶτα and there is no verb in verse 24 in the Greek text, it is sometimes argued that τὸ τέλος should be understood as referring to the general resurrection of the dead who would thus constitute the third τάγμα. This understanding of τέλος is, however, rarely attested in Greek literature. See F. F. Bruce, *1 and 2 Corinthians*, New Century Bible Commentary (London: Oliphants, 1971), 146-47 and Hill, "Paul's Understanding," 309. For the use of τέλος, see G. Delling, "τέλος," in *TDNT*, 8:49-59. Cf. Hans Leitzmann, *An die Korinther* (Tübingen: J. C. B. Mohr, 1940), 80 and Johannes Weiss, *Der erste Korintherbrief* (Göttingen: Vandenhoeck & Ruprecht, 1977), 358, who argue otherwise.

[27]It is sometimes argued that because the temporal adverb εἶτα appears between παρουσία in verse 23b and τέλος in verse 24a, at Christ's coming he will reign for an unspecified length of time with all those who are in Christ. This reign supposedly corresponds to the millennium mentioned in Rev. 20:4-6. Although it is evident that there is an interval between the first and the second τάγμα, it is not certain from this verse whether there will be also an interval between the parousia and the end. The temporal adverb εἶτα can introduce either what is subsequent or what is immediately consequent (cf. Mark 8:25, John 13:5, 19:27, 20:27, 1 Cor. 15:5, 7, 1 Thess. 4:17, 1 Tim. 2:13, 3:10, and James 1:16). The sequence denoted by εἶτα is sometimes without a chronological reference at all (cf. Heb. 12:9). Thus, Brown, *Acts-1 Corinthians*, 389, states that "the only way to find a millennium in 1 Cor. 15:23-25 is to put it there." Similarly, Bruce, *1 and 2 Corinthians*, 147; Geerhardus Vos, *The Pauline Eschatology* (Grand Rapids: Eerdmans, 1952), 243; Robertson and Plummer, *1 Corinthians*, 354; and Hill, "Paul's Understanding," 309. Otherwise, Schweitzer, *Mysticism*, 88-89; Clarence Tuchker Craig, *The First Epistle to the Corinthians*, Interpreter's Bible (New York: Abingdon-Cokesbury, 1953), 237-38; and Wilber B. Wallis, "The Problem of an Intermediate Kingdom in 1 Corinthians 15:20-28," *JETS* 18 (Fall 1975): 229-42.

and processes described in verses 24b through 28 revolve around this end (τέλος), revealing what will have happened for the kingdom and dominion of Christ by the time of its arrival. Until this end, however, the Son must reign in order to subdue πάντα under his feet (v. 25). The πάντα includes all dominion, authority, power, and even the last enemy, death (v. 26).

Christ's reign until the end is described in terms of Ps. 110:1 and Ps. 8:6 (vv. 25, 27). Psalm 110, which is often called a "royal psalm," is cited or alluded to elsewhere in the New Testament to denote the present lordship of the exalted Christ.[28] Interestingly, Psalm 8, also cited elsewhere in the New Testament, reflects upon the creation account and the place of man in creation.[29] According to this Psalm, man is entrusted with dominion over all things. Paul, like the writer to the Hebrews (Heb. 2:9), applies the psalmist's language to Christ as the last Adam, the one who retrieved the situation which the first Adam lost.[30] This implies that the Adam-Christ typology is still in the background. When the subjection of πάντα is completed and the last enemy destroyed, Christ will have fully accomplished his redemptive work. Then comes the end (τέλος).

1 Cor. 15:42-49

After further defending the resurrection of the dead by mentioning the practice of baptism for the dead (15:29-34), Paul begins another major section of the chapter with hypothetical questions (15:35): "But someone may ask, 'How are the dead raised? With what kind of body will they come?'" Verses 36 through 57 are basically Paul's answers to these questions. Paul's answer involves (1) the analogy of nature (15:36-41), (2) a transitional summary statement that leads into the Adam-Christ typology (15:42-44), and (3) the Adam-Christ typology (15:45-49).

The analogy of nature is drawn from plants (15:37-38), animals (15:39), and planets (15:40-41). By this analogy Paul basically argues (1) that there is difference between what is sown in the ground (seed) and what is raised from it (plant), (2) that God gives a different kind of body to different species as He chooses, and (3) that there are different kinds of bodies and degrees of glory

---

[28]Matt. 22:44 (Ps. 110:1), Heb. 5:6 (Ps. 110:4).
[29]Matt. 21:16 (Ps. 8:2), Heb. 2:6-8 (Ps. 8:4-6).
[30]Bruce, *1 and 2 Corinthians*, 147.

of the body. As the conjunction οὕτως καί in verse 42 indicates, Paul now applies what is made obvious by the analogy of nature to explaining the resurrection of the dead: οὕτως καὶ ἀνάστασις τῶν νεκρῶν. The nature of the resurrection of the dead is similar to the growth of the seed in that the body (or plant) that arises from death is something different from the body (or seed) which was initially placed into the ground. What is sown is perishable, in dishonor, and in weakness, but what is raised is imperishable, in glory, and in power (15:42b-43). Paul's argument reaches its climax and provides a transition in verse 44 as he introduces a contrast between the "soulish body" (σῶμα ψυχικόν)[31] and the "spiritual body" (σῶμα πνευματικόν) upon which the rest of the argument (15:45-49) is founded.[32] Since Paul has demonstrated the existence of more than one kind of σῶμα, he can readily argue for the existence of another kind of σῶμα (15:44b): "If there is a soulish body, there is also a spiritual body."

To explain the difference that exists between these two σώματα, Paul once more turns to the Adam-Christ typology (15:45-49).

(Gen. 2:7b LXX)
ἐγένετο ὁ ἄνθρωπος εἰς ψυχὴν ζῶσαν.

(1 Cor. 15:45-49)
45a. ἐγένετο ὁ πρῶτος ἄνθρωπος Ἀδὰμ εἰς ψυχὴν ζῶσαν.
45b.   ὁ ἔσχατος Ἀδὰμ   εἰς πνεῦμα ζῳοποιοῦν.

46a ἀλλ᾽ οὐ πρῶτον τὸ πνευματικὸν,
46b ἀλλὰ τὸ ψυχικόν, ἔπειτα τὸ πνευματικόν.

---

[31]The phrase σῶμα ψυχικόν is often translated as "physical body." This translation, however, prompts an unneccessary contrast between "physical" and "spiritual" in a sense of Platonic dualist understanding of the nature of man. The better translation is, therefore, either "soulish body" or "natural body."

[32]Bultmann, *Theology*, 1:204, argues that Paul is here using the adjective ψυχικόν and πνευματικόν in a gnostic sense, but Scroggs, *Last Adam*, 85, n. 27, insists that these terms are "not foreign to an apocalyptic thinking Jew who understood man apart from the eschatological gift of the Spirit to be a distorted being, ignorant of the secret counsels of God." He thus claims that σῶμα ψυχικόν is the distorted human existence of every man after the fall and σῶμα πνευματικόν the new humanity seized by the Spirit. See also Robinson, *Body*, 20, 32, 80.

47a   ὁ πρῶτος ἄνθρωπος ἐκ γῆς χοϊκός,
47b   ὁ δεύτερος ἄνθρωπος ἐξ οὐρανοῦ.

48a   οἷος ὁ κοϊκός   τοιοῦτοι καὶ οἱ χοϊκοί,
48b καὶ οἷος ὁ ἐπουράνιος τοιοῦτοι καὶ οἱ ἐπουράνιοι.

49a καὶ καθὼς ἐφορέσαμεν   τὴν εἰκόνα τοῦ χοϊκοῦ,
49b   φορέσομεν και τὴν εἰκόνα τοῦ ἐπουρανίου.

He establishes the basis for the contrast between Adam and Christ by quoting Gen. 2:7 (15:45). His quotation is, however, quite free and the second half is entirely missing from the Old Testament text. The purpose of adding πρῶτος and Ἀδάμ is probably to set up a typological contrast with the last (ἔσχατος) Adam, Christ. The addition of the second half, ὁ ἔσχατος Ἀδάμ εἰς πνεῦμα ζῳοποιοῦν, is probably Paul's haggadic midrash based on Gen. 2:7.[33] Whereas the first man Adam is a ψυχή ζῶσα, the last Adam is a πνεῦμα ζῳοποιοῦν. Interestingly, in this verse the contrast is made not between σῶμα and ψυχή (or πνεῦμα), as one would naturally expect if Paul is thinking in terms of a Platonic dualist anthropology, but it is made between ψυχή and πνεῦμα. This implies that when Paul describes Christ as πνεῦμα, he does not think of the disembodied existence of Christ. He simply indicates that while the first man is animated by ψυχή, the last Adam is animated by πνεῦμα.[34] The Adam-Christ typology in verse 45, therefore, describes the two σώματα already mentioned in verse 44 by further clarifying the meaning of ψυχικόν and πνευματικόν. This fact is supported also by verse 46 in which Paul emphasizes the temporal sequence of τὸ ψυχικόν and τὸ πνευματικόν. Significantly, Paul here uses the two adjectives ψυχικόν and πνευματικόν not in the masculine gender, as if they refer to two men, but in the neuter. This indicates that he is still thinking of two σώματα.[35] If so, the temporal

---

[33]Quek, "Adam and Christ," 69; Scroggs, *Last Adam*, 86-87. For discussion of midrash as an exegetical method utilized by the New Testament writers, see Ellis, *Old Testament*, 91-101.

[34]See Conzelmann, *1 Corinthians*, 283; Barrett, *First Adam to Last*, 74; Davies, *Paul and Rabbinic Judaism*, 57; Ellis, "Sōma," 142; Bultmann, *Theology*, 1:203-09; Robinson, *Doctrine of Man*, 109-11; Stacey, *Pauline View of Man*, 146-50; and Robinson, *Body*, 80.

[35]Barrett, *First Adam to Last*, 75; idem, "The Significance of the Adam-Christ Typology for the Resurrection of the Dead: 1 Co 15, 20-22. 45-49," in *Résurrection*

sequence probably refers to the order of two σώματα, that is, two kinds of human existence. In a sense this sequence is already implied in verse 36 where Paul indicates the necessity of death of the seed (σῶμα ψυχικόν) before it rises to life (σῶμα πνευματικόν). In the following verse (15:47) Paul contrasts the two men, Adam and Christ, who represent the two σώματα, by referring again to Gen. 2:7: ὁ πρῶτος ἄνθρωπος ἐκ γῆς χοϊκός, ὁ δεύτερος ἄνθρωπος ἐξ οὐρανοῦ. The word χοῦς suggests ἐπουράνιος as its counterpart. The first man was "out of the earth" (ἐκ γῆς) and its counterpart, the second man, is "out of heaven" (ἐξ οὐρανοῦ). In the last two verses (15:48-49) Paul identifies Adam and Christ with their respective followers. As those who are of dust share the nature of the first man Adam who is also of dust, so those who are of heaven share that of the last or second man Christ who is of heaven. The believers who once bore the image of the man of dust now bear the image of the one of heaven (τοῦ ἐπουρανίου).[36]

In conclusion, Paul describes the nature of the resurrection body (σῶμα πνευματικόν), in the framework of the Adam-Christ typology, by a series of contrasts with the present, soulish body (σῶμα ψυχικόν) in Adam. The contrasts between the two can be summarized as follows:

the nature of the soulish body[37]	the nature of the resurrection body
perishable (ἐν φθορᾷ)	imperishable (ἐν ἀφθαρσίᾳ)
in dishonor (ἐν ἀτιμίᾳ)	in glory (ἐν δόξῃ)
in weakness (ἐν ἀσθενείᾳ)	in power (ἐν δυνάμει)
soulish body (σῶμα ψυχικόν)	spiritual body (σῶμα πνευματικόν)
first Adam (ὁ πρῶτος Ἀδάμ)	last Adam (ὁ ἔσχατος Ἀδάμ)
living soul (ψυχὴ ζῶσα)	immortalizing Spirit (πνεῦμα ζῳοποιοῦν)
first man (ὁ πρῶτος ἄνθρωπος)	second man (ὁ δεύτερος ἄνθρωπος)
from the earth (ἐκ γῆς)	from heaven (ἐξ οὐρανοῦ)
of dust (χοϊκός)	of heaven (ἐπουράνιος)

---

du Christ et des Chrétiens (Rome: Abbaye de S. Paul, 1985), 113; and Scroggs, *Last Adam*, 87.

[36] The word φορέω reveals textual variations. The subjunctive mood φορέσ-ωμεν is supported by the majority of the important texts such as 𝔓[46] A C D F G Ψ 075 0243 33 1739 𝔐. Despite this many scholars prefer the future indicative that is attested only by less reliable texts such as B I 6 630 945[v.l] 1881. Although the future tense may fit more easily the context of 1 Corinthians 15, it is difficult to ignore the witness of good texts. Moreover, the idea that the subjunctive conveys is also Pauline (cf. Rom. 12:2, 2 Cor. 4:16, and Col. 3:10). See Scroggs, *Last Adam*, 89, n. 35.

[37] See p. 48, n. 31 above.

image of the one of dust   image of the one of heaven
(εἰκόν τοῦ χοϊκοῦ)   (εἰκόν τοῦ ἐπουρανίου)

Rom. 5:12-21

In Romans 5 Paul basically speaks of the reconciliation of sinners and their eschatological hope for eternal life in Christ. In this respect, he continues the discussion of the previous chapters and at the same time lays a foundation for the argument of the following chapters.[38] In Romans 1-4 he argued for universal sinfulness (1:18-3:20) and justification by faith (3:21-31). To support his argument, he referred to the faith of Abraham (4:1-25). Now in Romans 5, as the phrase δικαιωθέντες ἐκ πίστεως with the inferential conjunction οὖν (5:1) indicates, he discusses the results of justification by faith. The sinners are now reconciled to God (5:1, 10a, 11). They have a hope for eschatological glory (5:2-4, 10b). The basis of their reconciliation is God's love demonstrated in the death of Christ (5:6-10) and the basis of their hope is God's love in the Holy Spirit (5:5). To explain further the redemptive work of Christ and its effect on humanity Paul turns to the Adam-Christ typology (5:12-21).

Paul's use of the Adam-Christ typology in this passage differs from that in 1 Corinthians 15 in a number of ways: (1) The expressions are more specific.[39] For example, whereas in 1 Corinthians 15 Paul simply states ἄνθρωπος, here he adds εἷς.[40] When referring to the person or act of Adam and Christ, Paul also uses the definite article.[41] (2) Adam's sin, missing in 1 Corinthians 15, is repeatedly stressed as the cause of death for all men. For example, Rom. 5:12 states that through sin came death (διὰ τῆς ἁμαρτίας ὁ θάνατος) and thus death spread to all men because all men had sinned" (καὶ

---

[38]Cf. Scroggs, *Last Adam*, 77 and John Murray, *The Epistle to the Romans*, New International Commentary on the New Testament (Grand Rapids: Eerdmans, 1959), 211-12.

[39]Cf. Quek, "Adam and Christ," 77, n. 27.

[40]δι ἑνὸς ἁμαρτήσαντος (5:16a), ἐξ ἑνός (5:16b), δι ἑνὸς παραπτώματος (5:18a), and δὶ ἑνὸς δικαιώματος (5:18b).

[41]τοῦ ἑνὸς ἀνθρώπου (5:15d), διὰ τοῦ ἑνός (5:17), διὰ . . . τοῦ ἑνός (5:19), and τῷ τοῦ ἑνὸς παραπτώματι (5:15c, 17a).

οὕτως εἰς πάντας ἀνθρώπους ὁ θάνατος διῆλθεν, ἐφ᾽ ᾧ πάντες ἥμαρτον).[42]
(3) Another distinction in Romans 5 is the shift of attention from the "person"
of Adam and Christ to their respective acts.[43] Adam's act of "transgression"
(παράπτωμα), "sin" (ἁμαρτία), and "disobedience" (παρακοή) is repeatedly
contrasted to Christ's act of "grace" (χάρισμα), "righteousness" (δικαιοσύνη), and "obedience" (ὑπακοή). Finally, (4) a strong emphasis is placed
upon the effect of one man's act upon all/many men. Throughout the whole
passage the words εἷς and οἱ πολλοί/πάντες repeatedly occur in parallel.[44]

The meaning of the phrase ἐφ᾽ ᾧ in Rom. 5:12 has been much debated.
The debate is usually centered around the construction of ἐφ᾽ ᾧ and the
question of whether it refers to an individual sin or to corporate sin in Adam.
Various views have been offered. Broadly speaking, these views fall into two
groups:[45] (1) those who take ἐφ᾽ ᾧ as a causal conjunction and (2) those who
take it as a relative clause. The first group regards ἐφ᾽ ᾧ as equivalent to ἐπὶ
τούτῳ ὅτι (inasmuch as, in so far as, or on condition that) or ὅτι or διότι
(because, since). A decision still needs to be made whether it means (a)
because all sinned personally or (b) because all sinned in Adam when he
sinned. The second group finds an antecedent in Adam, death, or law.[46]
Adam as the antecedent may well support the idea of all men's involvement in
his sin, but it is too far separated from the relative pronoun. The law as the

---

[42]See also v. 15, "Many died through one man's transgression"; v. 17, "Because
of one man's transgression, death reigned"; v. 18, "One man's transgression led to
condemnation"; and v. 19, "As by one man's disobedience many were constituted
sinners, so by one man's obedience many will be constituted righteous."

[43]Quek, "Adam and Christ," 72.

[44]See Rom. 5:12b, 15a, 15b, 16, 17, 18a, 18b, 19a, 19b.

[45]For a summary of various views, see C. E. B. Cranfield, "On Some of the
Problems in the Interpretation of Romans 5:12," *SJT* 22 (1969): 324-41; idem, *A
Critical and Exegetical Commentary on the Epistle to the Romans*, International
Critical Commentary (Edinburgh: T. & T. Clark, 1975), 274-81; Sapp, "Adam
Christology in Paul," 212-31; and David Turner, "Adam, Christ, and Us: The Pauline
Teaching of Solidarity in Romans 5:12-21" (Th.D. diss., Grace Theological Semi-
nary, 1982), 131-82.

[46]For Adam as the antecedent, see Lucien Cerfaux, *Christ in the Theology of St.
Paul*, trans. Geoffrey Webb and Adrian Walker (New York: Herder and Herder,
1959), 232. For death as the antecedent, see J. Héring, *Le royaume de Dieu et sa
venue: Étude sur l'espérance de Jésus et de l'apôtre Paul* (Neuchatel: Delachaux &
Niestlé, 1959), 157. For law as the antecedent, see F. W. Danker, "Romans V.12. Sin
under Law," *NTS* 14 (April 1968): 424-39.

antecedent also makes some sense, but it comes only after the relative pronoun. Death comes near to the relative pronoun, but when taken as the antecedent, it does not make a clear sense. Therefore, it seems best to take the phrase as a causal conjunction, denoting the corporate sin in Adam. The corporate sin in Adam is supported both grammatically and contextually. Grammatically, an aorist in the dependent clause following an aorist in the main clause is ordinarily to be translated as a pluperfect: "So death came to all men because all had sinned," thus indicating some sort of involvement in Adam's sin.[47] The context of Rom. 5:12-21 also strongly suggests the corporate sin in Adam, particularly in view of 5:12ab, 13-14, and 19.[48]

Rom. 5:12-21 not only compares and contrasts Christ's act to that of Adam but also stresses its surpassing effect. The introductory formula ὥσπερ/ὡς . . . οὕτως καί (5:12, 15) indicates the comparison between Adam and Christ. But in Rom. 5:12 the *protasis* (ὥσπερ . . .) contains no *apodosis* (οὕτως καί).[49] Although some scholars argue that καὶ οὕτως (5:12) is the *apodosis*,[50] it is more likely an inferential conjunction and should be translated as "and thus." The comparison begun in verse 12 resumes in verse

---

[47]See Sapp, "Adam Christology in Paul," 226-30.

[48]For a similar conclusion, see F. F. Bruce, *The Letter of Paul to the Romans: An Introduction and Commentary*, 2nd ed., Tyndale New Testament Commentaries (Grand Rapids: Eerdmans, 1985), 122-23; Ellis, *Paul's Use*, 60; John Murray, *Romans*, 182-86; Ridderbos, *Paul*, 96; Quek, "Adam and Christ," 77, n. 28; Versteeg, *Adam*, 22; and Sapp, "Adam Christology in Paul," 225-31. Some scholars, however, insist that this phrase denotes a personal sin. For example, see Ernst Käsemann, *Commentary on Romans*, trans. ed. Geoffrey W. Bromiley (Grand Rapids: Eerdmans, 1980), 148; Cranfield, "Some of the Problems," 324-41; Brandenburger, *Adam und Christus*, 171; James D. G. Dunn, *Romans 1-8*, Word Biblical Commentary (Waco, TX: Work Books, 1988), 273-74; A. M. Hunter, *The Epistle to the Romans*, Torch Bible commentaries (London: SCM, 1955), 59-60; Bultmann, *Theology*, 1:252; and Werner Georg Kümmel, *Man in the New Testament*, rev. ed., trans. John J. Vincent (Philadelphia: Westminster, 1963), 64-67.

[49]Robertson, *Grammar*, 438; Davidson, *Typology*, 300; Cranfield, *Romans*, 272, n. 5; and Quek, "Adam and Christ," 70. A good survey and discussion on the subject are provided in David Turner, "Adam, Christ, and Us: The Pauline Teaching of Solidarity in Romans 5:12-21" (Th. D. diss., Grace Theological Seminary, 1982), 27-37.

[50]For example, see Cerfaux, *Christ*, 230-31; Scroggs, *Last Adam*, 79-80, n. 13; and John T. Kirby, "The Syntax of Romans 5:12: A Rhetorical Approach," *NTS* 33 (April 1987): 283-86.

18 and continues to the end of Romans 5.[51] As Cranfield has rightly pointed out, Paul argues from the relationship of "Adam and all men" for the relational structure of "Christ and all men."[52] In other words, what is true of Adam is also true of Christ. As (ὥσπερ) Adam's act was determinative for all (many) men who belong to him, so (οὕτως καί) Christ's act determines the destiny of all (many) men who belong to him.

Although Adam and Christ stand in correspondence as corporate figures, they are in stark contrast with respect to their acts. The introductory formulas οὐχ ὡς . . . οὕτως καί (5:15a, 16a) and τὸ μέν . . . τὸ δέ (5:16) clearly indicate the contrast between the two men. The contrasts between Adam's act of disobedience and Christ's act of grace (obedience) are as follows:

Adam's Act of Disobedience	Christ's Act of Grace/Obedience
(1) Many men died (v. 15a)	(1) Grace abounded for many (v.15b)
(2) It led to judgment/condemnation (vv. 16b, 18a)	(2) It led to Justification/acquittal/life (vv. 16c, 18b)
(3) Sin/death reigns (vv. 17a, 21a)	(3) Believers/grace reign(s) (vv. 17b, 21b)
(4) Many were constituted sinners (v. 19a)	(4) Many were constituted righteous (v. 19b).

Christ's act is not simply compared or contrasted to that of Adam, but its surpassing effect is emphatically stressed. The introductory formula εἰ . . . πολλῷ μᾶλλον (5:15, 17) clearly demonstrates this: "If (εἰ) through one man's transgression many died, much more (πολλῷ μᾶλλον) have the grace of God and the free gift . . . abounded for many (5:15). . . . If (εἰ) through one man's transgression death reigned through that one man, much more (πολλῷ μᾶλλον) will those who receive the grace and the free gift reign in life through the one man Jesus Christ (5:17)." The adverbial clause οὐ δέ plus ὑπερεπερίσσευσεν in the main clause (5:20) also express the surpassing effect of Christ's act: "Where sin increased, grace abounded all the more." In Christ's act of righteousness Adam's act of sin is not merely counter-balanced

---

[51]See Dunn, *Romans*, 282-83; J. A. Ziesler, *Paul's Letter to the Romans* (Philadelphia: Trinity, 1989), 151; John Murray, *The Imputation of Adam's Sin* (Grand Rapids: Eerdmans, 1959), 199; and Quek, "Adam and Christ," 71.

[52]Cranfield, *Romans*, 295.

but "is in fact counteracted and annulled, overcome, surpassed, defeated and done away with."[53]

Implicit Passages

Other passages in which Paul seems to allude to Adam include Phil. 2:5-11, Col. 1:15-20, 3:9-10, Rom. 1:18-32, Gal. 3:27-29, and Eph. 4:22-24.[54] One of the key factors in determining an allusion to Adam in these passages is Paul's conception of the image of God.[55] Since the concept of the image of God is reminiscent of the Genesis account of God's creation of Adam (Gen. 1:26-27)[56] and since Paul specifically designates Christ as the Last Adam (1

---

[53]Karl Barth, *A Shorter Commentary on Romans*, trans. D. H. van Daalen (London: SCM, 1959), 63.

[54]The list may also include Rom. 7:7-13, 8:29, 2 Cor. 4:4-5:21, and Eph. 5:31-33 in conjunction with 2 Cor. 11:2-3 (cf. 1 Tim. 2:11-14). For an argument for Adam in Rom. 7:7-13 and 8:29, see Dunn, *Theology*, 98-100; Käsemann, *Romans*, 244; and A. J. M. Wedderburn, "Adam in Paul's Letter to the Romans," in *Studia Biblica 1978 III. Papers on Paul and Other New Testament Authors*, ed. E. A. Livingstone, Journal for the Study of the New Testament Supplement Series 3 (Sheffield: JSOT, 1980), 419-22. For Adam in 2 Cor. 4:4-5:21, see E. Earle Ellis, "The Structure of Pauline Eschatology (II Corinthians v. 1-10)," in *Paul and His Recent Interpreters* (Grand Rapids: Eerdmans, 1979), 35-48; C. Marvin Pate, *Adam Christology as the Exegetical & Theological Substructure of 2 Corinthians 4:7-5:21* (Lanham, NY: University Press of America, 1991); and Scroggs, *Last Adam*, 96. Ellis, *Paul's Use*, 129, also recognizes an extension of the Adam-Christ parallel to Eve and the Church in Eph. 5:31-33 and possibly in 2 Cor. 11:2-3. Some of these passages are discussed in the following chapters (2 Cor. 4:4-5:21 in ch. 4 and Eph. 5:31-33 along with 2 Cor. 11:2-3 in ch. 5).

[55]The term εἰκών occurs eight times in Paul's letters: twice to designate Christ as the image of God (2 Cor. 4:4, Col. 1:15), four times to describe believers being transformed to Christ's image (Rom. 8:29, 1 Cor. 15:49, 2 Cor. 3:18, Col. 3:10), once to denote man as being the image and glory of God (1 Cor. 11:7), and finally in connection with man's rebellion and rejection of God where δόξα and εἰκών are related (Rom. 1:23).

[56]Although Paul nowhere specifically designates Adam as the image of God, he certainly alludes to it by stating that man is the "image" (εἰκών) and "glory" (δόξα) of God (1 Cor. 11:7). He was also probably aware of Adam's original place in the creation when he quoted Psalm 8 which speaks of man's being crowned with glory

Cor. 15:45), he may have Adam in mind when he designates Christ as the image of God or speaks of believers being transformed to that image.[57]

The allusion to Adam in Phil. 2:5-11 is apparent,[58] even if the passage goes beyond that analogy.[59] The following reasons are suggested: (1) The phrase ἐν μορφῇ θεοῦ in verse 6 echoes Gen. 1:26 that speaks of God's creation of man in His own image. Although Paul uses the term μορφή rather than εἰκών which the LXX renders for the Hebrew term צלם, its meaning is basically the same.[60] (2) Christ's action described in verse 6 is reminiscent of Adam's attempt in Gen. 3:5.[61] Unlike Adam, however, Christ did not grasp or

---

and honor and being placed over all creatures. The absence of a specific reference to Adam as the image of God is probably due to his strong emphasis on Christ as the image of God.

[57]A. E. J. Rawlinson, *The New Testament Doctrine of the Christ*, The Bampton Lectures (London: Longmans, 1926), 132; G. Kittel, "εἰκών," in *TDNT*, 2:395-96; Matthew Black, "The Pauline Doctrine of the Second Adam," *SJT* 7 (June 1954): 174-76; Scroggs, *Last Adam*, 97-100; Jervell, *Imago Dei*, 174-75, 200-01; Ridderbos, *Paul*, 70-71, 224-25; and Shedd, *Man in Community*, 156. However, see Kim, *Origin*, 137-62, 193-268.

[58]So, Dunn, *Theology*, 281-88; Ladd, *Theology*, 460-61; Morna D. Hooker, "Philippians 2.6-11," in *From Adam to Christ: Essays on Paul* (Cambridge: Cambridge University Press, 1990), 96-100; Kim, *Origin*, 265; N. T. Wright, *The Climax of the Covenant: Christ and the Law in Pauline Theology* (Minneapolis, MN: Fortress, 1992), 57-58; G. Howard, "Phil. 2:6-11 and the Human Christ," *CBQ* 40 (July 1978): 368-87; Barrett, *First Adam to Last*, 69-72; Oscar Cullmann, *The Christology of the New Testament*, rev. ed., trans. Shirley C. Guthrie and Charles A. M. Hall (Philadelphia: Westminster, 1963), 176-78; Andrews, *Meaning of Christ*, 158-61; Ellis, *Paul's Use*, 129, n. 6; and Ziesler, *Pauline Christianity*, 43.

[59]Cf. Wright, *Climax*, 58, who insists that Phil. 2:5-11 is an example of the phenomenon of multiple "intertextual echo." He says that it echoes Psalm 8, Genesis 1, Isa. 45:23 (Phil. 2:10-11), and even Daniel 7. For a list of other suggestions of allusive background in Phil. 2:5-11 and the respective scholars, see Dunn, *Theology*, 282, n. 68.

[60]See R. P. Martin, *Carmen Christi: Phil. ii. 5-11 in Recent Interpretation and in the Setting of Early Christian Worship*, 2nd ed., Society of New Testament Studies Monograph Series, vol. 4 (Cambridge: Cambridge University Press, 1983), 102-19; Kim, *Origin*, 200-04; and Cullmann, *Christology*, 176. Paul might have employed the term μορφή here to contrast Christ's "being in the form of God" with his act of "taking the form of a slave" described in the next verse. Cf. Dunn, *Theology*, 284 and Barrett, *First Adam to Last*, 71.

[61]Hooker, "Philippians 2.6-11," 96-98.

hold on to equality with God but emptied himself and took the form of a servant, being born in the likeness (ἐν ὁμοιώματι) of men.[62] (3) The passage has a parallel even to Romans 5 in that both passages emphasize Christ's obedience even unto death (Phil. 2:8, Rom. 5:19).[63] (4) Hooker suggests that the statement of Christ's name being placed above every name (2:9-11) also reflects Adam's original place in the creation or at least ideas which developed from it.[64] This analogy with Adam is, however, doubtful because Phil. 2:9-11 is probably connected to Isa. 45:23 rather than to Psalm 8 and the "name" is "Yahweh."[65]

Although less apparently than in the Philippian passage, an Adam typology also probably underlies Col. 1:15-20.[66] It states that Christ, like Adam, is the image of God (1:15) and that in contrast to the rebellion of the creation in Adam, Christ brings about the reconciliation of all things through his death (1:20).[67] In this respect, Col. 1:20 corresponds to Rom. 5:12-21 where an explicit reference to Adam and Christ also occurs in conjunction with the theme of redemption and reconciliation through the death of Christ.

Col. 3:9-11, Gal. 3:27-29, and Eph. 4:22-24 may also allude to Adam.[68] The key element in these passages is the imagery of "putting off the old man" and "putting on the new man." Although Paul's expressions concerning the

---

[62]The interpretation of the phrase οὐχ ἁρπαγμὸν ἡγήσατο, whether it should be understood as "res rapienda" or as "res rapta," has been a puzzling question for many scholars. Although the issue is important for the question of Christ's pre-existence and his divine nature, much of its discussion is beyond the scope of this study. For an analytical summary of various views, see Wright, *Climax*, 62-82 and R. P. Martin, *Carmen Christi*, 134-53.

[63]Barrett, *First Adam to Last*, 69-72.

[64]Cf. Hooker, "Philippians 2.6-11," 99.

[65]Cf. David B. Capes, *Old Testament Yahweh Texts in Paul's Christology* (Tübingen: J. C. B. Mohr, 1992), 157-60.

[66]Many scholars believe that this passage, like Phil. 2:5-11, is a pre-formed non-Pauline hymn. For example, Ernst Käsemann argues that Col. 1:15-20 was originally gnostic material that was later incorporated into a baptismal hymn. See E. Käsemann, "Eine urchristliche Taufliturgie," in *Festschrift Rudolf Bultmann* (Stuttgart and Cologne, n.p., 1949), 133-48. Otherwise, Kim, *Origin*, 144-59 and Davies, *Paul and Rabbinic Judaism*, 41-44.

[67]Barrett, *First Adam to Last*, 86.

[68]Whiteley, *Theology*, 1:113; Cullmann, *Christology*, 174; and Alan Richardson, *An Introduction to the Theology of the New Testament* (New York: Harper & Row, 1958), 246.

"old man" and the "new man" often emphasize the ethical aspect of the transformation, they also imply the objective basis of this transformation: Adam is the old man and Christ the new man.[69] As believers put on the new man, Jesus Christ (Gal. 3:27, Rom. 13:14), they become "one new man" in Christ (Eph. 2:15, Gal. 3:28) where there is "neither Jew nor Greek, neither slave nor free, no male and female, for you all are one in Christ Jesus" (Gal. 3:28, cf. Col. 3:11). The reference to the believer's transformation according to the image (κατ᾽ εἰκόνα) of God (Col. 3:10) also seems to allude to Adam in Gen. 1:26-27.

M. D. Hooker, supported by Barrett, Wedderburn, and Dunn, vigorously argues for an allusion to Adam in Rom. 1:18-32.[70] The suggested evidence includes the following: (1) The passage, although influenced by the theme and language of Ps. 106:20, clearly reflects the language of Genesis 1. (2) The statement, "claiming to be wise, they became fools" (1:22), echoes Adam's temptation in Gen. 3:5-6: To covet wisdom was a temptation to become like God. (3) The phrase ἤλλαξαν τὴν δόξαν τοῦ ἀφθάρτου θεοῦ ἐν ὁμοιώματι εἰκόνος φθαρτοῦ ἀνθρώπου (1:23) may also contrast Adam in God's image with Adam after the fall. Since the term ἄνθρωπος is used in the singular while the following words are in the plural, the "likeness of the image of corruptible man" may denote the image of the fallen man, Adam. Bearing the image of Adam is clearly in view at 1 Cor. 15:47-49 where Paul states that believers once bore the image of the man of dust (τὴν εἰκόνα τοῦ χοϊκοῦ).

In the light of the above analysis, one can reasonably conclude that the Adam-Christ typology not only provides a basic exegetical key to the interpretation of a number of key passages but also serves as a fundamental substructure upon which Paul builds his theology, especially his teaching

---

[69]Cullmann, *Christology*, 174.

[70]Hooker's two articles, "Adam in Romans 1" and "A Further Note on Romans 1," in *From Adam to Christ: Essays on Paul* (Cambridge: Cambridge University Press, 1990), 73-85, 86-87; Barrett, *First Adam to Last*, 17-19; Wedderburn, "Adam," 413-19; Dunn, *Theology*, 91-93. Also see Jervell, *Imago Dei*, 312-31. Otherwise, see Joseph A. Fitzmyer, *Romans*, Anchor Bible Commentary (New York: Doubleday, 1993), 274 and Scroggs, *Last Adam*, 75, n. 3.

about redemption and resurrection.[71] What specific implications does this
conclusion have for Paul's understanding of Christ and of man?

Implications

Adam and Christ as Individual Persons

Paul presents Adam and Christ as the two decisive individuals in human
history. He repeatedly stresses their humanity by designating them as "a
man," "the one man," "the first man," "the second man," "the man of dust," or
"the man of heaven."[72] He sees Christ even in his exalted nature as a man
(ἄνθρωπος) and calls him "the first born of many brethren," indicating his
continuing humanity after the resurrection.[73] Although the resurrected Christ
radically differs from his earthly mortal nature, he is still a man.[74]

Paul's Adam-Christ typology is, in fact, built upon the assumption of
the historicity and humanity both of Adam and of Christ.[75] Paul's affirmation
of the historicity of Adam is most clearly seen in his frequent use of the
Genesis accounts. He states (1) that Adam was the first man, (2) that he
became a ψυχή ζῶσα, (3) that he was from the earth, a man of dust, and (4)
that he is the one whose sin, trespass, and disobedience brought sin,
condemnation, and death upon all men.[76] Paul also alludes to the creation of

---

[71]Numerous scholars have recognized the significance of the Adam Christology
in Paul. For example, Black, "Second Adam," 173, claims that "the Second Adam
doctrine provides St. Paul with the scaffolding, if not the basic structure, for his redemption and resurrection Christology." Kim, *Origin*, 264, states that "the Adam-
Christ typology is one of the fundamental theological motifs in Paul and is used in
association with various motifs for various purposes." Wright, *Climax*, 18, also says,
". . . questions about the use of Adam in Pauline christology bring us at once to some
quite central Pauline texts . . . . These questions, and texts, introduce us to some current debates whose significance goes beyond their own immediate context." See also
Ellis, *Pauline Theology*, 55-57; Davies, *Paul and Rabbinic Judaism*, 53; Oudersluys,
"Paul's Use," 1; and Shedd, *Man in Community*, 107-25, 151-56.

[72]1 Cor. 15:21, 45, 47-49, Rom. 5:12-21.

[73]1 Cor. 15:47, 49, Rom. 8:29; cf. 1 Tim. 2:5.

[74]Scroggs, *Last Adam*, 93-94.

[75]Davidson, *Typology*, 299; Ellis, *Paul's Use*, 128-29.

[76]1 Cor. 15:15, 47, Rom. 5:12-21; cf. Gen. 1:20, 2:7, 3:14-19.

Adam in the image of God, to the priority of Adam over Eve in creation, and to the role of the serpent in the temptation.[77] His reference to Psalm 8 also implies Adam's original place in the creation.[78]

Paul's acceptance of the historicity of Jesus Christ is also apparent. He accepts the death, burial, and resurrection of Jesus as historical facts.[79] In the list of resurrection appearances in 1 Cor. 15:5-8 he identifies the exalted Christ with the Jesus who died on the cross.[80] In numerous other texts in his letters Paul presents Christ as a historical person. For example, (1) Jesus was born of woman, under the Law (Gal. 4:4). (2) He was an Israelite according to the flesh (Rom. 9:5), of the family of David (Rom. 1:3) and (3) had a brother called James (Gal. 1:19). (4) He carried on a ministry among the Jews (Rom. 15:8), (5) had twelve disciples (1 Cor. 15:5), and (6) instituted the Last Supper (1 Cor. 11:23-26). Paul also presupposes the humanity of Jesus in his statement that Jesus was born in the likeness of men (ἐν ὁμοιώματι ἀνθρώπων) (Phil. 2:7) and in the likeness of sinful flesh (ἐν ὁμοιώματι σαρκός) (Rom. 8:3). If he regards the second man Christ as historical, he must equally regard the first man Adam as historical; otherwise, the comparison and the contrast that he establishes between the two makes no sense. The theory that Paul employs Adam only as a convenient theological symbol, therefore, hardly does justice to his consistent, repeated, and coupled historical references to Adam and to Christ.[81]

---

[77]1 Cor. 11:7-9, 2 Cor. 11:3, 1 Tim. 2:13-14; cf. Gen. 1:16-27, 2:21-22, 3:1-5.

[78]1 Cor. 15:27, Eph. 1:22; cf. Rom. 1:20.

[79]1 Cor. 15:4; cf. 1 Cor. 15:20, 2 Cor. 13:4, Phil. 2:8, Col. 1:18.

[80]See Acts 9:5, 22:8, 26:15 where, according to Luke, Paul identifes the exalted Christ with Jesus of Nazareth.

[81]For example, C. H. Dodd, *The Epistle to the Romans*, Moffatt New Testament Commentary (London: Collins, 1959), 79, says: "Paul's doctrine of Christ as the 'second Adam' is not so bound up with the story of the Fall as a literal happening that it ceases to have meaning when we no longer accept the story as such. Indeed, we should not too readily assume that Paul did so accept it. The subtler minds of his age (like Philo of Alexandria, and the Egyptian Greek who wrote the Hermetic tract Poimandres) treated it as a symbolic allegory and Paul's too was a subtle mind." Similarly, Richardson, *Theology*, 248 and Vincent Taylor, *The Person of Christ* (London: Macmillan, 1958), 48. However, Versteeg, *Adam*, 52-58, vigorously refutes this view and points out the serious consequences that such a non-historical understanding of Adam brings upon Paul's Adam-Christ typology and thus for his theology.

Adam and Christ as Corporate Persons

Paul understands Adam and Christ not only as two great individuals but also as corporate beings in whom the whole humanity is included, the old humanity in Adam and the new humanity in Christ. His conception of the resurrection of Christ as the beginning of the new creation and the manifestation of the presence of the coming Messianic age in terms of the Adam-Christ typology clearly reflects this understanding.

Terms that he uses for the resurrection of Christ signify a new beginning. He designates Christ as the "first fruits (ἀπαρχή) of those who have fallen asleep," the "first-born (πρωτότοκος) from the dead," the "beginning" (ἀρχή), and the "first-born (πρωτότοκος) among many brethren."[82] The term ἀπαρχή suggests not only priority in time but also inclusiveness. It suggests that Christ's resurrection is the first resurrection of the dead but not the last. As "first fruits" (ἀπαρχή), it embraces the resurrection of believers. The term πρωτότοκος likewise denotes priority in time, but when Paul designates Christ as "first-born (πρωτότοκος) among many brethren," it also implies the priority in rank or dignity and includes the larger group.[83] This sense is underscored in his designation of Christ as the head (κεφαλή) of the body, that is, the church (Col. 1:18). The resurrection of the individual Christ has inaugurated a new world (κόσμος) of reality that necessarily implicates his corporate body, that is, the church.[84] It also has manifested the presence of the coming age (αἰών μέλλων).[85]

The concepts of the "world" (κόσμος) and the "age" (αἰών) are important for understanding Paul.[86] Although Paul uses these terms in various senses, generally speaking, he employs the term "age" (αἰών) more in a temporal sense and "world" (κόσμος) more in a spatial sense.[87] When he uses these terms, he thinks in terms of two worlds or two ages, the present age

---

[82]1 Cor. 15:20, 23, Col. 1:18, Rom. 8:29.

[83]Rom. 8:29, Col. 1:18. See Ridderbos, *Paul*, 56; Scroggs, *Last Adam*, 94; and Wilhelm Michaelis, "πρωτότοκος," in *TDNT*, 6:876-79.

[84]See pp. 108-11 (ch. 3) below.

[85]Cf. Ellis, *Pauline Theology*, 10-11.

[86]For the discussion of Paul's usage of κόσμος and αἰών, see Ridderbos, *Paul*, 91-93; Ladd, *Theology*, 397-400; Shedd, *Man in Community*, 111-25, 151-56; Hermann Sasse, "αἰών," in *TDNT*, 1:197-208; idem, "κόσμος," in *TDNT*, 3:883-95; and Bultmann, *Theology*, 1:254-59.

[87]Ridderbos, *Paul*, 91. Cf. Shedd, *Man in Community*, 113.

set over against the coming age, that is, the Messianic age (Col. 1:13). Paul regards the present age as evil (Gal. 1:4) and life outside of Christ as "walking according to the age of this world" and "according to the prince of the power of the air, the spirit that is now at work in the sons of disobedience" (Eph. 2:2). Paul also states that Christ died to deliver sinners from the present evil age into the kingdom of Christ (Gal. 1:4, Col. 1:13). The term κόσμος not only refers to a created world or human living space in a physical sense,[88] but also often denotes the domain of demonic powers, which Paul describes as "angels," "principalities," "powers," "the world rulers of this darkness," and "the evil spirits in heavenly places."[89] It also refers to the human situation or mankind qualified by sin and thus subject to judgment.[90] It is at this point that κόσμος approximates to αἰών in usage.[91] Paul sees in the resurrection of Christ a new world and the manifestation of the coming age. The new world in Christ is so radically different from this world that it could be called a new creation.[92] Thus, Paul claims: "Therefore, if any one is in Christ, he is a new creation (καινὴ κτίσις); the old has passed away, behold, the new has come" (2 Cor. 5:17, Gal. 6:15). He knows that those who are included in Christ's resurrection have already been transferred from this age to the coming age. They no longer belong to this age but to the coming age. Thus, they are exhorted not to be conformed to this age (Rom. 12:2).

Paul's conception of new creation, two worlds, and two ages can be most clearly understood in the framework of his Adam-Christ typology. Paul envisions in Adam and Christ two creations, two worlds, and two ages. Understanding the resurrection of Christ as the beginning of the new creation, he sets this new creation in Christ over against the old creation in Adam. He then views human history as extending from the first creation into the new creation.[93] In a temporal sense, history consists of two distinguishable ages (αἰῶνες), the present (or this) age and the coming age. At the beginning of each age stand, respectively, Adam and Christ, Adam representing the present

---

[88]Rom. 1:20, 4:13, 1 Cor. 14:10, Eph. 1:4.

[89]Rom. 8:38, 1 Cor. 15:24, Col. 2:14, Eph. 6:12.

[90]Rom. 3:16, 19, 2 Cor. 5:19, 1 Cor. 1:21, Rom. 3:6, 1 Cor. 11:32. See Bultmann, *Theology*, 1:254-55; Ridderbos, *Paul*, 92; and Ladd, *Theology*, 398.

[91]1 Cor. 1:20, 2:6, 3:19, Eph. 2:2. See Bultmann, *Theology*, 1:255-56 and Ladd, *Theology*, 398.

[92]Ellis, *Pauline Theology*, 8; Davies, *Paul and Rabbinic Judaism*, 37; and C. H. Dodd, *The Bible and the Greeks* (London: Hodder and Stoughton, 1954), 106.

[93]Oudersluys, "Paul's Use," 10.

age and Christ the coming age. It is probably in this sense that he calls Adam the "first man" (ὁ πρῶτος ἄνθρωπος) and Christ the "second man" (ὁ δεύτερος ἄνθρωπος).[94] For Paul the coming age is also the eschatological age that has been inaugurated with the coming of Christ the Messiah and manifested in his resurrection. In this sense Christ is also the "last Adam" (ἔσχατος ᾿Αδάμ).[95]

As the inaugurator of the ages, Adam and Christ not only represent the humanity that belongs to their respective ages, Adam representing the old humanity and Christ the new humanity, but also determine the destiny of their respective humanities. This is clearly in view in Rom. 5:12-21 and 1 Cor. 15:21-22. In these passages Paul states (1) that sin came into the world through Adam and death through sin (Rom. 5:12), (2) that Adam's trespass led to condemnation for all men (Rom. 5:15-18), and (3) that his disobedience constituted many sinners (Rom. 5:19). In contrast, it is said that (1) through Christ came the resurrection of the dead (1 Cor. 15:21), (2) that his act of righteousness leads to acquittal and life for all men (Rom. 5:18), and (3) that his obedience constitutes many righteous (Rom. 5:19). Käsemann succinctly expresses the destiny motif in this passage as he comments on Rom. 5:15-17:

> Predominant here is the antithetical correspondence according to which Adam and Christ are both bearers of destiny for the world although they do not have the same significance in their functions. The bearer of eschatological salvation is the only alternative to the first Adam. These two--and basically these two alone--have determined the world as a whole.[96]

Corporate Dimension of Human Solidarity

As Adam and Christ determine the destiny of their respective people, they also qualify their mode of existence. Thus, Paul states that whereas Adam's disobedience brought humanity under the reign of sin, death, and law, Christ's obedience resulted in the reign of righteousness, life, and grace (Rom. 5: 17, 20-21). He also indicates that the whole of humanity now exists corporately either in Adam or in Christ (1 Cor. 15:22). The humanity that

---

[94]1 Cor. 15:45a, 47.
[95]1 Cor. 15:45b.
[96]Käsemann, *Romans*, 153.

belongs to the present age exists in Adam while the humanity that belongs to the coming age exists in terms of its destiny in Christ. Furthermore, when he speaks of the two σώματα in 1 Cor. 15:44-46, he suggests two kinds of human existence. In this passage, the existence in Adam is described as σῶμα ψυχικόν and the existence in Christ as σῶμα πνευματικόν. The characteristic difference between the two is that while the former is empowered by ψυχή, the latter is empowered by πνεῦμα.[97]

Unfortunately, Paul does not explain how Adam and Christ determined the destiny and the mode of existence of the whole of humanity. Some evidence, however, indicates that he assumes some sort of solidarity relationship between Adam and all men and also between Christ and all men.[98] The following indications are noticeable: (1) The repeated emphasis of the effect of the one man's act upon the many/all men in Rom. 5:15-19 and in 1 Cor. 15:22 implies some kind of solidarity relationship.[99] (2) The statements that sin was in the world before the law was given and death reigned from Adam to Moses (Rom. 5:13-14) and that "as by (διά) one man's disobedience many were constituted sinners, so by (διά) one man's obedience many will be constituted righteous" (Rom. 5:19) also indicate a solidarity of humanity with either Adam or Christ.[100] (3) The solidarity relationship is, however, most clearly seen in 1 Cor. 15:22: "As all in Adam (ἐν Ἀδάμ) die, so also all in Christ (ἐν Χριστῷ) shall be made alive." It is significant that Paul here replaces the preposition διά with ἐν. While διά with the genitive case signifies the agency of Adam and Christ, ἐν with the locative case indicates Adam and Christ as spheres of human existence.[101] This means that in 1 Cor. 15:22 Adam and Christ are more than representative figures. They are corporate persons who include in themselves their respective followers.

------

[97]See pp. 49-50 above.

[98]Ellis, *Paul's Use*, 60G; Oudersluys, "Paul's Use," 6.

[99]Paul's emphasis on the relationship of the one and the many is apparent: Rom. 5:15, "If many died through one man's trespass, much more have the grace of God and the free gift in the grace of one man Jesus Christ abounded for many"; Rom. 5:18, "As one man's trespass led to condemnation for all men, so one man's act of righteousness leads to acquittal and life for all men"; Rom. 5:19, "As by one man's disobedience many were constituted sinners, so by one man's obedience many will be constituted righteous"; also 1 Cor. 15:22, "As all in Adam (one man) die, so also all in Christ (one man) shall be made alive."

[100]Ridderbos, *Paul*, 96-98; Ellis, *Paul's Use*, 60; Ladd, *Theology*, 403-04.

[101]For a further discussion, see pp. 13-14, 16 (ch. 1) above.

(4) Expressions such as "bearing the image," "putting off," and "putting on" further indicate the solidarity of humanity with either Adam or Christ.[102] Although not frequent in number, some Pauline texts designate Christ as the "image of God."[103] This designation probably implies Paul's understanding of the resurrected Christ as the true eschatological humanity.[104] Bearing Christ's image then denotes believers' participation in his resurrected humanity. Paul specifically states in 1 Cor. 15:49 that believers will bear the image of Christ, as they once bore the image of Adam.[105] He also reiterates that believers have put off the old man and put on the new man, "which is being renewed in knowledge after the image of its creator" (Col. 3:9-10). The old man probably refers to Adam and the new man to Christ.[106] As the result of having put off the old man and put on the new man, believers became "one," "one new man," or "one body" in Christ.[107] These expressions strongly suggest a corporate solidarity of believers with Christ and with one another.

The implication of this conclusion is very significant for the present study because (1) it suggests that Paul understands Christ not only as an individual but also as a corporate person and (2) it also suggests the corporate solidarity of human existence. Two questions now arise regarding the background of Paul's conceptions: (1) Where did Paul derive his conception of Christ as the last Adam? In other words, what is the origin of Paul's Adam Christology? This question includes the origin of his Adam-Christ typology. (2) Where did he derive his conception of Adam and Christ as corporate persons? If it was derived from an assumption of human solidarity, what prompted him to such an assumption? The following study seeks to answer some of these questions.

---

[102]1 Cor. 15:49, Eph. 4:22, 24, Col. 3:9-10, Gal. 3:27.

[103]The explicit reference to Christ as the image of God occurs in 2 Cor. 4:4 and Col. 1:15. Christ as the image is also implied in other passages such as 2 Cor. 3:18 and Rom. 8:29. Note also references to Christ as the glory of God or to the believer's participation in God's glory at 2 Cor. 3:7-4:6, Rom. 8:17, Phil. 3:20-21, and Col. 3:4.

[104]So, Scroggs, *Last Adam*, 100-08.

[105]Also, Rom. 8:29, 2 Cor. 3:19, Col. 3:10,

[106]See pp. 57-58 above.

[107]Gal. 3:27-28, Col. 3:9-11, Eph. 2:15-16, 22, 24.

Possible Backgrounds

The conception of Christ as the last (second) Adam is unique to Paul. Apart from possible allusions in Mark 1:12-13, in Luke 3:38, 4:3, and in Heb. 2:5-9,[108] it does not occur elsewhere in the New Testament. Other expressions that Paul employs to describe Adam and Christ are also unique. Although he is certainly dependent on the Genesis accounts for his depiction of Adam, the specific expressions and concepts that he applies to Adam and Christ go beyond the terms in Genesis. Moreover, apart from Genesis 1-3, Adam rarely occurs in the Old Testament. These facts have led many scholars to suggest other backgrounds for Paul's conception. The following specific backgrounds have been advocated: (1) the gnostic "Primal Man" myth, (2) Jewish Adam speculations, (3) the "Son of Man," (4) the Old Testament conception of "corporate personality," and (5) Paul's Damascus vision of Christ.

The Gnostic "Primal Man" Myth

Some scholars argue that Paul derived his Adam Christology from the hellenistic "Primal Man" (*Urmensch*) myth that was transmitted to him by a first-century form of Gnosticism, by the mystery religions, or by a gnostic-influenced Judaism or Christianity. This view was pioneered by R. Reitzenstein and W. Bousset, assumed by R. Bultmann and his students, and most extensively defended by E. Brandenburger.[109] One of the key sources that these scholars rely on is the tractate *Poimandres*. According to its description, a pre-temporal, divine, bisexual man (ἄνθρωπος) who was the "image" and the "form" of God and who was closely connected with the

---

[108]Cf. Ellis, *Paul's Use*, 96; idem, *Old Testament*, 108; and Davies, *Paul and Rabbinic Judaism*, 42-43.

[109]Reitzenstein, *Hellenistic Mystery-Religions*, 426-96, esp. 436-50; Bousset, *Kyrios Christos*, 178, 188-200, 274-75; Bultmann, *Theology*, 1:174-75, 251, 289-90; idem, "Adam and Christ according to Romans 5," in *Current Issues in New Testament Interpretation: Essays in Honor of Otto A. Piper*, ed. William Klassen and Graydon F. Snyder (New York: Harper & Row, 1962), 154; Käsemann, *Leib und Leib Christi*, 163-64; and Brandenburger, *Adam und Christus*. See also J. M. Creed, "The Heavenly Man," *JTS* 26 (January 1925): 113-36 and Hamerton-Kelly, *Pre-existence*, 132-44.

creation of the world (1:12) fell into the physical world, a world of mindless matter (1:14). As a result, his nature became twofold: mortal in the body, but immortal in the essential man, that is, in "mind" (νοῦς) (1:15). This man, however, can reclaim his original state only through "knowledge" (γνῶσις) (1:26) by which his "mind" will be stripped of all the "bodily senses" and will ascend at the death of the physical body (1:24-26).

This "Primal Man" myth allegedly originated in the Orient and penetrated into the various hellenistic religions including hellenistic Judaism[110] where it existed in two forms: (1) It was mixed with the biblical Adam stories. (2) It was combined with the Jewish Messiah, producing an eschatological figure such as the "son of man." Philo is claimed to be the supreme witness to the first form. In his interpretation of Genesis 1 and 2, Philo indeed speaks of two types of men (ἄνθρωποι), the heavenly man and the earthly man. The heavenly man, who appears in Gen. 1:26-27, is created in the image of God and is non-corporeal and by nature immortal. The earthly man, who appears in Gen. 2:7, is created from the clay and is corporeal and by nature mortal. This mortal man, however, has an immortal "soul" or "mind" that God breathed into him.[111] In Philo's thought, the heavenly man is the heavenly "archetype" or "idea" after which the earthly man is shaped.[112] The heavenly man, therefore, existed before the earthly man. When Philo speaks of the "first man," however, he means the earthly man rather than the heavenly.[113]

From this background the above-mentioned scholars explain both the nature of Paul's Corinthian opponents and the specific expressions and

---

[110]Reitzenstein, *Poimandres*, 81; idem, *Hellenistic Mystery-Religions*, passim; and Bousset, *Kyrios Christos*, 190-98.

[111]*Leg. All.* 1. 31-32, 89, 2.4, *Opif.* 69, 134-35.

[112]*Leg. All.* 2.4, *Opif.* 69, 134. Philo's interpretation of the creation as whole is Platonic in nature. He claims that God first created incorporeal ideas and then molded the corporeal world after the pattern of the incorporeal. See *Opif.* 36, 129, *Leg. All.* 1.1, 19, 21-24.

[113]*Opif.* 136, 140, 148. Interestingly, Philo uses rabbinic concepts to describe the first man. He gives three reasons for the superiority of the first man to his off-spring. (1) He was created from purer material. (2) God molded him out of the best selected clay. (3) God excelled in skill to create the man in perfect proportions. Moreover, He breathed in the man the divine breath. As the result, the first man had senses more perceptive than those of present mankind. See *Opif.* 136-38, 140, 145, 148.

concepts that he applies to Adam and to Christ.[114]   Their argument can be summarized as follows: (1) The "Primal Man" myth underlies 2 Cor. 4:4, Col. 1:15-20, and Phil. 2:5-11 in which Paul speaks of Christ's pre-existence as the image or form of God, of his close connection with the creation of the world, and of his incarnation, death, and exaltation.   (2) Paul's designation of Adam and Christ as ἄνθρωπος, "the first man" and "the second man," "the man from the earth" and "the man from heaven," or "the man of dust" and "the man of heaven" demonstrates that he thinks in terms of the gnostic two ἄνθρωποι, Christ as the heavenly man and Adam as the earthly man.[115]   (3) His reference to the order of τὸ πνευματικόν and τὸ ψυχικόν in 1 Cor. 15:46 also indicates that he adopts the Philonic two ἄνθρωποι, but reverses the order to refute the belief of his gnostic opponents.[116]   According to Brandenburger, these opponents are almost identical to those indicated in 2 Tim. 2:18 who claim that the resurrection has already happened.   (4) The contrast between ψυχή and πνεῦμα (1 Cor. 15:45) further reflects the gnostic dualist anthropology.[117] Finally,   (5) Paul's conception that Adam's sin brought sin and death to all men and that all men are "in Adam" or "in Christ" is foreign to "genuine Judaism" and therefore must have been derived from a gnostic myth that

---

[114]Cf. Bousset, *Kyrios Christos*, 178, 188-98; Conzelmann, *1 Corinthians*, 284-86; Käsemann, *Leib und Leib Christi*, 56; Brandenburger, *Adam und Christus*, 68-131, 158-264; Birger A. Pearson, *The Pneumatikos-Psychikos Terminology in 1 Corinthians: A Study in the Theology of the Corinthian Opponents of Paul and Its Relation to Gnosticism*, SBL Dissertation Series 12 (Missoula, MT: University of Montana for the Society of Biblical Literature, 1973), 24; and de Boer, *Defeat of Death*, 128-29.

[115]Brandenburger, *Adam und Christus*, 68-77 and C. H. Kraeling, *Anthropos and Son of Man: A Study in the Religious Syncretism of the Hellenistic Orient* (New York: AMS, 1966), 161.   Cf. Carsten Colpe, "ὁ υἱὸς τοῦ ἀνθρώπου," in *TDNT*, 8:475.

[116]Cf. *Opif.* 134 and *Leg. All.* 1.31, 92-94, 2.4.   Brandenburger, *Adam und Christus*, 70-76, argues that Paul corrects the Corinthians' gnostic doctrine which affirmed the heavenly-pneumatic and the earthly-psychic Anthropos as the first and the second respectively.   See Barrett, "Adam-Christ Typology," 114-15 and Davies, *Paul and Rabbinic Judaism*, 51-52, who disagree with Brandenburger and yet recognize Paul's correction of the doctrine which Philo occasionally advances.

[117]Cf. Brandenburger, *Adam und Christus*, 74; Rudolf Bultmann, "Gnosis," *JTS* 3 (April 1952): 14-16; and Boussett, *Kyrios Christos*, 258-65.

speaks of the "Primal Man" as a giant cosmic figure or from mystery religions that speak of the deification of believers.[118]

Although it may be difficult to deny completely the hellenistic influences in Paul, this view is certainly subject to criticism. The most extensive criticism against this view has been brought by Colpe and Wedderburn.[119] Their criticism includes the following: (1) The "Primal Man" is a composite figure produced over long periods of time and of space.[120] Moreover, since all written gnostic materials used in support of the myth are post-Pauline, there is no clear evidence for a pre-Christian gnostic conception of the "Primal Man."[121] (2) For Paul, both Adam and Christ are concrete historical persons whereas the "Primal Man" is an abstract, non-historical construct.[122] (3) Paul contrasts two men, Adam and Christ, whereas the gnostic myth speaks of two phases of activity of the one "Primal Man."[123] (4)

---

[118]Cf. Brandenburger, *Adam und Christus*, 68, 72, 230; W. Schmithals, *Gnosticism in Corinth: An Investigation of the Letters to the Corinthians*, trans. John E. Steely (Nashville, TN: Abingdon, 1971), esp. 141-55, 259-75; and Bultmann, "Adam and Christ," 154.

[119]Carsten Colpe, *Die religionsgeschichtliche Schule: Darstellung und Kritik ihres Bildes vom gnostischen Erlösermythus*, Forschungen zur Religion und Literatur des Alten und Neuen Testaments 60 (Göttingen: Vandenhoeck & Ruprecht, 1961) and Wedderburn, "Adam and Christ," who specifically counter-attacks Brandenburger's argument. See also E. M. Yamauchi, *Pre-Christian Gnosticism* (Grand Rapids: Eerdmans, 1973); Kim, *Origin*, 162-80; and Machen, *Origin*, 244-90.

[120]Colpe, *Religionsgeschichtliche Schule*, 191, succinctly describes this aspect: "The gnostic redeemer myth arose sometime in the distant past somewhere in the vast reaches of the Orient, which can only be imagined a little more precisely as 'Iran'; then wandered through space and time, in order to leave behind a few mosaic pieces now in this, now in that circle of tradition, e.g., in Wisdom poetry, Philo, Adam-speculation and apocalypticism, then grew once again in a grand unity in Manichaeism and with the Mandeans finally disintegrated into its components" (translation provided in Kim, *Origin*, 163). See also Scroggs, *Last Adam*, ix and Black, "Second Adam," 177.

[121]Colpe, *Religionsgeschichtliche Schule*, 207; Black, "Second Adam," 177; Ellis, *Paul's Use*, 65; Kim, *Origin*, 175-76; Wedderburn, "Adam and Christ," 115-64; and Conzelmann, *1 Corinthians*, 284.

[122]Ellis, *Paul's Use*, 129; Kim, *Origin*, 177; and Black, "Second Adam," 171-72.

[123]Ellis, *Paul's Use*, 129; Oudersluys, "Paul's Use," 10; Black, "Second Adam," 171-72; and Whiteley, *Theology*, 116-17.

Paul's use of the term ἄνθρωπος does not point to a gnostic "Primal Man," but simply emphasizes the common humanity of Adam and of Christ and stresses their link to the rest of the humanity. (5) The expressions that Paul applies to Christ such as the "second man," "last Adam," "man from heaven," "man of heaven," and "life-giving Spirit" are the result of antithetical typology that is derived from the Genesis accounts of Adam rather than the influence of the Philonic two ἄνθρωποι.[124] (6) The phrases τὸ πνευματικόν and τὸ ψυχικόν in 1 Cor. 15:46 seem to indicate the temporal sequence of the two bodies (σώματα) rather than the ontological order of the two ἄνθρωποι.[125] Otherwise, it would be difficult to explain why they are used in the neuter. Finally, (7) contrary to Brandenburger's assumption, the Corinthian opponents can hardly be the same as those in 2 Tim. 2:18.[126]

The Jewish Adam Speculations

Dissatisfied with attempts to find the background in the gnostic "Primal Man" myth, several scholars have argued that Paul's conception of Christ as the last Adam can be better explained from Old Testament and Jewish backgrounds. These scholars include W. D. Davies, R. Scroggs, and A. J. Wedderburn.[127] Their arguments, when put together, basically run as follows: (1) Paul thinks in terms of two ages and of a new creation. He perceives the resurrection of Christ as a new beginning and the radical nature of existence in Christ as a new creation (καινὴ κτίσις). He explains this new creation in Christ against the background of the creation described in Genesis and of the

---

[124]Brandenburger, *Adam und Christus*, 68-157, argues that Paul's Adam-Christ typology is not his own construction, but his adoptation and adaptation of the two Adam-ἄνθρωποι doctrine which his opponents in Corinth held. Hamerton-Kelly, *Pre-existence*, 132-43, also draws a similar conclusion. However, see Ellis, *Paul's Use*, 129.

[125]Cf. Barrett, *First Adam to Last*, 74-75; Wedderburn, "Adam and Christ," 97; and Kim, *Origin*, 177. See pp. 49-50 above.

[126]Ellis, *Prophecy and Hermeneutic*, 103, writes: "In I Corinthians . . . there are individual dissensions (1:12, ἕκαστος) and erring children but no opponents nor, in the strict sense, false teachers." See also Wedderburn, "Adam and Christ," 46-48 and Kim, *Origin*, 168.

[127]Davies, *Paul and Rabbinic Judaism*, 36-57; Scroggs, *Last Adam*; and Wedderburn, "Adam and Christ."

Jewish conception of the Messianic age that allegedly corresponds to the Genesis creation.[128] (2) Since the idea that Adam brought sin and death upon his descendants occurs in the literature of early Judaism, Paul's conception of Adam's fall as the cause of sin and death of all men is best understood against this background. Some early Jewish writings teach (a) that Adam's fall brought sin and death to all men,[129] (b) that the effects of his fall extended even to the animal world,[130] and (c) that when he sinned, the whole creation eventually became involved in corruption.[131] (3) In Judaism there was also an expectation of the Messiah who would inaugurate the Messianic age and restore the original state that was lost through Adam's fall. Paul's conception of the last Adam corresponds to these ideas.[132] (4) Along with the Jewish tradition that condemns Adam exists another tradition that glorifies him. In the Old Testament Apocrypha and Pseudepigrapha Adam is described as the first father of Israel, a king, or the image and the promise of eschatological humanity. He is sometimes related to the angels.[133] The exaltation of Adam in rabbinic literature is more fascinating. He is described not only as a king, the father of Israel, or a priest, but his wisdom, glory, and physical body are

---

[128]Davies, *Paul and Rabbinic Judaism*, 36-37; Scroggs, *Last Adam*, 61-74; and Wedderburn, "Adam and Christ," 67-73. For a list of evidences in the Jewish writings that show the expectation of a restoration of the primal state, see Wedderburn, "Adam and Christ," 68-73.

[129]This is most explicitly expressed in *4 Ezra*: "And to him thou commandedst one only observance of thine, but he transgressed it. Forthwith thou appointedst death for him and for his generations" (3:7) and "O thou Adam, what hast thou done? For though it was thou that sinned, the fall was not thine alone, but ours also who are thy descedants" (7:118). See also *4 Ezra* 3:26, 4:30, *Sir.* 14:17, *2 Bar.* 17:3, 19:8, 23:4, 54:15, and 56:6. For the well-known rabbinic tradition about six things that Adam lost because of his sin, namely, the lustre on the face of man, his eternal life, his upright stature or height, the fruit of the earth, the fruit of trees, and the luminaries, see *Gen. R.* 12:6. Occasionally, the blame goes to other than Adam, usually Eve, the serpent, or the devil. See *Sir.* 25:24, *Vit. Ad.* 16:4, *Apoc. Mos.* 7:1-3, 9:2, 14:2, 21:5-6, and *Wis.* 2:23-24 (cf. 2 Cor. 11:3, 1 Tim. 2:14). Cf. Wedderburn, "Adam and Christ," 57-62; Scroggs, *Last Adam*, 18-20, 32-38; and Ellis, *Paul's Use*, 61-63.

[130]*Jub.* 3:28-29.

[131]*4 Ezra* 6:55, 59, 7:11-12, 8:1, 44, *m. San.* 4.5, *Gen. R.* 28.6 and 23.6.

[132]*4 Ezra* 7:29-30, 12:32-34, *2 Bar.* 29:3, 30:1, 40:1-3, and 72:1-6. Cf. Ellis, *Paul's Use*, 56-58.

[133]*Sir.* 49:16, *1 Enoch* 37:1, *2 Enoch* 33:10, 58:1-2, *Jub.* 2:14, *2 Enoch* 30:12, *4 Ezra* 6:53-54, *Vit. Ad.* 12:1-17:3, *2 Enoch* 30:11, and *1 Enoch* 69:11.

described as extraordinary.[134] This fact clearly demonstrates that in early Judaism there were two trends of thought about Adam: condemnation and exaltation.[135] Paul's conception of Christ as the last Adam must have been influenced by one or both of these traditions.

This view seems to do more justice to Paul than the gnostic "Primal Man" perspective for the following reasons: (1) It draws Paul closer to his Jewish heritage. He was after all, by his own claim, "a Hebrew of Hebrews and in regard to the law, a Pharisee" (Phil. 3:5). (2) As discussed above,[136] when Paul speaks of Adam and Christ, he clearly thinks in terms of the creation and the Messianic age. His frequent references to the creation accounts well demonstrate this. For him, Christ is the Messiah whom Judaism expected to come at the *eschaton*. The coming of the Messiah, therefore, signifies for Paul the arrival of the Messianic age and the beginning of the redemption process. (3) This view also successfully demonstrates that, contrary to Brandenburger's claim, the conception of Adam's fall as the cause of sin and death of all men was after all not a strange idea to Judaism.

There are, however, a couple of points unfavorable to this view: (1) Most apocryphal and pseudepigraphal writings in support of this view are either contemporary with or later than Paul, and no written rabbinic materials existed until at least a century after Paul's death.[137] (2) According to Scroggs and Wedderburn, the idea that Adam could be related to the Messiah appears to be lacking in Judaism, although a few texts point in this direction.[138] This leads one to wonder whether Paul derived from Judaism his idea that the Messiah is the eschatological Adam.

The "Son of Man"

Some scholars claim that the second man or last Adam is basically

---

[134]For specific references, see Davies, *Paul and Rabbinic Judaism*, 45-46 and Scroggs, *Last Adam*, 41-52.

[135]Scroggs, *Last Adam*, 1-15, argues that both ideas already existed in the Genesis.

[136]See pp. 61-63 above

[137]Ellis, "NT Teaching on Hell," 205-06, esp. n. 18.

[138]Scroggs, *Last Adam*, 29, 56; Wedderburn, "Adam and Christ," 82.

Paul's substitute for Jesus' self-designation the "Son of Man."[139] Most of them believe, however, that Paul's understanding of the last Adam combines the "Son of Man" conception with other motifs. Rawlinson, for example, argues that Paul combines the apocalyptic "Son of Man" tradition with the biblical description of *pre-fall* man as having been made in the image of God.[140] Barrett, however, insists that the "Son of Man" is combined with Jewish meditations on *post-fall* Adam.[141] Matthew Black, meanwhile, argues for a combination of the early Christian "Son of Man" eschatology with rabbinic speculations about both *pre-* and *post-fall* Adam.[142] Those who find the "Son of Man" in Paul's second man or last Adam build their case on the following grounds: (1) Paul uses the term ἄνθρωπος, which is equivalent to the Hebrew "son of man," interchangeably with the names of Adam and Christ,[143] (2) In 1 Cor. 15:27 he cites Ps. 8:6 ("son of man," 8:4), which, on

---

[139]Rawlinson, *NT Doctrine*, 122-23; T. W. Manson, *The Teaching of Jesus*, 2nd ed. (Cambridge: Cambridge University Press, 1935), 233-34; Black, "Second Adam," 173; Cullmann, *Christology*, 166-81. See also Barrett, *First Adam to Last*, 75-76; idem, "Adam-Christ Typology," 117-18; Ellis, *Paul's Use*, 96-97; Wedderburn, "Adam and Christ," 86-114; and Colpe, "ὁ υἱὸς τοῦ ἀνθρώπου," 470-72.

The origin of the "Son of Man" has been much debated. Some scholars argue that it was derived from the "Primal Man" myth. For example, see Kraeling, *Anthropos and the Son of Man: A Study in the Religious Syncretism of the Hellenistic Orient* (New York: AMS, 1966), 166-90; F. H. Borsch, *The Son of Man in Myth and History* (Philadelphia: Westminster, 1967), 240-56; Cullmann, *Christology*, 166-81; and J. Jeremias, "Ἀδάμ," in *TDNT*, 1:142-3. This claim, however, has been vigorously criticized by Colpe, Kim, and Wedderburn. See Colpe, "ὁ υἱὸς τοῦ ἀνθρώπου," 408-14; Kim, *Origin*, 180-83; and Wedderburn, "Adam and Christ," 93-114. Also, see J. A. Emerton, "The Origin of the Son of Man Imagery," *JTS* 9 (October 1958), 231 and B. Lindars, "Re-Enter the Apocalyptic Son of Man," *NTS* 22 (October 1976), 52-72.

[140]Rawlinson, *NT Doctrine*, 122-36.

[141]Barrett, *First Adam to Last*, 75-76; idem, "Adam-Christ Typology," 117-18. Cf. Wedderburn, "Adam and Christ," 114.

[142]Black, "Second Adam," 172-75, 179.

[143]It is argued that the Aramaic idiom בר־אנשׁ or בר־אנשׁא, which stands behind ὁ υἱὸς τοῦ ἀνθρώπου in the Gospels, means "man" and therefore can denote ἄνθρωπος in Greek (cf. Mark 10:45, 1 Tim. 2:5). So when Paul designates Christ as ἄνθρωπος (Rom. 5:15, 1 Cor. 15:21, 47), he renders בר־[א]נשׁא in idiomatic Greek, avoiding the literal ὁ υἱὸς τοῦ ἀνθρώπου, which would be incomprehensible and misleading to his Gentile audience. See Colpe, "ὁ υἱὸς τοῦ ἀνθρώπου," 8·401-5, 70; Manson, *Teaching of Jesus*, 212-33; and Jeremias, "Ἀδάμ," in *TDNT*, 1:142-43.

the one hand, is linked to the "son of man" in Dan. 7:13-14 and, on the other hand, looks back to Gen. 1:26-27, which describes Adam's creation in God's image and with dominion over creation.[144]   (3) He describes the second man as the "man from heaven" (1 Cor. 15:47), which corresponds to the "son of man" in Dan. 7:13. (4) He identifies the Messiah as the "second man" (1 Cor. 15:45). To these reasons Rawlinson adds that Paul's whole eschatological outlook agrees with the apocalyptic "Son of Man" tradition of the Gospels.[145]

This view has been criticized by Anton Vögtle, Seyoon Kim, and Margaret Thrall.[146] Their criticisms include the following: (1) Paul never uses the term ἄνθρωπος as a title of Christ like the "Son of Man" in the Gospels.[147] (2) He cites Ps. 8:6 but not Ps. 8:4 where the phrase "son of man" occurs.[148] Furthermore, (3) Jesus' self-designation as the "Son of Man" cannot explain Paul's specific parallelism and contrast between the two men, Adam and Christ.[149] Kim, however, admits that in view of Heb. 1:13-2:9,[150] if Psalm 8 and 110 were very early joined together as a scriptural witness to the exaltation of the "Son of Man" as the Lord and if Ps. 8:4 led Paul to cite Ps. 8:6 in 1 Cor. 15:27, it is then possible that in the "man" or "son of man" of Ps. 8:4, which clearly alludes to the creation of man in Gen. 1:26-27, Paul saw Christ as "the last Adam" who has recovered the glory and dominion lost in Adam.[151]

---

[144]Cf. Heb. 2:6-9. So Ellis, *Paul's Use*, 96-97; Black, "Second Adam," 173; F. F. Bruce, *The Epistle to the Hebrews, International Commentary on the New Testament* (Grand Rapids: Eerdmans, 1964), 34-36; Richardson, *Theology*, 138-39; Rawlinson, *NT Doctrine*, 124-25.

[145]Rawlinson, *NT Doctrine*, 124-25.

[146]Anton Vögtle, *'Der Menschensohn' und die paulinische Christologie* (Rome: Pontifical Bible Institute, 1963); 199-218; Kim, *Origin*, 184-85; Margaret E. Thrall, "The Origin of Pauline Christology," in *Apostolic History and the Gospel: Biblical and Historical Essays Presented to F. F. Bruce on His 60th Birthday*, ed. W. Ward Gasque and Ralph P. Martin (Grand Rapdis: Eerdmans, 1970), 306-07. This view is also rejected by Whiteley, *Theology*, 117; R. H. Fuller, *The Foundation of New Testament Christology* (New York: Charles Scribner's Sons, 1965), 233-34; and Käsemann, *Romans*, 144-45.

[147]Vögtle, *Menschensohn*, 208-09; Kim, *Origin*, 184-85.

[148]Kim, *Origin*, 185; Vögtle, *Menschensohn*, 207.

[149]Vögtle, *Menschensohn*, 207.

[150]See Eph. 1:20, 22.

[151]Kim, *Origin*, 185-86.

The Old Testament Conception of "Corporate Personality"

There are still others who claim that behind Paul's understanding of Adam and of Christ lies the Old Testament conception of "corporate personality."[152] The term "corporate personality" refers to the Old Testament teaching regarding the relationship between the individual and the group. The conception basically involves four aspects: (1) identification, (2) extension, (3) realism, and (4) oscillation.[153] It is claimed that in the Old Testament the individual man is never considered as an isolated unit. He lives in constant interaction with others within a given community. As such, he is often identified with the group to which he belongs. Moreover, the individual man is thought of as extending himself beyond his physical contours to include those who belong to him. This extension goes beyond his own time both in the past and the future. The most striking example is found in the relationship of the father to his household and of the king to his nation. The father and the king are considered as encompassing in themselves the household and the nation respectively. In other words, they are head persons with whom their respective group is identified. Because of this real, dynamic unity between the two, the act of the head person often affects all those who belong to him. This is witnessed in a number of biblical passages in which the sin of the

---

[152]H. W. Robinson, *Doctrine of Man*, 121; Jean de Fraine, "Adam and Christ as Corporate Personalities," *TD* 10 (Spring 1962): 99-102; idem, *Adam and the Family*, 142-52; Ellis, "Biblical Interpretation," 716-25; idem, *Old Testament*, 110-12; Moule, *Origin*, 45-56, 94-95; Quek, "Adam and Christ," 73; Shedd, *Man in Community*, 97-125, 150-73.

For the discussion of the conception of "corporate personality," see H. W. Robinson, *Corporate Personality*; J. A. T. Robinson, *Body*; Aubrey R. Johnson, *The One and the Many in the Israelite Conception of God*. 2nd ed. (Cardiff: University of Wales Press, 1961); idem, *Sacral Kingship in Israel* (Cardiff: University of Wales Press, 1955); de Fraine, *Adam and the Family*, 13-48; Shedd, *Man in Community*, 3-41; Ellis, *Old Testament*, esp. 110-16; idem, *Pauline Theology*, 8-13; and idem, "S ma," 138-40.

[153]H. W. Robinson, *Corporate Personality*, 27-34; Johnson, 1-13; Shedd, Man in Community, 5-41; de Fraine, *Adam and the Family*, 20-48; Ellis, Pauline *Theology*, 9-10.

leader is punished[154] or the righteousness of the leader rewarded in the persons of those who belong to him.[155] The punishment and the blessing often extend even to their future generations (cf. Ex. 20:5-6). The relationship between the individual person and the group is, however, not rigid. There exists an oscillation or fluidity from individual to group and vice versa without either a sharp distinction or a loss of personal distinction between the two. This conception is probably presupposed, as H. W. Robinson and others claim,[156] in the Psalms where the "I" refers not only to an individual but also to the nation,[157] in Isaiah where "the suffering servant" apparently has both an individual and a corporate dimension,[158] and in Daniel where an individual, "one like a son of man," is apparently identified with the collective people of God, "the saints."[159]

---

[154]The most striking examples are that of Korah, Achan, and David. Cf. Num. 16:1-50, Josh. 7:1-26, 2 Sam. 12:7-15. See also discussions in Shedd, *Man in Community*, 12-26; de Fraine, *Adam and the Family*, 71-81, 96-100; Ellis, "The Biblical Concept of the Solidarity of the Human Race as Seen in Blessing and Punishment" (B.D. thesis, Wheaton College, 1953); and Joel S. Kaminsky, *Corporate Responsibility in the Hebrew Bible*, Journal for the Study of the Old Testament Supplement Series 196 (Sheffield: Sheffield Academic, 1995), 55-113. Cf. J. R. Porter, "The Legal Aspects of the Concept of 'Corporate Personality' in the Old Testament," *VT* 15 (July 1965): 361-80, who assesses the examples differently.

[155]For example, the following generations were blessed because of Noah, Lot, David, and Josiah. Cf. Gen. 6:9, 19:12-29, 1 Kings 15:1-5, 2 Kings 8:19, 22:16-22. See the discussion in Shedd, *Man in Community*, 17-19 and de Fraine, *Adam and the Family*, 64-71, 92-96.

[156]For example, see Ellis, *Pauline Theology*, 8-9; Johnson, *One and the Many*, 10-13; H. W. Robinson, *Corporate Personality*, 37-42; de Fraine, *Adam and the Family*, 43-46, 182-233; Shedd, *Man in Community*, 38-41; and Kim, *Origin*, 247

[157]For example, Ps. 44:4-8, 81:1-10, 129:1-3. Cf. S. Mowinckel, *The Psalms in Israel's Worship*, vol. 1, trans. D. R. Ap-Thomas (Nashville, TN: Abingdon, 1962), 42-80 and Aubrey R. Johnson, *The Cultic Prophet and Israel's Psalmody* (Cardiff: University of Wales Press, 1979), 6-12.

[158]For example, Isa. 42:1-4, 49:1-6, 50:4-9, 52:13-53:12. Cf. C. R. North, *The Suffering Servant in Deutro-Isaiah: An Historical and Critical Study* (London: Oxford University Press, 1956), 192-239; Johannes Lindblom, *The Servant Songs in Deutro-Isaiah: A New Attempt to Solve an Old Problem* (Lund: C. W. K. Gleerup, 1951), 7-51.

[159]Dan. 7:13-14, 27.

The argument that this Old Testament conception underlies Paul's Adam-Christ typology is as follows.[160] Paul regards Adam and Christ not only as individual but also corporate persons who include in themselves their respective people. Thus, as clearly indicated by the expressions such as "all in Adam" and "all in Christ" (1 Cor. 15:22), he expresses "the most comprehensive human solidarity as one that embraces in two groups the whole of humanity, man-in-Adam and man-in-Christ."[161] As corporate persons, their acts immediately affect those who belong to them. Thus, Adam's fall, on the one hand, brought sin and death to all men, and his disobedience constituted all men sinners (Rom. 5:12, 19). Christ's act of righteousness, on the other hand, led to acquittal and life for all men, and his obedience constituted many righteous (Rom. 5: 18-19). Since Paul regards Adam and Christ as concrete historical figures and their acts as historical facts, his conception involves ontological realism. That means that the whole of humanity of the past, present, and future is in a real sense involved in Adam's sin, and believers are involved in Christ's righteousness.[162] Romans 5 clearly reflects this perspective as does 1 Cor. 15:49 where Paul implies that humanity is identified either with Adam or with Christ.

If this Old Testament conception of man is valid, it may well explain the basis for Paul's underlying assumption of the solidarity of the human race in Adam and in Christ. But the validity of the conception as well as the appropriateness of the terminology have been criticized by some scholars.[163] J. S. Kaminsky summarizes the criticisms as follows:[164]

---

[160]See de Fraine, *Adam and the Family*, 142-52; Ellis, *Old Testament*, 112; idem, *Pauline Theology*, 10-13; Shedd, *Man in Community*, 107-25, 151-56; and Bruce, *Romans*, 119-20.

[161]Ellis, *Pauline Theology*, 10.

[162]Shedd, *Man in Community*, 108, 150-56; Ellis, *Paul and His Recent Interpreters*, 33. Cf. F. R. Tennant, *The Sources of the Doctrines of the Fall and Original Sin* (n.p., 1903; reprint, New York: Schocken Books, 1968), 261 and Davies, *Paul and Rabbinic Judaism*, 32.

[163]See particularly J. R. Porter, "Corporate Personality," 361-80; J. W. Rogerson, "The Hebrew Conception of Corporate Personality: A Re-Examination," *JTS* 21 (April 1970): 7-10; Cyril S. Rodd, "Introduction to *Corporate Personality in Ancient Israel*," rev. ed., by H. W. Robinson (Edinburgh: T. & T. Clark, 1981), 13; and Stanley E. Porter, "Two Myths: Corporate Personality and Language/Mentality Determinism," *SJT* 43 (1990): 289-307.

[164]Kaminsky, *Corporate Responsibility*, 18-19.

(1) This theory [corporate personality] creates a false dichotomy between the idea of the individual and the idea of the group and leaves one with the impression that Israelite society had little awareness of the individual until the later biblical period (Mendenhall).[165] (2) The various cases that are discussed under the rubric of corporate personality are sometimes better explained by different ideas such as bloodguilt, ancient conceptions of property rights, and violation of holiness taboos (Daube and Porter).[166] (3) The concept of corporate personality grew out of certain anthropological ideas that are now recognized to be fallacious (Evans-Pritchard, Rogerson, Snaith, Smith).[167] (4) Robinson used the term in an imprecise way and thus employed different senses of the term to solve different types of problems. In doing so he emptied the term of any clear meaning and thus of any usefulness (Rogerson)[168]

Several scholars responded to these criticisms. (1) In response to the first criticism, Ellis rightly points out that the Old Testament conception of "corporate personality" reflects a "more balanced appreciation of both an individual and a corporate existence of man."[169] The critics often assume that the conception of "corporate personality" ignores or denies the significance of the individual person.[170] The conception does not imply that individuality is absorbed or lost in the group or that the ancient Israelites could not recognize one's physical boundaries. It simply states (a) that since in the Old Testament man is thought of as extending himself beyond his physical boundaries to include those who belong to him, his existence has a corporate dimension, (b) that there is a great fluidity or oscillation between the individual and the group, and (c) that the existence and the significance of the individual person

---

[165]G. E. Mendenhall, "The Relation of the Individual to Political Society in Ancient Israel," in *Biblical Studies in Memory of H. C. Alleman*, ed. J. M. Meyerson, O. Reimherr, and H. N. Bream (Locust Valley, NY: Augustin, 1960), 89-108.

[166]D. Daube, *Studies in Biblical Law* (Cambridge: Cambridge University Press, 1947), 154-89; Porter, "Corporate Personality," 361-80.

[167]E. E. Evans-Pritchard, *Nuer Religion* (New York: Oxford University Press, 1956), 123-43; Rogerson, "Corporate Personality," 7-10; Z. Smith, *Map Is Not Territory: Studies in the History of Religions* (Leiden: E. J. Brill, 1978), 274-88; and N. H. Snaith, Review of The One and the Many, by A. R. Johnson, *JTS* 44 (January-April 1943): 81-84.

[168]Rogerson, "Corporate Personality," 2, 14.

[169]Ellis, *Pauline Theology*, 9-10. Cf. Kaminsky, *Corporate Responsibility*, 188.

[170]For example, see Mendenhall, "Relation of the Individual to Political Society," 91 and Rogerson, "Corporate Personality," 3-7.

are often determined by the group to which he belongs or with which he is identified. (2) Kaminsky points out a couple of problems with Porter's criticism: (a) "Porter's critique of Robinson has not eliminated the notion of corporateness by providing other alternate explanations that are non-corporate; rather, his argument has begun to reveal some of the factors that participate in cases that are clearly corporate in nature." (b) "By attributing the corporate elements in these cases to early religious beliefs and by separating these cases from the legal domain, Porter creates a false dichotomy and leaves one with the sense that there is a sharp contrast between the legal sphere in which individualism reigns supreme and the religious sphere in which certain older corporate ideas seems to persist."[171] (3) Against Rogerson's criticism, Ellis comments that modern theories "may have stimulated" Robinson's recognition of corporate ideas in Scripture, but were not responsible for his and others' exegetical conclusions. Rogerson needed "a more persuasive explanation of the texts and that he did not give."[172] Contrary to Rogerson's claim, a close look at Robinson's work reveals that he uses the work of L. Lèvy-Bruhl and E. Durkheim only to illustrate the psychological possibility of a fluid movement between the group and the individual as opposed to the modern sharp antithesis between them. He was, after all, not a social anthropologist who attempted to establish or prove a sociological theory.[173] He simply utilized some current scholarship to support his exegesis of the Old Testament texts. Therefore, the fact that L. Lèvy-Bruhl's theory is now recognized to be fallacious by modern sociologists does not warrant Rogerson's dismissal of the exegetical work of Robinson and others. After all, modern theories may also involve a fallacy. (4) Rogerson's comments on the ambiguity of the term "corporate personality" may have some validity. Scholars who continue to use the term probably need to define precisely what they mean by it. The issue at stake is, however, not the appropriateness of the terminology, but the validity of the conception. Over all, Rogerson has rightly raised a flag against an uncritical use of the conception, but he definitely overreacted when he discredited altogether the careful exegetical work of H. W. Robinson, A. R. Johnson, and R. P. Shedd

---

[171]Kaminsky, *Corporate Responsibility*, 20.

[172]Ellis, *Prophecy and Hermeneutic*, 170, n. 89.

[173]See H. W. Robinson, *Corporate Personality*, 31-32.

Paul's Damascus Vision of Christ

Seyoon Kim offers yet another intriguing suggestion. He claims that Paul's Adam christology is ultimately rooted in his Damascus vision of Christ.[174] His basic contention is that, contrary to common belief,[175] Paul derived his Adam christology from his perception of Christ as the image (εἰκών) of God. Kim writes that Paul conceived Christ as the image of God, understood in terms of Ez. 1:26-28, when he encountered Christ on the Damascus road, and that this perception naturally led him to Gen. 1:26-27 and to the contrast between Adam and Christ. According to Gen. 1:26-27, Kim continues, Adam was created in the image of God, but because of his fall he lost the divine image. Seeing Christ as the image of God, Paul could therefore think of him as the Adam of the new humanity in contrast to the old humanity in Adam. Thus Paul places Adam and Christ in an antithetical typology, the Adam of *Urzeit* and the Adam of *Endzeit* respectively. The various antithetical expressions are results of this Adam-Christ typology.[176] In order to establish this argument, Kim had to prove that the conception of Christ as the image of God was unique to Paul and it did not occur prior to him. Thus, he rejected the view of Jervell and others who believed that such passages as 2 Cor. 4:6, Col. 1:15-20, and Phil. 2:5-11 were pre-Pauline.[177]

Kim's contribution to the study of the background of Paul's thought is significant. First of all, he rightly recognizes the dominant role of the Damascus vision of Christ in Paul's life and thought. He also recognizes Paul as an original thinker. He even raises some serious questions against the claim of non-Pauline authorship of several critical passages. It is, however, still questionable whether Paul could have derived his Adam christology, apparently a more dominant theme in Paul than the image of God, from the image christology, a less dominant one. Since both ideas are based on Gen. 1:26-27 and are closely interrelated, it is difficult to determine the priority between the two. Moreover, since Paul's Damascus encounter of Christ is a pivotal event that changed his entire life and thought, everything that comes after it could eventually be related to it in one way or another.

---

[174]Kim, *Origin*, 135-268. See also Thrall, "Origin of Pauline Christology," 308-09.

[175]See pp. 55-56 above.

[176]Kim, *Origin*, 260-67.

[177]Ibid., 141-62.

From the above discussion, the following conclusion can be drawn as to the origin of Paul's conception and the relation of Adam and Christ in Paul's writings. First of all, although there are some similarities in language and expressions between Paul and the gnostic "Primal Man" myth, it is unlikely that Paul derived his conception of Christ as the last (second) Adam from that source. The various conceptions and expressions that Paul applies to Adam and Christ can be better explained, as Wedderburn argues,[178] in the light of his Old Testament, Jewish, and Christian backgrounds. Within this general framework, the specific sources discussed above probably contributed in various ways to Paul's conceptions and expressions. It is possible that the Jewish conception of the Messiah and the schema of the primal time (*Urzeit*) and the end time (*Endzeit*) provided a framework for Paul's thought. Also, Paul's Damascus vision of Christ assured him of the resurrection and the exaltation of Christ. As a result, he came to realize that Jesus was the Messiah who in Judaism was expected to come at the *eschaton* and to conquer all the enemies under his feet. To describe the exaltation and the present lordship of Christ, he employs Ps. 8:6 and 110:1. In view of the use of these verses in Heb. 2:6-9, Paul seems to share some common traditions with other New Testament writers. He was probably aware of the synoptic tradition of the "Son of Man." However, it is unlikely, although not impossible in view of his use of Psalm 8, that he actually substituted his last Adam for the synoptic "Son of Man." In the resurrection of Christ Paul saw a new beginning (ἀρχή) which he perceived in terms of a new creation. This perception quickly led him to the Genesis accounts of creation. As he placed the new creation over against the old creation, he eventually set Christ over against Adam. Based on his midrash on Gen. 2:7 (1 Cor. 15:44-45), he draws antithetical contrasts between Adam and Christ that are direct results of this Adam-Christ typology. In Rom. 5:12-21 he applies the Adam-Christ typology to his teaching about redemption. Here the focus of attention shifts from the persons of Adam and Christ to their respective acts. In explaining the determining act of Adam, he seems to share ideas about Adam often found in late Judaism. His description of Adam is, however, focused on the negative side. This is probably to heighten the contrast between Adam and Christ. This does not mean, therefore, that he was unaware of or ignored traditions about the pre-fall Adam. His designation of Christ as the image of God and of man as the image of God (1 Cor. 11:7) rather implies his

---

[178]Wedderburn, "Adam and Christ," 248.

awareness of the pre-fall condition of Adam. As he applies the Adam-Christ typology to his teaching about redemption and resurrection, he clearly assumes some sort of solidarity of humanity. This assumption can probably be best explained in terms of the Old Testament conception of "corporate personality."

CHAPTER 3

THE CHURCH AS THE BODY OF CHRIST

The term σῶμα ("body") is of special interest for this study because it has been one of the key elements in the studies of Pauline anthropology.[1] It has been used, in relation to the nature of an individual, to support either a monistic or a dualistic view of man.[2] It also has been employed in the discussion of the individual and the corporate dimensions of man.[3] Although both issues are still open to much debate, the following study limits its investigation to the second issue with the primary interest in its reference to a corporate reality.

In Paul's letters σῶμα in its corporate sense denotes primarily the sexual union and the church as the body of Christ.[4] The explicit references to the church as the body of Christ[5] occur in 1 Cor. 12:27, Eph. 1:22-23, 5:30, and

---

[1]For discussions on σῶμα, see R. Bultmann, *Theology*, 1:192-203; Gundry, *Sōma*; J. A. T. Robinson, *Body*; Eduard Schweizer, "σῶμα," in *TDNT*, 7:1024-94; Jewett, *Anthropological Terms*, 201-304; Stacey, *Pauline View of Man*, 181-93; Dunn, *Theology*, 51-78; Ridderbos, *Paul*, 114-26; and Ellis, "Sōma," 132-44. For a helpful survey of the studies of σῶμα in Paul's letters, see Jewett, *Anthropological Terms*, 210-50.

[2]For σῶμα in support of a monistic view, see Bultmann, *Theology*, 1:192-203; Conzelmann, *Theology*, 176-78; Ellis, "Sōma," 133-38; and Stacey, *Pauline View of Man*, 181-92. However, see Gundry, *Sōma*, 29-80, 135-244, who vigorously argues against Bultmann and claims that σῶμα basically signifies a dualism, and Cooper, *Body, Soul, Life Everlasting*, 253, who takes a more philosophical approach to the problem and draws a conclusion similar to that of Gundry.

[3]Bultmann, for example, argues that σῶμα basically denotes an individual existence of man as the "object-self," but Robinson insists on solidarity as the keynote. See Bultmann, *Theology*, 1:195-203 and J. A. T. Robinson, *Body*, 21, 26-33.

[4]Since the last chapter is devoted to the discussion of σῶμα in reference to sexual union, this chapter discusses primarily Paul's use of the term in reference to the church as the body of Christ.

[5]A few significant works on this subject are as follows: Käsemann, *Leib und Leib Christi*; idem, "The Theological Problem Presented by the Motif of the Body of Christ," in *Perspectives on Paul*, trans. Margaret Kohl (Philadelphia: Fortress, 1971): 102-21; Percy, *Leib Christi*; Schweizer, *Church*; A. Wikenhauser, *Die Kirche als der mystische Leib Christi nach*

Col. 1:24. Beside these explicit references, possible allusions occur in 1 Cor. 6:15, 17, 10:16, 11:24-29, Eph. 4:12, and Col. 2:17. The church is also identified as "one body in Christ" (Rom. 12:5; cf. Eph. 3:6), "the body" (Eph. 5:23, Col. 1:18), or simply as "one body" without a reference to Christ (1 Cor. 10:17, Eph. 2:16, 4:4, Col. 3:15). Paul's designation of Christ as the head of the church occurs exclusively in Ephesians and Colossians (Eph. 1:22, 4:15-16, 5:23, Col. 2:19).

The interpretation of these passages involves several critical issues. For example, (1) should one understand the expression "body of Christ" realistically or metaphorically? (2) Does the "body of Christ" refer to the individual body of Christ, to the church, or to both? (3) What is the relationship between the individual body of Christ and his body that is the church? (4) How can or should one harmonize Paul's designation of the church as the body of Christ and of Christ as the head of the church? (5) What is the relation of water and Spirit baptism and of the Lord's Supper to the body of Christ? (6) What are the sources from which Paul possibly derived his expression and conception? Answers to these questions are important for determining what specific implications Paul's designation of the church as the body of Christ has for his understanding of the nature of man, his anthropology.

Analysis of Paul's Usage

Passages in 1 Corinthians

Four passages in 1 Corinthians deserve careful investigation. They are 1 Cor. 6:13-20, 10:14-22, 11:17-34, and 12:12-27. Although the explicit reference to the church as the body of Christ occurs only in 1 Cor. 12:12-27,

---

dem Apostel Paulus (Münster: Aschendorff, 1940); S. Hanson, The Unity of the Church in the New Testament: Colossians and Ephesians (Lexington, KY: American Theological Library Association, 1963); J. A. T. Robinson, Body; L. Cerfaux, The Church in the Theology of St. Paul, trans. Geoffrey Webb and Adrian Walker (New York: Herder and Herder, 1959); Best, One Body; T. Soiron, Die Kirche als Leib Christi (Düsseldorf, 1951); E. Mersch, The Whole Christ: The Historical Development of the Doctrine of the Mystical Body in Scripture and Tradition, trans. John R. Kelly (Milwaukee, WI: Bruce, 1938); J. J. Meuzelaar, Der Leib des Messias: Eine exegetische Studie über den Gedanken vom Leib Christi in den Paulusbriefen (Kampen: Kok, 1979); P. S. Minear, Images of the Church in the New Testament (Philadelphia: Westminster, 1960), 173-220; and Ridderbos, Paul, 362-95.

other passages are also significant because they have specific bearings on the interpretation of 1 Cor. 12:12-27. The following analysis, therefore, begins with 1 Cor. 12:12-27 and then proceeds to other passages.

1 Cor. 12:12-27

This passage is a part of Paul's discussion concerning spiritual gifts, which embraces chapters 12 through 14. It directly follows a section that addresses the unity of the church in the diversity of the spiritual gifts (12:1-11),[6] which is demonstrated by the analogy of a human body (12:12-27).

The analogy runs basically as follows: 1 Cor. 12:12 compares the unity and the diversity of the church to one body that has many members: "For just as the body is one and has many members, and all the members of the body, though many, are one body, so also is Christ." Interestingly, the analogy is made here to Christ rather than to the church. If Paul used σῶμα simply as a metaphor to illustrate the unity and the diversity of the church, he should have said, "so also is the church" or "so also is the body of Christ." But he states, "so also is Christ." This is significant because it indicates not only that σῶμα is more than a mere metaphor but also that there exists a special relationship between Christ and the church.

1 Cor. 12:13 provides the basis for the idea expressed in verse 12.[7] Paul states, "For in one Spirit we were all baptized into one body (εἰς ἓν σῶμα ἐβαπτίσθημεν), Jews or Greeks, slaves or free, and all were made to drink one Spirit." A similar expression occurs in Rom. 6:3 and in Gal. 3:27-29, but there Paul says that believers are baptized into Christ (εἰς Χριστόν), which he further defines as "baptism into his death" (Rom. 6:3) and as "putting on Christ" (Gal. 3:27). In view of these verses, "baptism into one body" must mean basically the same as "baptism into Christ" or "putting on Christ"[8] If

---

[6]The phrases τὸ αὐτὸ πνεῦμα (12:4, 8, 9, 11), τὸ ἓν πνεῦμα (12:9, 11), ὁ αὐτὸς κύριος (12:5), and ὁ αὐτὸς θεός (12:6) stress the unity while the terms διαιρέσεις (12:4, 5, 6), ἕκαστος (12:7, 11), ἕτερος (12:9), and ἄλλος (12:8, 9, 10) denote the diversity of the church.

[7]Ridderbos, *Paul*, 372; Moule, *Origin*, 71. For the discussion of this verse in relation to baptism, see Cerfaux, *Church*, 270-72; G. R. Beasley-Murray, *Baptism in the New Testament* (London: Macmillan, 1962), 170-71; Rudolf Schnackenburg, *Baptism in the Thought of St. Paul*, trans. G. R. Beasley-Murray (New York: Herder and Herder, 1964), 26-29; Dunn, *Theology*, 443-59; and Ridderbos, *Paul*, 396-414.

[8]Cf. Gal. 3:27, Rom. 13:14, Eph. 4:24, Col. 3:10. So, Ellis, *Pauline Theology*, 80.

so, "one body" in verse 13 signifies nothing other than Christ himself. Furthermore, verse 13 says that "*in one Spirit* (ἐν ἑνὶ πνεύματι) we were all baptized into one body . . . and all were made to drink *one Spirit* (ἐν πνεῦμα)." This statement probably signifies that believers are incorporated into the body of Christ by baptism in the Spirit rather than by water baptism.[9]

1 Cor. 12:14-26 further amplifies the analogy and explains in greater detail both the unity and the diversity of the church. Verse 14 stresses the diversity of the body: "For the body is not of one member but of many." Accordingly, the following verses (vv. 15-19) recognize the unique significance of each member of the body. In verse 20, however, the attention shifts from the diversity to the unity of the body: "Now there are many members, yet one body." Accordingly, the following verses (vv. 21-26) emphasize the mutual dependence of the diverse members both in honor and in suffering. Since Paul speaks of various parts of the body simply to demonstrate their mutual dependence, one should not stretch the analogy too far by identifying whom in the church each part of the body represents.

1 Cor. 12:27 sums up the analogy by stating most explicitly that believers are "(the) body of Christ (σῶμα Χριστοῦ) and individually members of it." The interpretation of this verse involves two grammatical issues: (1) the absence of the definite article before σῶμα and (2) the meaning of the genitive Χριστοῦ. A number of scholars insist that because there is no definite article before σῶμα, verse 27a cannot mean, "You are the body of Christ." Thus, Moule opts to translate σῶμα Χριστοῦ as "a body of Christ."[10] Synge, however, rejects this translation by saying that it suggests that Christ has more than one mystical body. He instead translates it as "like a Body of Christ."[11] This translation also has a problem because, while striving to be faithful to the grammar, it does more damage by adding a new element.[12]

---

[9]Cf. Tit. 3:5, 1 Cor. 6:11. So, Ellis, *Pauline Theology*, 30-31, 45, 79; Shedd, *Man in Community*, 183-84; Dunn, *Theology*, 450-52; Beasley-Murray, *Baptism*, 171; and Rudolf Schnackenburg, *The Church in the New Testament* (New York: Herder & Herder, 1965), 168. Otherwise, see Cerfaux, *Church*, 268-86; Schweitzer, *Mysticism*, 260-63; and Wikenhauser, *Pauline Mysticism*, 109-32.

[10]Moule, *Origin*, 72. See also Cerfaux, *Church*, 277 and A. J. M. Wedderburn, "The Body of Christ and Related Concepts in 1 Corinthians," *SJT* 24 (February 1971): 79.

[11]F. C. Synge, *St. Paul's Epistle to the Ephesians: A Theological Commentary* (London: S.P.C.K., 1959), 38.

[12]Synge treats the concept of the body of Christ merely as a simile and insists that Paul uses σῶμα to denote not an organism but a community. Consequently, he interprets all the relevant passages in Paul according to this presupposition. For example, he interprets 1 Cor.

Paul does not say, "You are ὡς σῶμα Χριστοῦ," but simply, "You are σῶμα Χριστοῦ." The absence of the article is probably, as Griffiths argues, due to the predicative use of σῶμα.[13]

Moule also argues that Χριστοῦ is used here as genitive of possession and thus the phrase σῶμα Χριστοῦ means a body that belongs to Christ, referring primarily to the congregation.[14] This kind of interpretation may be grammatically possible in Rom. 12:5 where Paul speaks of "one body in Christ" (ἓν σῶμα ἐν Χριστῷ), but it is not warranted in 1 Cor. 12:27, particularly in view of verses 12 and 13. There is simply no clear indication in this passage that σῶμα refers to anything other than to the body of Christ.

1 Cor. 6:13-20

A possible allusion to the church as the body of Christ occurs in this passage where Paul strongly condemns sexual immorality.[15] He roots the condemnation in his understanding of the body (σῶμα), arguing that sexual sins are abhorrent for believers not only because they involve a sin against one's "own body" (1 Cor. 6:18) but also because the resulting "one body" created by such an act clashes inevitably with the "one spirit" created by the union with the Lord (1 Cor. 6:16-17). Paul bases this argument on Gen. 2:24 where it says, "The two shall become one flesh (σάρξ)."

The "body" (σῶμα) in this passage has a couple of specific implications for Paul's understanding of man. First, it is used almost interchangeably with

---

12:27 as "You are, as a community of Christ, like a body" and Rom. 12:5 as "We who are many (and yet a community) are like one body in Christ." He also does a violent emendation to the interpretation of Eph. 5:22-33 and the passages in which Paul identifies Christ as the head. See Synge, *Ephesians*, 64.

[13]J. G. Griffiths, "A Note on the Anarthrous Predicate in Hellenistic Greek," *ExpTim* 62 (July 1951): 314-16. See also Schweizer, *Church*, 41 and Best, *One Body*, 105. Examples without the article are found in 1 Cor. 3:9 (θεοῦ οἰκοδομή) and 3:16 (ναὸς θεοῦ) (cf. 3:17) while the article before σῶμα appears in Rom. 7:4, 1 Cor. 10:16, and Eph. 4:12. For the absence of the article in the predicate, see the discussion in Robertson, *Grammar*, 767-69, 794.

[14]Moule, *Origin*, 72. See also Meuzelaar, *Leib des Messias*, 6 and Gundry, *Sōma*, 231-36.

[15]In Paul, sexual immorality concerns not only fornication with a prostitute but also an incestuous relationship, homosexual sodomy, and lesbianism. For example, see 1 Cor. 5:1, 6:9, 11, 13, and Rom. 1:26-27.

σάρξ.[16] This is apparent in verse 16 where Paul states, "He who joins himself to a harlot becomes one body (σῶμα) with her" and cites Gen. 2:24, "The two shall be one flesh (σάρξ)." The same identification of these two words occurs in a similar context in Eph. 5:22-23. Second, it appears to signify a whole person.[17] For example, in verse 14 where one might expect "our bodies," Paul employs the personal pronoun "us": "God . . . will raise *us* up." By so doing, he eventually makes σῶμα equivalent to a "person." Similarly, the statement, "*Your bodies* are members of Christ" (1 Cor. 6:15), is essentially no different from saying, "*You* are . . . members of it [Christ's body]."[18] Also in verse 19 where one might expect, "*Your bodies* are not your own," he states, "*You* are not your own."[19]

1 Cor. 6:13-20 contains two statements that probably allude to the church as the body of Christ. The first occurs in verse 15, "Your bodies are members of Christ." Understood in the light of 1 Cor. 12:12, 27, this statement is almost the same as saying, "You are members of Christ" or "You are members of the body of Christ." The second assertion occurs in verse 17, "He who joins himself to the Lord becomes one spirit with him" (1 Cor. 6:17). "One spirit with him [the Lord]" is a direct parallel to "one body with her [a harlot]" (6:16) and it probably means either "spiritual body"[20] or the "corporate Body of Christ created by the Holy Spirit."[21] If so, it alludes to the church as the body of Christ.

1 Cor. 10:14-22

While warning against idolatry, Paul refers to the church as "one body"

---

[16]Σῶμα and σάρξ are often used interchangeably, but they are not completely identical. Paul probably follows the example of the LXX in which בשׂר is rendered sometimes σῶμα and some other times σάρξ, with no difference in meaning. For discussion on this matter, see Bultmann, *Theology*, 1:199-203, 239-46; J. A. T. Robinson, *Body*, 26-33; Ellis, "Sōma," 133-34; and Stacey, *Pauline View of Man*, 181-93.

[17]Bultmann, *Theology*, 1:192, 194-95; J. A. T. Robinson, *Body*, 26-33; Ellis, "Sōma," 133-34; Best, *One Body*, 74; Brown, *Acts-1 Corinthians*, 324-26. However, see Gundry, *Sōma*, 135-56.

[18]1 Cor. 12:27; cf. Eph. 5:30.

[19]Cf. J. A. T. Robinson, *Body*, 29 and Ellis, "Sōma," 133.

[20]Conzelmann, *Theology*, 180; idem, *1 Corinthians*, 112; Bultmann, *Theology*, 1:209; J. A. T. Robinson, *Body*, 52; Shedd, *Man in Community*, 160.

[21]Ellis, "Sōma," 140.

(10:17). His warning against idolatry begins with a reference to an Old Testament incident. He says that the Israelites who were baptized into Moses and who ate the supernatural food and drank the supernatural drink which came from the Rock (Christ) were nevertheless destroyed when they indulged in idolatry (10:1-13).[22] Having stated that "these things are warnings for us" (10:6) and "were written down for our instruction" (10:11), he applies this Old Testament incident directly to the Corinthian situation to warn the Corinthian believers against idolatry (10:14-15).

In the following verses (10:16-22), he explains why believers should avoid idolatry by referring to the institution of the Lord's Supper.[23] By drinking the cup and breaking the bread believers participate in the blood and the body of Christ (10:16). Similarly, by partaking of the table of demons, they become partners (κοινωνούς) with demons (10:20).[24] In other words, participation in the body of Christ creates a union with Christ while participation in the pagan sacrifice creates a union with demons. In Paul's thought, these two unions are so real and mutually exclusive that believers cannot partake of the table of the Lord and that of demons at the same time (10:21).

Paul's language in this passage clearly refers to the institution of the Lord's Supper and thus may have to be understood in harmony with it. This means that participation in the body and the blood primarily refers to the individual body of Christ that was sacrificed on the cross and to his blood that was shed as atoning blood.[25] Since believers have already become "one

---

[22]Baptism and the Eucharist motives certainly underlie this passage. See Ernst Käsemann, "Pauline Doctrine of The Lord's Supper," in *Essays on New Testament Themes*, trans. W. J. Montague (Philadelphia: Fortress, 1982), 113-19; Ridderbos, *Paul*, 419-20; E. Schweizer, "πόμα," in *TDNT*, 6:146-48; and Dunn, *Theology*, 448, 614-15.

[23]For Paul's teaching on the Lord's Supper, see Bultmann, *Theology*, 1:144-52, 311-14; J. Jeremias, *The Eucharistic Words of Jesus* (London: SCM, 1966); Käsemann, "Lord's Supper," 108-35; Oscar Cullmann, "The Meaning of the Lord's Supper in Primitive Christianity," in *Essays on the Lord's Supper*, ed. F. J. Leenhardt, trans. J. G. Davies (Richmond, VA: John Knox, 1958), 5-23; Conzelmann, *1 Corinthians*, 200-01; Dunn, *Theology*, 599-623; Ridderbos, *Paul*, 414-28; E. Schweizer, *The Lord's Supper according to the New Testament*, trans. J. M. Davies (Philadelphia: Fortress, 1967); and Whiteley, *Theology*, 178-85.

[24]Partaking of the table of devils probably refers to cult-meals. See Best, *One Body*, 88; A. D. Nock, "Early Gentile Christianity," in *Essays on the Trinity and the Incarnation*, ed. A. E. J. Rawlinson (London: Longmans, 1928), 124-26; and W. L. Willis, *Idol Meat in Corinth: The Pauline Argument in 1 Corinthians 8 and 10* (Chico, CA: Scholars, 1985), 7-64, 188-92.

[25]Ridderbos, *Paul*, 374; Moule, *Origin*, 72-73. Cf. Conzelmann, *1 Corinthians*, 172.

body" in Christ by baptism in the Spirit (1 Cor. 12:13, Tit. 3:5), the participation in the body of Christ by partaking of the Lord's Supper does not mean the creation of a new or different union with Christ. The Supper rite is simply a "visual manifestation and proclamation of an already existing reality."[26] Believers are one body because there is one bread. By partaking together of this one bread, they proclaim their existing unity with Christ.

By connecting the notion of unity with the word "body," however, Paul seems to go beyond the usual meaning of the body in the Lord's Supper.[27] This is apparent in verse 17, "We who are many are one body."[28] This statement is basically the same as that in 1 Cor. 12:12-13 or Rom. 12:5. The "one body" in this verse, therefore, may also refer to the body of Christ, that is, the church. If so, Christ's individual body and his corporate body are not viewed as two different bodies but as one body.

1 Cor. 11:17-34

Paul's reference to the institution of the Lord's Supper occurs again in this section of 1 Corinthians, but in a different context. According to 11:21-22, some Corinthian believers abused the Lord's Supper by eating and drinking without considering other members of the church (11:20-21).[29] This selfish act eventually led the church to divisions and thus broke the unity of the church (11:18).

Paul responds to this problem by reminding them of the significance of the Lord's Supper and of the seriousness of their sin. He points out that Jesus himself instituted the Supper and interpreted it as a sign of his sacrificial death

---

[26]Ellis, "Sōma," 141. See also Best, *One Body*, 106-07 and Shedd, *Man in Community*, 189-94.

[27]Conzelmann, *1 Corinthians*, 172, elaborates this: "'Body' is not simply the correlate of 'blood.' He is thinking already of the 'body of Christ,' the church. This explains also the reversal of bread and cup: Paul is aiming at an interpretation of the community by means of the Lord's Supper." Cf. Moule, *Origin*, 72.

[28]Many scholars see here a transition to the identification of the church with the historical and glorified body of the Lord in the literal sense. See J. A. T. Robinson, *Body*, 57-58; Percy, *Leib Christi*, 44; and Cerfaux, *Church*, 276-82. Otherwise, see Moule, *Origin*, 72.

[29]It seems that the Corinthian believers observed the Lord's Supper with a communal meal. Paul's rebuke (vv. 21-23) and recommendation (vv. 33-34) strongly suggest that the Corinthians abused the communal meal which preceded the Supper rite. See Ellis, *Pauline Theology*, 112-13 and Schweizer, *Lord's Supper*, 5-6.

(11:23-26).[30] By participating in the Supper, believers proclaim the Lord's death until he comes (11:26). Therefore, "he who eats the bread or drinks the cup of the Lord in an unworthy manner is guilty of profaning the body and the blood of the Lord" (11:27); "he who eats and drinks without discerning the body eats and drinks judgment upon himself" (11:29). Consequently, he writes, many became weak, ill, and some died (11:30).

Within this context, Paul mentions the "body" three times: "my body for you" (11:24), "profaning the body" (11:27), and "discerning the body" (11:29).[31] Scholars wonder whether the body here refers to the bread which signifies the individual body of Christ sacrificed on the cross or to the church. The "body" in verses 24 and 27 seems to refer to the individual body of Christ that was sacrificed on the cross. The reasons are as follows: (1) "This is my body for you" is a traditional statement that Paul received from the early church which signifies Jesus' death.[32] (2) The body and the blood occur in a direct parallel to the bread and the cup (10:24-25, 27). And (3) verse 26 specifically states that by eating the bread and drinking the cup, believers proclaim the Lord's death.[33]

The case in 1 Cor. 11:29 is, however, more complicated. It is difficult, if not impossible, to determine whether the body denotes the individual body of Christ or the church. If it refers to the individual body of Christ, it is parallel to 11:27 where Paul speaks of the body and the blood of Christ. In this verse, then, the bread and the individual body of Christ are closely identified, implying that believers actually eat the body of Christ when they eat the bread.[34] There are, however, a number of problems with this understanding: (1) Unlike John's Gospel,[35] eating the body of Christ is a very

---

[30]Cf. Mark 14:22-25, Matt. 26:26-29, Luke 22:15-20.

[31]A textual variation occurs in verse 29. Some manuscripts add τοῦ κυριοῦ to the body. See a[2] C[3] D[3] D F G (Ψ 1241[s]) 1881[c] 𝔐 vg[c]. The text without τοῦ κυριοῦ is, however, supported by more reliable texts such as 𝔓[46] a[*] A B C[*] 6 33 1739 1881[*] pc vg[st].

[32]As the words παραλαμβάνειν and παραδιδόναι clearly indicate, verses 23-25 are a piece of fixed, pre-Pauline tradition. See Conzelmann, *1 Corinthians*, 195-96; Brown, *Acts-1 Corinthians*, 356-57; and Ellis, "Traditions in 1 Corinthians," 486-87.

[33]So, Schweizer, *Church*, 45-46. However, see Ellis, "Sōma," 141, who argues that "when 'my body for you' (11:24-26) is understood in the light of 10:16-17, the rite identifies the body of Christ with the corporate Christ, inclusive of the congregation."

[34]Cf. Brown, *Acts-1 Corinthians*, 349.

[35]For example, John 6:51 says: "I am the living bread which came down from heaven; if any one eats of this bread, he will live for ever; and the bread which I shall give for the life of the world is my flesh."

strange idea for Paul. It never occurs elsewhere in his letters, and such an understanding ignores the present context. (2) In 11:29 Paul mentions only the body and not the cup. Moreover, in 11:24-25 he specifically states that believers partake of the Lord's Supper "in remembrance of me [Jesus]."[36] The main concern of the passage is the abuse of the Lord's Supper, namely, by ignoring other members of the body at the Supper. In response to this particular problem, Paul refers to the institution of the Lord's Supper and in 11:27-29 he seems to apply its significance to the Corinthian situation. If so, his statement, "not discerning the body" (11:29), must have something to do with that situation and must refer to the church that is elsewhere identified as the body of Christ.[37]

A sharp distinction between the individual body of Christ and the body referring to the church is as difficult here as it is in 1 Cor. 10:14-22 and it may run counter to Paul's whole line of exhortation. Moule also recognizes this:

> It is not improbable that Paul is here deliberately using *sōma* with a *double entendre*, to mean not only the body of Jesus sacrificed on the cross and participated in at the Lord's Supper through the Spirit, but also the body which is the Church: the selfishness and greed which he is castigating in 1 Corinthians 11 constitute a failure to discern both the physical body of Christ as surrendered on the cross and the metaphorical body of Christians gathered at the Lord's Supper.[38]

Passage in Romans

Rom. 12:3-8

The general context of Rom. 12:3-8 is similar to that of 1 Cor. 12:12-27. The reference to the church as "one body in Christ" occurs in Rom. 12:4-5: "For as in one body we have many members . . . so we, though many, are one body in Christ and individually members of one another." This statement immediately follows a reference to humility appropriate to believers (12:3)

---

[36]Cf. Conzelmann, *1 Corinthians*, 198. For the origin of the meaning of the phrase, "Do this in remembrance of me," see Jeremias, *Eucharistic Words*, 237-55.

[37]Cf. 1 Cor. 12:27, Eph. 1:22-23, 5:30, Col. 1:24. So, Shedd, *Man in Community*, 160-61 and Scott, *Christianity*, 189-90. Cf. Schweizer, *Church*, 45-46.

[38]Moule, *Origin*, 73.

and precedes a suggestion of proper ways of using the various gifts (12:6-8).

The most significant difference of Rom. 12:4-5 from 1 Cor. 12:27 is this: In 1 Cor. 12:27 believers are said to be "the body of Christ and individually members of it [the body of Christ]"; however, in Rom. 12:4-5, they are described as "one body in Christ, and individually members one of another." Moule argues that since the body is said to be in Christ, "it is not, strictly speaking, that Christ is here identified with the body."[39] "One body in Christ" may not be the same as the "body of Christ." But Paul's expressions are rather fluid. In Ephesians he both identifies the church as the body of Christ and at the same time distinguishes Christ from the church by designating him as the head of the church.[40] In a similar manner, in 1 Corinthians he identifies believers, that is, the church, variously as the "body of Christ," as "members of Christ," and as "in Christ."[41] Although there may be fine differences in expression between Rom. 12:5 and 1 Cor. 12:27, these two verses do not speak of two different realities, but of the same reality from a different perspective.[42] The church is from one standpoint the "body of Christ" and from another, "one body in Christ." The difference is perhaps one of emphasis: While Paul emphasizes the unity of believers with Christ in 1 Corinthians 12, he seems to lay more stress on the unity of believers with one another in Rom. 12:5, as he does in 1 Cor. 10:17.

Passages in Ephesians

References to the church as the body of Christ occur also in Ephesians and Colossians, but with a few distinctive ideas.[43] In Ephesians they are as follows.

---

[39]Ibid., 72. See also Jewett, *Anthropological Terms*, 303 and Best, *One Body*, 106. Cerfaux, *Church*, 277-78, finds here a development from the notion of life in Christ (Rom. 12:5) to the body of Christ (1 Cor. 12:27).

[40]For example, see Eph. 1:22-23, 5:23, and Col. 1:18.

[41]1 Cor. 12:27, 6:15, 15:22, 16:22.

[42]See Best, *One Body*, 106 and Cerfaux, *Church*, 277-78.

[43]Cf. Moule, *Origin*, 74; Käsemann, "Theological Problem," 120-21; and Shedd, *Man in Community*, 161.

Eph. 1:22b-23

Paul refers to the church as the body of Christ in his prayer for the Ephesian believers (1:15-23). Within this context, he cites Ps. 8:7[44] and states, "He [God] . . . gave him [Christ] [to be] the head (κεφαλή) over all things for the church, which is his body, the fullness that is filled all in all (τὸ πλήρωμα τοῦ τὰ πάντα ἐν πᾶσιν πληρουμένου)" (1:22-23). As elsewhere, Paul designates the church as the body of Christ, but introduces a few distinctive ideas that are not found in 1 Corinthians or in Romans. For example, (1) he uses the specific word ἐκκλησία to designate the community of believers and identifies it as the body of Christ. (2) He implies that Christ is the head of all things, denoting the cosmic dominion and the rulership of Christ.[45] (3) He also introduces the idea of fullness (πλήρωμα) in relation to Christ and to the church.[46]

----

[44]Cf. 1 Cor. 15:27, Heb. 2:8.

[45]The word κεφαλή occurs first in 1 Cor. 11:3, "The head of every man is Christ," and takes on decisive theological significance in Ephesians and Colossians when referred to Christ in his relation to the church. Cf. Eph. 4:15, 5:23, Col. 1:18, 2:10, and 2:19. On κεφαλή, see Ridderbos, *Paul*, 378-87; Ellis, *Pauline Theology*, 41; Schlier, "κεφαλή," in *TDNT*, 3:673-81; S. Bedale, "The Meaning of κεφαλή in the Pauline Epistles," *JTS* 5 (October 1954): 211-15; and W. Grudem, "Does κεφαλή Mean 'Source' or 'Authority over' in Greek Literature? A Survey of 2,336 Examples," *TJ* 6 NS (Spring 1985): 38-59.

[46]Cf. Eph. 3:19, 4:10, 13, Col. 1:19, 2:9, 10. The meaning of the last phrase, τὸ πλήρωμα τοῦ τὰ πάντα ἐν πᾶσιν πληρουμένου, is much debated. The interpretation of this phrase centers around πληρουμένου, whether one should take it as passive or as middle with an active sense. If taken as middle with an active sense, it refers to Christ as himself filling the fullness of things. When an active sense is required, however, Paul usually uses the active voice (cf. Eph. 4:10). If taken as passive, it may imply that "the fullness of Christ is filled by the church. In other words, the fullness of Christ (the head) is progressively completed as the church (his Body) grows (i.e., Armitage Robinson). This is, however, a strange idea to Paul. He states that the fullness of God dwells in Christ (Co. 1:19, 2:9) and this fullness is the standard which the church is to attain (Eph. 3:19, 4:13, Col. 2:10). According to Eph. 4:10, it is Christ who fills all things. The fullness of Christ is, therefore, not dependent on the growth of the church. See the discussion in Armitage Robinson, *Ephesians*, 42-45, 255-59; Wilfred L. Knox, *St. Paul and the Church of the Gentiles* (Cambridge: Cambridge University Press, 1939), 186; J. A. T. Robinson, *Body*, 67-72; and Best, *One Body*, 139-46; cf. Gerhard Delling, "πλήρωμα," in *TDNT*, 6:298-311; R. Yates, "A Re-examination of Ephesians 1:23," *ExpTim* 83 (February 1972): 146-51; G. Howard, "The Head/Body Metaphors of Ephesians," *NTS* 20 (April 1974): 350-56; and C. F. D. Moule, "'Fullness' and 'Fill' in the New Testament," *SJT* (March 1951): 79-86. J. A. T. Robinson, *Body*, 66, argues that an unnecessary confusion has been caused by treating κεφαλή and πλήρωμα either as complementary (Armitage Robinson) or

These distinctions are, however, not contradictory to 1 Corinthians and Romans but rather complementary.   The basic thought in Ephesians and Colossians is the same as that of 1 Corinthians and Romans: The church is the body of Christ (Eph. 1:23, 4:13) and believers are members of his body or of the same body (σύσσωμα) in Christ (Eph. 5:30, 3:6). To this basic thought, Paul introduces a new concept that Christ is the head of the church.   An exegetical confusion arises when one attempts to harmonize these two images as if they are one and the same.[47] Although they are closely connected with each other, each one has an "independent significance and an independent existence."[48] In Eph. 4:15-16 and Col. 2:19 the head appears to be regarded as a specific organ of the body, but Paul does not say here "the head, from which," but "the head, from whom," that is, from Christ. Moreover, he represents the church not merely as the remaining parts of the body belonging to the head but as the whole body. The designation of Christ as the head of the church is, therefore, not contradictory to the concept of the church as the body of Christ but rather complementary.

Eph. 2:14-16

Paul's reference to "one body" occurs in verse 16: "(that he) might reconcile both [Jew and Gentile] to God in one body (ἐν ἑνὶ σώματι) through the cross."[49] Scholars differ as to whether "one body" in this verse refers only to the individual body of Christ sacrificed on the cross or to the church. Percy and Schnackenburg, for example, argue that "one body" signifies the body of Christ given up on the cross in the sense of "his flesh" (Eph. 2:15) or "his body of flesh" (Col. 1:22).[50] This view, however, has a number of problems: (1) If Paul was referring to the individual body of Christ, he would have

---

identical (F. C. Synge). He insists that although the two terms are closely related, they are nevertheless independent and presuppose different metaphors.

[47]Cf. Percy, *Leib Christi*, 52-54 and Ridderbos, *Paul*, 379-83.

[48]Ridderbos, *Paul*, 381.

[49]Ellis, *Pauline Theology*, 80, insists that this passage is an implicit commentary on Isa. 57:19. Cf. N. A. Dahl, "Christ, Creation and the Church," in *The Background of the New Testament and Its Eschatology*, ed. W. D. Davies and D. Daube (Cambridge: University Press, 1964), 436-37.

[50]Percy, *Leib Christi*, 39, 42; Schnackenburg, *Church*, 174-75; cf. Cerfaux, *Church*, 326 and Ridderbos, *Paul*, 377, n. 58.

spoken of "his body" rather than "one body."[51] (2) The underlying idea of the passage, as is clearly indicated by the continual contrast between "two" (or "both") and "one" in verses 14-16, is that the two groups of people become one in Christ. Paul explains this unity as "one" (2:14), "one new man" (2:15), and "one body" (2:16). The "one body" is clearly parallel to "one" and "one new man" and all three expressions must, therefore, be interpreted as referring to the same entity.[52] Moreover, (3) the phrase "in one body" occurs also in Col. 3:15, and there it clearly refers to the church. It is likely, therefore, that the "one body" in Eph. 2:16 alludes primarily, though implicitly, to the church as the body of Christ.

Eph. 3:6

In a similar context to the previous passage, Paul states that "the Gentiles are fellow heirs (συγκληρονόμα), members of the same body (σύσσωμα), and partakers (συμμέτοχα) of the promise in Christ Jesus through the gospel." The underlying idea is basically the same as that of Eph. 2:16, namely, the unity of Jew and Gentile in Christ. Although it is grammatically possible to construe the phrase "in Christ Jesus" only with the "promise," it is more likely that the phrase modifies all three nouns συγκληρονόμα, σύσσωμα, and συμμέτοχα. If so, the phrase σύσσωμα . . . ἐν Χριστῷ Ἰησοῦ is not much different from "one body in Christ" in Rom. 12:5 or "one in Christ Jesus" in Gal. 3:28, and refers to the church as the body of Christ.

Eph. 4:4, 11-16

The general context of the passage is very similar to the contexts of 1 Corinthians 12 and Romans 12, namely, the unity of the church expressed in the diversity of the spiritual gifts. The recurring word "one" (ἕν or εἷς) in Eph. 4:4-5 clearly refers to the unity while the various offices mentioned in verse 11 denotes the diversity.[53] The common purpose of the diverse gifts is

---

[51]Moule, *Origin*, 77; Best, *One Body*, 153.

[52]Eph. 4:24, Col. 3:10, Gal. 3:27. Cf. Ridderbos, *Paul*, 378 and Best, *One Body*, 153.

[53]The unity is stressed by "one body," "one Spirit," "one hope," "one Lord," "one faith," "one baptism," and "one God" while various offices "apostles," "prophets," "evangelists," "pastors," and "teachers" (cf. 1 Cor. 12:18) denote the diversity.

"for the equipping of the saints, for the work of ministry, for the building (εἰς οἰκοδομήν) of the body of Christ" (4:12). Although it is uncertain what "one body" in 4:4 specifically refers to,[54] the "body of Christ" in 4:12 clearly denotes the church.

In this passage Paul also identifies Christ as the head.[55] The head (Christ) not only is the standard of the growth of the body (church) but also supplies all the spiritual needs for its growth (4:16).[56] By combining the analogy of the body with those of "head" and "building" (4:12, 16),[57] he emphasizes the growing aspect of the body: "Until we all attain . . . to the mature adulthood (ἄνδρα τέλειον), to the measure of the stature of the fullness of Christ" (4:13). In the following verse (4:15) he says, "We are to grow up in every way into him who is the head, that is, Christ." The full-grown man in his maturity is apparently compared with Christ. The church must grow to the fullness of Christ. In order to do that, every part of the body, joined and knit together, must work properly and depend on the head.[58] In this passage, therefore, Paul emphasizes not only the unity of believers with one another but also their ultimate unity with Christ who is individually the head.

Eph. 5:23, 30

An explicit reference to the church as the body of Christ occurs in this passage in a general context similar in some respects to that of 1 Cor. 6:12-20. Both passages deal with the sexual union on the basis of Gen. 2:24. In this passage, however, the comparison is between the union of husband and wife and that of Christ and the church. Paul applies Gen. 2:24 to the church as the

---

[54]"One body" in verse 4 occurs in a passing manner. Moule, *Origin*, 78, argues that the fact that "one Lord" is separate and subsequent lends weight to taking "one body" as equivalent to the body of Christ mentioned in verse 12. If so, it also refers to the church.

[55]Cf. Eph. 1:22, 5:23, Col. 1:18, 2:10, 2:19.

[56]Here it looks as if the head is a part of the body analogy. But as Meuzelaar points out, Paul uses the masculine relative pronoun instead of the feminine pronoun that one might expect if the feminine noun κεφαλή was intended to be taken into the body analogy. See Meuzelaar, *Leib des Messias*, 121-22. On the relationship between the head and the body, see Ridderbos, *Paul*, 376-83 and Howard, "Head/Body Metaphors," 350-56.

[57]The idea of "building" in connection with that of growth is introduced in Eph. 2:20-22 (cf. 1 Cor. 3:9, 2 Cor. 5:1).

[58]Cf. Col. 2:19.

bride of Christ and compares the unity between Christ and the church to that of "one flesh" effected through marriage.[59] The basic idea is twofold: (1) The church is the body of Christ, and (2) Christ is the head of that body. The "head" in this passage denotes Christ as the bridegroom of the church.[60] The statement in Eph. 5:30, "We are members of his body," is reminiscent of 1 Cor. 6:15, "Your bodies are members of Christ" and of 1 Cor. 12:27, "You are . . . members of it [Christ's body]." These texts imply, therefore, that believers are members of the body of Christ, regarded as the church.

Passages in Colossians

References to the church as the body of Christ and the designation of Christ as the head also occur in Colossians, often in a very similar manner to the passages in Ephesians. They appear in the following texts.

Col. 1:18

The expression in Col. 1:18, "He [Christ] is the head of the body, the church," is similar to that of Eph. 1:22-23. Like the Ephesian passage, Paul designates ἐκκλησία as the body of Christ and Christ as its head. However, there are a few distinctive aspects of this passage: (1) Although Col. 1:18 implies that Christ is the leader of the church, it seems to lay more stress on the pre-eminence of Christ. For example, it describes Christ not only as the "head" (κεφαλή) of the church, but also as the "beginning" (ἀρχή) and as the "first-born (πρωτότοκος) from the dead." As the phrase ἵνα γένηται ἐν πᾶσιν αὐτὸς πρωτεύων (1:18b) indicates, Paul employs these terms to denote the priority and the pre-eminence of Christ in all things.[61] (2) His reference is more compact, but less clear than that in Eph. 1:22-23. For example, Col.

---

[59]For the discussion of the church as the bride of Christ, see Claude Chavasse, *The Bride of Christ: An Enquiry into the Nuptial Element in Early Church* (London: Faber and Faber, 1940), 66-85; Richard A. Batey, *New Testament Nuptial Imagery* (Leiden: E. J. Brill, 1971); Shedd, *Man in Community*, 164; and Best, *One Body*, 169-83.

[60]Cf. 1 Cor. 11:3, 7-9, where Paul speaks of the headship of Christ over the church and of the husband over his wife on the basis of the priority of male in creation. See Ellis, *Pauline Theology*, 41, esp. n. 62.

[61]Cf. Ridderbos, *Paul*, 382 and Bedale, "Meaning of κεφαλή," 213-15.

1:18 states that Christ is ἡ κεφαλὴ τοῦ σώματος τῆς ἐκκλησίας. It is not clear whether one should understand this phrase as meaning that "Christ is the head of the body of the church" or that "Christ is the head of the body, the church." If the first view is taken, the "body of the church" seems to imply the community of believers in the sense of the Stoic metaphor that refers to the body of people in a political sense. Then, the "head" means simply a "leader." Although this construction is grammatically possible, it is less likely in view of other similar passages.[62] The phrase τῆς ἐκκλησίας is more likely in apposition with τοῦ σώματος.[63] If so, the "head" implies the headship of Christ over the church regarded as his body.

Col. 1:24

This passage, one of the most enigmatic verses in the Pauline letters, states that Paul's sufferings "complete what is lacking in Christ's afflictions for the sake of his body, which is the church."[64] Although what exactly is lacking in Christ's afflictions and how Paul's sufferings complete it are subject to much debate,[65] this verse at least clearly identifies Christ's body with the church.[66]

Col. 2:16-19

Possible allusions to the body of Christ occur in Col. 2:17 and 19, a passage in which Paul deals with heretical teachers who insist on various religious practices (2:16). Against these heretics, he explains that believers who were buried and raised up with Christ in baptism are no longer obligated to such practices because Christ canceled in his death the bondage of legal demands. Furthermore, "they are only a shadow of what is to come." Paul

---

[62]Cf. Eph. 1:22-23, 5:23, Col. 1:24, and 2:19.

[63]Cf. Col. 1:24, Eph. 1:22-23, and 5:23.

[64]Here the appositional understanding of Col. 1:18 is confirmed.

[65]For a review of various interpretations of this verse, see R. Yates, "A Note on Colossians 1:24," *EvQ* 42 (April-June 1970): 88-92.

[66]See Acts 9:4-5 (cf. 22:7-8, 26:14-15): "Saul, Saul, why are you persecuting me?" Paul never persecuted Jesus personally, but Jesus regards Paul's persecution of the church as a persecution of himself.

then adds the enigmatic phrase τὸ δὲ σῶμα τοῦ Χριστοῦ (2:17). The meaning
of this phrase has been much debated. Many scholars find in this verse a
σκιά-σῶμα contrast like the one found in Philo or Josephus,[67] and translate
the phrase, "The substance belongs to Christ."[68] Even J. A. T. Robinson, who
takes Paul's expression "body of Christ" more seriously and realistically,
thinks that σῶμα is used only here in a non-human sense.[69] Although the
word σῶμα is clearly contrasted to the word σκιά, one cannot simply ignore
the literal meaning of σῶμα. The phrase τὸ σῶμα τοῦ Χριστοῦ means "the
body of Christ."[70] The body of Christ is the reality of what is to come.
Whether this body refers to the individual body of Christ sacrificed on the
cross or to the church is, however, not clear.

The reference in verse 19 is more explicit. The expression is very
similar to that of Eph. 4:15-16. Although in Col. 2:19 Paul refers to the head
and to the body without a reference to Christ or to the church, it is obvious
from the context that the head refers to Christ and the body to the church. The
main emphasis of the passage is the body "holding fast" to its head for
growth.

Col. 3:15

In this verse a reference to "one body" occurs in passing. While
speaking of the peace of Christ, Paul states, ". . . to which you were called in
one body (ἐν ἑνὶ σώματι)." Whether "one body" refers to the individual
body of Christ or to the church is not clear. In view of 1 Cor. 12:13 and Eph.
2:16 where similar expressions occur, however, it seems to denote the body
regarded as the church.[71]

The following conclusions may be drawn from the above analysis of the
passages in which Paul explicitly or implicitly refers to the church as the body
of Christ: (1) Paul's designation of the church as σῶμα appears in various
forms. For example, he refers to the church as "the body of Christ," "one

---

[67]Cf. Philo, *Conf.* 190, *Post.* 112, and Josephus, *War* 2.2.5.

[68]For example, see Moule, *Origin*, 75.

[69]J. A. T. Robinson, *Body*, 27, n. 1.

[70]Even though the conjunction δέ appears, it seems better to take τοῦ Χριστοῦ simply as
genitive, thus meaning "the body of Christ, rather than supplying a verb, thus meaning "The
body is of Christ."

[71]"Baptized into one body" (1 Cor. 12:13), "reconcile us. . . in one body" (Eph. 2;16).

body in Christ," "the body," or simply as "one body" without a specific reference to Christ.[72] (2) The various expressions are, nevertheless, closely related to one another and basically refer to the same reality. For example, the statement, "So we, though many, are one body in Christ" (Rom. 12:5) is the same as saying, "We who are many are one body" (1 Cor. 10:17). The same expression occurs also in 1 Cor. 12:12-13 where the one body is clearly identified as Christ himself. The statement, "Your bodies are members of Christ" (1 Cor. 6:15) is basically the same as saying, "We are members of his body" (Eph. 5:30) or "You are . . . members of it [the body of Christ]" (1 Cor. 12:27). Furthermore, "We were all baptized into one body" (1 Cor. 12:13) is probably not much different from saying, "You were called in one body" (Col. 3:15). (3) The basic denotation of the body of Christ, regarded as the church, is the unity and the communion that exist between Christ and the church. Even when the church is described simply as "one body" without a specific reference to Christ, it is not a body apart from Christ.[73] (4) Since the church and Christ are so closely connected in Paul, it is often difficult, if not impossible, to make a sharp distinction between the body referring to the individual body of Christ and the body referring to the church. This is most apparent in 1 Cor. 10:14-22 and 11:17-34. (5) Paul's designation of the church as the body of Christ seems more than a mere metaphor.[74] It involves an ontological reality. Paul's conception of the union between Christ and the church is so real that he expresses it in various physical terms. It is as real as the physical union created by sexual intercourse and as the union with demons created by the physical participation in the pagan sacrifice.[75] Finally, (6) in Ephesians and Colossians, the body of Christ is combined with other ideas such as "head," "building," and "fullness."[76] These ideas are often used to

---

[72]1 Cor. 12:27, Eph. 1:22-23, 5:30, Col. 1:24, Rom. 12:5 (cf. Eph. 3:6), Eph. 5:23, Col. 1:18, 1 Cor. 10:17, Eph. 2:16, 4:4, Col. 3:15.

[73]Cf. 1 Cor. 12:13, Rom. 12:5, Gal. 3:27-28, and Eph. 3:6.

[74]So, E. P. Sanders, *Paul and Palestinian Judaism: A Comparison of Patterns of Religion* (Minneapolis, MN: Fortress, 1977), 455; Schnackenburg, *Church*, 170; J. A. T. Robinson, *Body*, 50-51; E. L. Mascall, *Christ, the Christian and the Church: A Study of the Incarnation and Its Consequences* (London: Longmans, 1946), 112, 116; Ellis, "Sōma," 141; Käsemann, "Lord's Supper," 109, 118, 132; and idem, "Theological Problem," 103, 105. Otherwise, cf. F. W. Dillistone, "How is the Church Christ's Body?" *TToday* 2 (April 1945): 56-58; Minear, *Images*, 173-220; Best, *One Body*, 98-101, 112-13; Moule, *Origin*, 70; Gundry, *Sōma*, 231, 234-35; and Ridderbos, *Paul*, 376.

[75]Cf. 1 Cor. 6:13-20, 10:14-22.

[76]Cf. Eph. 1:22-23, 4:11-16, 5:23, Col. 1:18-19, 2:19.

emphasize the mutual dependence and the growing aspect of the church.[77]

Implications

Paul's designation of the church as the body of Christ denotes primarily the unity of believers with Christ.[78] What is then the exact nature of this unity between believers and Christ that the body of Christ qualifies? In what sense is the church the body of Christ? The answer to this question may be difficult, but it is important for determining what implications this unity has for Paul's understanding of Christ, of the church, and particularly of man.

Various Understandings

Broadly speaking, there are two views of Paul's designation of the church as the body of Christ: (1) Some understand it in a metaphorical sense and (2) others in a realistic sense.[79] The point of departure for the metaphorical view is the distinction between the individual body of Christ and his body that is the church.[80] Scholars who support this view argue that the phrase "body of Christ" is simply a metaphor that refers to the collection of believers.[81] They regard the church as the body of Christ only because it has a special relationship with him and not because it is a manifestation of the body of Christ in a realistic sense. Consequently, the relationship between Christ and the church, regarded as the body of Christ, has no physical dimension. In

---

[77]Cf. Eph. 1:22-23, 4:12-16, Col. 2:19.

[78]Ridderbos, *Paul*, 375; Best, *One Body*, 93. However, cf. Meuzelaar, *Leib des Messias*, 1-19, who insists that it is not so much a matter of the relationship of believers with Christ as it is of the relationship of believers to one another. He argues that the body of Christ is simply a metaphor that Paul employs for a practical purpose, that is, to appeal for the unity of Jews and Gentiles in the church.

[79]For discussion of various views, see Ridderbos, *Paul*, 363-69 and Jewett, *Anthropological Terms*, 201-27.

[80]For example, see Gundry, *Sōma*, 228-29; Best, *One Body*, 100-01; and Moule, *Origin*, 70-82. Moule, however, acknowledges that "1 Cor. 12:12-13 and 1 Cor. 6:15 are difficult to interpret otherwise than as symptoms of a mode of thought which viewed Christ himself as an inclusive Person, a Body, to be joined to which was to become part of him" (81).

[81]For example, see Gundry, *Sōma*, 223-44; Moule, *Origin*, 81; and Ziesler, *Pauline Christianity*, 54.

addition, there is no pre-existing body of Christ into which believers enter. Since believers constitute the church, without them there is no body of Christ that is the church.[82]

Now, a question arises. If the relationship between the church and Christ is not physical, what is it? Various suggestions have been offered. Traditionally, the phrase "body of Christ" has been understood as denoting the pneumatic existence of the church.[83] The church is the body of Christ because Christ constitutes it by his Spirit and enlivens it by his indwelling. The union between Christ and the church is, therefore, of a spiritual nature. Ridderbos, following Percy, however, criticizes this view, saying that it is based on the analogy of a dualistic body/soul anthropology that according to him, is foreign to Paul.[84] He also rejects the idea that the Spirit constitutes the body of Christ. Based on the exegesis of 1 Cor. 12:13, he argues that the Spirit is "not thought of here as the factor constituting the body, . . . but as the gift in which believers share in virtue of their incorporation into the body."[85]

E. Best argues that the phrase "body of Christ" is a metaphor that denotes a corporate personality which believers form with Christ.[86] He insists that since Paul employs various metaphors, including "body of Christ," to depict different aspects of this conception and since the physical union with Christ is unthinkable, the church is "not really or ontologically the actual body of Christ."[87] Best may be right in recognizing that a basic conception underlies the various Pauline expressions, but his treatment of the phrase as a metaphor simply because a physical union between Christ and the church is incomprehensible to him is not convincing.[88] Interestingly, J. A. T. Robinson, who shares a similar definition of σῶμα, draws a conclusion quite different from that of Best. For him, the church is really and ontologically the body of

---

[82]See Gundry, *S ma*, 223-24 and Moule, *Origin*, 71-81.

[83]For example, see C. H. Dodd, "Matthew and Paul," *ExpTim* 58 (1947): 293-98; H. A. A. Kennedy, *The Theology of the Epistles* (London: Duckworth, 1919), 148; and Gundry, *S ma*, 228.

[84]Ridderbos, *Paul*, 364-65, 372-73; Percy, *Leib Christi*, 10-44.

[85]Ridderbos, *Paul*, 372-73. See also Best, *One Body*, 97, 110.

[86]Best, *One Body*, 95-159. Cf. Ellis, *Pauline Theology*, 44 and Shedd, *Man in Community*, 164-65. Concerning the conception of "corporate personality," see pp. 75-79 (ch. 2) above.

[87]Best, *One Body*, 99-100.

[88]Ibid., 75.

Christ.[89] Jewett's criticism of Best's view is also noteworthy. He states that Best's view "tends to reduce Paul's σῶμα concept down to the common denominator of mid [twentieth]-century ecumenical piety," and "it avoids those uncomfortable aspects of Paul's usage which years of research have uncovered."[90]

H. Ridderbos offers yet another explanation.[91] He argues that the unity of Christ and the church, expressed as the "body of Christ," has its ground "in the church's belonging to Christ in the redemptive-historical sense, in the inclusion of 'the many' in the one." "In virtue of this common belonging to and inclusion of 'the many' in Christ," he continues, "individual believers are qualified as members of Christ and the church as his body."[92] In other words, believers have been included in the sacrificial death of Christ. As result, they now belong to and exist in Christ. They are in the new age. Ridderbos' view is very similar to that of Percy in that both explain the body of Christ in the redemptive-historical sense and thus in the sense of "in Christ."[93] Interestingly, however, Percy argues for the identification between the church and the individual body of Christ while Ridderbos argues for the distinction between them. Ridderbos insists that the inclusion in Christ is not the same as the identification of the church with the historical and glorified body of Christ.[94] Thus, he concludes: "The qualification of the church as the 'body of Christ' . . . clearly has a figurative, metaphorical significance, however real and literal the unity and communion with Christ expressed thereby is."[95]

Other scholars understand the body of Christ in a realistic sense. They identify the individual body of Christ with his body that is the church, arguing that the body of Christ as the church is fundamentally no other body than that

---

[89]J. A. T. Robinson, *Body*, 51-52; also, L. S. Thornton, *The Common Life in the Body of Christ*, 4th ed. (London: Dacre, 1963), 298.

[90]Jewett, *Anthropological Terms*, 223.

[91]Ridderbos, *Paul*, 369-87.

[92]Ibid., 375-76.

[93]Percy, *Leib Christi*, 20, 32; Ridderbos, *Paul*, 369-76. Their attempt to interpret the body of Christ in the sense of "in Christ" has been criticized by Best, *One Body*, 18-19, 93; Käsemann, "Theological Problem," 106; and Conzelmann, *Theology*, 265. Interestingly, Schweitzer, *Mysticism*, 117, 122-23, argues for precisely the opposite. According to him, "the expression 'being-in-Christ' is merely a brachyology for being partakers in the Mystical Body of Christ" (122-23).

[94]Ridderbos, *Paul*, 365-66, 376.

[95]Ibid., 376. The difference between Percy and Ridderbos may be rooted in the Reformation disputes between Lutheran and Reformed theology.

which died on the cross, rose again on the third day, ascended into heaven, and now lives on high.[96]   While these scholars identify the two bodies as being essentially the same, they often disagree as to how or in what sense the two bodies are identical.

A. Schweitzer offers the most radical explanation.[97] Drawing upon the apocalyptic conception of the predestined solidarity of the Elect with the Messiah and with one another,[98] he contends that the phrase "body of Christ" denotes the physical corporeity of believers with Christ and with one another that is achieved by water baptism.   By participating in this baptismal corporeity, he argues, believers become a part of the body of Christ.[99]   As a result, they even now share the resurrection corporeity with Christ.   In other words, they are already corporately in the resurrection mode of existence. Schweitzer's view certainly had a great impact on the subsequent studies of the subject, but it was not widely accepted because of its extremely realistic anticipation of the participation of believers in the resurrection corporeity of Christ.   Gundry, for example, points out that "to equate the present physical body of Christ with believers wreaks havoc with the temporal distinction Paul carefully makes between the pastness of Christ's resurrection and the futurity of believers' resurrection."[100]

John A. T. Robinson expresses a view similar to that of Schweitzer.[101] The basis for his argument is, however, not the apocalyptic conception of the corporeity of the Elect with the Messiah, but the Old Testament anthropology that in his view regards individual man as a whole [unified] person in solidarity.[102]   Understanding the term σῶμα also in this sense, he argues that believers participate corporately in the resurrection body of Christ and that the church is an extension of Christ's individual body.   For him, therefore, the

---

[96]For example, see Percy, *Leib Christi*, 44; J. A. T. Robinson, *Body*, 51, 57; Thornton, *Common Life*, 298; and Cerfaux, *Church*, 281.

[97]Schweitzer, *Mysticism*, 109-40.

[98]Schweitzer cites Dan. 7:27, *1 Enoch* 38:1-5, 62:7-8, 14-15, *4 Ezra* 9:38-10:57.

[99]Schweitzer, *Mysticism*, 117.

[100]Gundry, *S ma*, 228.   See also Jewett, *Anthropological Terms*, 215 and Ridderbos, *Paul*, 366, esp. n. 11.

[101]J. A. T. Robinson, *Body*, 49-72.

[102]Ibid., 11-16.   See also Best, *One Body*, 215-21 and Cerfaux, *Church*, 262-86. Cerfaux's view is, however, different from that of Robinson in that while Robinson stresses the wholeness of believers and Christ in their solidarity as one body, Cerfaux stresses the individuality of Christ's physical body to which believers are united.

body of Christ is nothing other than the extended individual body of Christ.[103] He finds the identification of the two bodies in Paul's reference to the Lord's Supper in 1 Corinthians 10 and 11. He recognizes, however, a logical jump in these passages from "feeding on" to "becoming" the body itself.[104] Claiming that only Paul could make that jump, he traces the ground for it to Paul's conversion encounter with the risen Christ Jesus who identified himself with the church.[105] For him, therefore, the union between Christ and the church is not only real but also physical. This understanding is evident in his statement: "It is almost impossible to exaggerate the materialism and crudity of Paul's doctrine of the Church as literally now the resurrection *body* of Christ." The union that the term σῶμα conveys is, he continues, "something *not corporate but corporal*."[106] For this reason, however, his view faces the same criticism that has been brought against Schweitzer's view.[107]

E. Percy also strongly argues for the identification of the church with the individual body of Christ.[108] The starting-point for his argument is the rejection of the view that explains the phrase "body of Christ" on the analogy of the dualistic body/soul anthropology. Understanding the term σῶμα in the light of Old Testament anthropology, particularly the Old Testament conception of "corporate personality," he argues that the union of Christ and the church qualified by the phrase "body of Christ" bears a redemptive-historical character in that believers ("the many") have been included in Christ ("the one"). They have been included in the death and the resurrection of Christ. They have participated in the bodily existence of Christ in which he suffered and died as the substitute for his own. As a result, they have been incorporated into Christ and thus now belong to him. Proceeding on the idea of believers' inclusion in and belonging to Christ, he comes to the conclusion that the body of Christ identical with the church is fundamentally no other body than that which died on the cross and rose again on the third day.[109] Ridderbos who closely follows Percy's view in most parts digresses from him at this point because for him the inclusion in the suffering and in the death of

---

[103] J. A. T. Robinson, *Body*, 51-52.

[104] Ibid., 57.

[105] Ibid., 57-58. Cf. Acts. 9:4-5, 7-8, 26:14-15.

[106] J. A. T. Robinson, *Body*, 50-51.

[107] For example, see Gundry, *Sōma*, 228-44, who most vigorously criticizes Robinson's view. Cf. Ellis, "Structure," 38-39.

[108] Percy, *Leib Christi*, 18-46.

[109] Ibid., 44.

Christ is not the same as becoming his body in the literal and historical sense of the word.[110]

R. Bultmann also takes Paul's designation of the church as the body of Christ in a real sense, but not in a physical sense.[111] He claims that the risen Christ has a non-physical, supramundane, and transcendental body, and it is this body that the phrase "body of Christ" denotes and into which believers enter.[112] Consequently, this body was there before believers came into being and remains there now above them. Bultmann's interpretation of Paul's "body of Christ" concept is clearly influenced by his extreme individualistic and existentialist understanding of man. He recognizes the communal element but plays it down as secondary. He also recognizes the physical aspect of σῶμα but never imparts any theological significance to such physicality.[113] In this respect, his view has been vigorously criticized.[114]

E. Käsemann differs slightly from the view of Bultmann.[115] He starts with Bultmann's idea that σῶμα signifies the whole [unified] person in historical existence, faced with the choice of either being determined by God or by sin. Realizing the danger of the extreme individualistic interpretation of Bultmann, however, he redefines the term σῶμα as the "possibility of communication" rather than as the "object-self."[116] In this way, he changes the existentialist interpretation of σῶμα from "relationship to one's object-self" to "relationship with others" and reverses the error of a private, existential exposition of the body of Christ without forsaking the transcendental interpretation. For him, therefore, the body of Christ is a transcendent, non-temporal sphere into which believers enter by the sacraments.[117] Ironically, he traces the background of this conception of the corporal unity between Christ and the church to the gnostic "Primal Man" myth.[118] Jewett points out that "the gnostic conception had no place for actual corporal unity since its underlying dualism involved a negation of the material world as the

---

[110]Ridderbos, *Paul*, 365-66.

[111]Bultmann, *Theology*, 1:306-14.

[112]Ibid., 1:310.

[113]Ibid., 192-203.

[114]For example, see J. A. T. Robinson, *Body*, 11-33; Gundry, *Sōma*, 217-22; and J. Macquarrie, *An Existentialist Theology: A Comparison of Heidegger and Bultmann* (London: SCM, 1965), 219-20.

[115]Käsemann, *Leib und Leib Christi*, 137-86; idem, "Theological Problem," 102-21.

[116]Käsemann, *Leib und Leib Christi*, 118-25.

[117]Ibid., 156-59, 151-55, 171-74, 139-44, 174-79.

[118]Ibid., 59-94, 168-71.

root of evil."[119] Gundry also states that "the physicality of the Body and the materialism of the sacraments by which believers enter the Body . . . are far too mundane to agree with an exclusively functional interpretation of *sōma* or a Gnostic background in the Ur-Anthropos, who was a *spiritual* light-being."[120]

This brief survey of various views shows that the determining factor in explaining Paul's designation of the church as the body of Christ is basically one's understanding of Paul's use of the term σῶμα, whether it refers to a part of man or to the whole person, whether it denotes the physical or the non-physical substance, and whether it refers to an individual person in isolation or in solidarity.[121] When σῶμα is understood as conveying the idea of physicality, one faces the difficulty of explaining the physical union between Christ and the church that the phrase "body of Christ" implies. The easiest solution may be to take Paul's expression simply as a metaphor referring to a non-physical reality and thus to separate the ecclesiastical body of Christ from his individual body. His expression is, however, simply too realistic to be regarded as a mere metaphor. Moreover, it is exegetically impossible to make a complete distinction in Paul between σῶμα that refers to the individual body of Christ and σῶμα that refers to his ecclesiastical body.

The Church as the Corporate Body of Christ

There is a fluidity in Paul between the individual body of Christ and his body designated as the church so that either to equate them or to distinguish completely between them creates a confused exegesis. Believers are in one sense identified with Christ, but in another sense distinguished from him.

---

[119]Jewett, *Anthropological Terms*, 217.

[120]Gundry, *Sōma*, 225-26. See also Jewett, *Anthropological Terms*, 219.

[121]Gundry, for example, understands σῶμα as referring to the physical part of a body/soul dualism while Bultmann, Käsemann, Robinson, and Cerfaux understand it as referring to the whole (unified) person. Gundry, Robinson, and Cerfaux emphasize the physicality of the body of Christ, but Bultmann plays it down as theologically insignificant. Bultmann and Cerfaux stress the individuality of Christ's body (Cerfaux, however, does not do the individualization on the existentialist base), Robinson and Käsemann stress the wholeness of believers and Christ in their solidarity. See Gundry, *Sōma*, 159-83, 217-44; Bultmann, *Theology*, 1:192-203; Käsemann, *Leib und Leib Christi*, 118-25; J. A. T. Robinson, *Body*, 26-33, 49-55; and Cerfaux, *Church*, 262-86.

They are identified with the individual body of Christ in his death.[122] They are baptized into Christ or into the body of Christ.[123] In other words, they have been joined to the Lord and have put on the new man (Christ).[124] As a result, they have become one spirit (body) with him and members of Christ or of the body of Christ. In this sense, they are really and ontologically the body of Christ.[125]

Although Paul identifies the church with Christ, he always maintains a distinction between them. For him, Christ is always an individual person with a distinct physical body. Even after the resurrection, although transformed into the glorious body, he is still an individual person who now lives on high and will some day come again to receive those who belong to him.[126] He likewise distinguishes the church from Christ in passages where he refers to the church as "one body in Christ"[127] and where he designates Christ as the head of the body.[128] Thus, it must be concluded that whereas for Paul the church is identified with the body of Christ, it (the church) is not identical to the individual physical body of Christ.

In what sense then is the church the body of Christ? To answer this question, one must first understand Paul's conception of Christ.[129] In Paul's letters Christ is depicted not only as an individual person, but also as a corporate being into whom believers are incorporated and in whom they find their existence. Although he is an individual person with a distinct physical body, his personhood is not limited by his individual being. He is often viewed as extending himself beyond his individual person to include those who belong to him.

Believers are incorporated into Christ when they participate in his death

---

[122]Rom. 7:4; cf. Rom. 6:3-8, Gal. 2:20, Col. 2:12.

[123]Rom. 6:3, Gal. 3:27, 1 Cor. 12:13.

[124]1 Cor. 6:17, Gal. 3:27, Rom. 13:14, Eph. 4:24, Col. 3:10.

[125]1 Cor. 6:15, 17, 12:27, Eph. 1:22-23, 4:12, 5:23, 30, Col. 1:18, 24. Cf. J. A. T. Robinson, *Body*, 51-52; Thornton, *Common Life*, 298; Ellis, "Sōma," 141; Shedd, *Man in Community*, 189-94; Percy, *Leib Christi*, 44; and Schweitzer, *Mysticism*, 127. Otherwise, Best, *One Body*, 99-100; Ridderbos, *Paul*, 365-66, 376; and Gundry, *Sōma*, 223-44.

[126]Cf. Phil. 3:21, 1 Cor. 15:42-49.

[127]Rom. 12:5, Eph. 3:6; cf. Gal. 3:28.

[128]Eph. 1:22, 4:15, 5:23, Col. 1:18, 2:10, 19.

[129]J. A. T. Robinson, *Body*, 48, claims: "Whatever the linguistic source or sources may have been from which Paul brought that most characteristic of all his expressions, τὸ σῶμα τοῦ Χριστοῦ, it should be axiomatic that it has to be elucidated and interpreted, not primarily in terms of these sources, but *in terms of his own Christology*."

by baptism in the Spirit. This is evident in 1 Cor. 12:13, Rom. 6:3, and Gal. 3:27 where Paul states that believers are baptized into Christ or into one body.[130] "To be baptized" in these verses probably has its primitive sense of immersion and the preposition "into" has a local and realistic meaning.[131] "To be baptized into Christ" means, therefore, "to enter into Christ." Water baptism by immersion effectively depicts and symbolizes this reality.[132]

Incorporated into Christ, believers form a corporate unity with him and Paul's designation of the church as the body of Christ basically denotes this unity. Paul states in 1 Cor. 12:13 that believers were baptized into one body that is nothing other than the body of Christ.[133] He therefore declares that they are "the body of Christ and individually members of it." (1 Cor. 12:27). This means that believers have entered into the body of Christ and thus become one body with him. The same idea is expressed in 1 Cor. 6:15-17 where he describes the unity of believers with Christ by the analogy of the sexual union. He states in verse 17 that "he who joins himself to the Lord (ὁ κολλώμενος τῷ κυρίῳ) becomes one spirit with him." The term κολλᾶσθαι, which is used also in Eph. 5:31 to signify the physical union between husband and wife in marriage, indicates a sort of physical union between believers and Christ.[134] He says that by this union, believers become "one spirit" with Christ. In other words, they become one corporate body with Christ that is animated by the Spirit. Thus, Paul states that their bodies are members of Christ (1 Cor. 6:15).[135] The unity of believers with Christ is also evident in 1 Cor. 10:16 where Paul states that by partaking of the bread, believers participate in the body of Christ. Although the Lord's Supper does not create a new unity with Christ, it certainly manifests in a visual fashion the unity that believers have established with Christ when "we all were baptized by (ἐν) one Spirit into one body" (1 Cor. 12:13).

As believers form a corporate unity with Christ, they also form a unity

---

[130]Rom. 6:3, Gal. 3:27, 1 Cor. 12:13.

[131]Hanson, *Unity*, 81. Cf. Schnackenburg, *Baptism*, 21-26.

[132]The relationship between faith and baptism and between water baptism and the Spirit that has been the subject of much debate is certainly beyond the scope of this study. For detailed discussion, see the discussions in Shedd, *Man in Community*, 181-89; Beasley-Murray, *Baptism*; Dunn, *Theology*, 443-59; Schnackenburg, *Baptism*, and Ridderbos, *Paul*, 396-414.

[133]Cf. 1 Cor. 12:12, Rom. 6:3, Gal. 3:27. See the discussion in Hanson, *Unity*, 75-86.

[134]Cf. Matt. 19:5. The term κολλᾶσθαι, which means "to cleave to," is used for intimate association in the form of sexual intercourse. See K. L. Schmidt, "κολλάω," in *TDNT*, 3:822-23 and Schweitzer, *Mysticism*, 127.

[135]Cf. 1 Cor. 12:27, Eph. 5:30.

with one another. Thus, Paul states that believers are "one body in Christ" and although many, are "one body" and "members of one another."[136] Jew and Gentile are "all one (man) in Christ Jesus," created as "one new man . . . in one body through the cross." Thus, the Gentiles are now "members of the same body in Christ."[137] In these verses, however, Paul does not speak of a body different from that which believers together form with Christ. There is perhaps a difference in emphasis that while the "body of Christ" stresses the corporate unity of believers with Christ, "one body in Christ" emphasizes their mutual unity with one another. Believers are, however, "one body" only because they are one body with Christ. In other words, the unity of believers with one another is derived from and dependent upon their corporate unity with Christ.

The church that Paul designates as the body of Christ is, therefore, the extended body of Christ. It is his corporate body that he forms with believers. Although this corporate body is closely connected with the individual physical body of Christ, it is not completely identical to it. Moreover, this corporate body may not be physical in nature if one defines the term "physical" strictly as the visual, material substance; nevertheless, it is an ontological reality as real as the physical body.

This understanding of Paul's designation of the church as the body of Christ is significant because it implies (1) that Christ is not only an individual but also a corporate person, (2) that the church is the body of Christ in a real sense, and more importantly, (3) that believers exist in a corporate solidarity with Christ and with other believers. On the one hand believers are distinct individuals, but on the other hand they are the corporate body of Christ. Paul claims that in this corporate body, there is neither Jew nor Greek, neither slave nor free, and no male and female because they are all one (man) in Christ Jesus.[138] This clearly demonstrates Paul's conception of man not only as an individual but also as a corporate being.

Possible Backgrounds

The designation of the church as the body of Christ is unique to Paul in

---

[136]Rom. 12:5a, 1 Cor. 10:17, 12:12, Rom. 12:5b.
[137]Eph. 2:15-16, Gal. 3:28, Col. 3:15, Eph. 3:6.
[138]Gal. 3:28; cf. Eph. 2:15-16, Col. 3:11, Rom. 10:12.

the New Testament. This fact has led many scholars to inquire into its origin. Possible backgrounds have been sought in hellenistic literature, in Jewish Apocalyptic and Rabbinic writings, in the Christian Eucharist or in Jesus' teaching, and also in the Old Testament.

The Stoic Metaphor

Some scholars contend that Paul's designation of the church as the body of Christ is adopted from the body metaphor that was widely used in the contemporary hellenistic world to denote the unity and the harmony of the city, of the state, or of the cosmos.[139] For example, W. L. Knox states that "the Church as a body, of which the individual believers were members, was derived from the Stoic commonplace of the state as a body in which each member had his part to play."[140] The evidence often cited in support of this view includes (1) Seneca's depiction of the Roman empire as a body of which Nero the emperor is later identified as the head; (2) Josephus' description of the dissenting parties in Jerusalem as one body; (3) the Stoic description of the cosmos as a single unified body that consists of units that are linked together; (4) Philo's representation of the High Priest as kinsman of the whole nation which is likened to a body; and most importantly, (5) the well-known fable of the belly and the members of Menenius Agrippa (c. 500 B.C.) which is similar to the body analogy in 1 Cor. 12:14-26.[141]

---

[139]Among supporters of this view are three different viewpoints: (1) A few argue that Paul's expression is purely a Stoic metaphor. For example, Meuzelaar, *Leib des Messias*, argues that the body of Christ is a mere metaphor used for the practical purpose of urging the unity of Jew and Gentile in the church. See also Knox, *Paul and the Church of the Gentiles* and George Johnston, *The Doctrine of the Church in the New Testament* (Cambridge: University Press, 1943). (2) Some think that the Stoic metaphor influenced only some of Paul's letters. For example, H. Schlier and A. Wikenhauser think that the popular Stoic metaphor greatly influenced Paul's usage in 1 Corinthians 12 and Romans 12, but not in Ephesians and Colossians. See H. Schlier, *Christus und die Kirche im Epheserbrief* (Tübingen: J. C. B. Mohr, 1930) and Wikenhauser, *Kirche*. Based on these observations, Cerfaux, *Church*, 266-82, suggests a development theory, according to which Paul adapted the Stoic metaphor by adding the element of the mystical life in Christ. (3) Others insist that the Stoic metaphor influenced only the phraseology but not the concept. For example, see Schweizer, "σῶμα," in *TDNT*, 7:1069.

[140]Knox, *Paul and the Church of the Gentiles*, 161.

[141]Seneca, *De Clem.* 1:5.1, 2:2.1; Josephus, *War* 4.406, 407; Philo, *Spec. Leg.* 3.131; *Livy* 2.32, Epictetus, *Dis.* 2.10.4-5. R. I. Hicks, "The Body Political and the Body

Despite certain verbal similarities, there are profound conceptual differences between the Stoic body metaphor and Paul's designation of the church as the body of Christ. For example, he does not compare the church simply to a body, but to the body of Christ. As T. W. Manson points out, the uniqueness of Paul's use of the phrase resides "not in the word σῶμα but in the qualifying genitive."[142] It is the body of a named individual person, that is, Christ. Although in Stoic usage a community is compared to a body, it is never considered to be the body of a named person in a real sense. Moreover, whereas the Stoic metaphor implies that the diverse people constitute one body because they are members of one another, for Paul believers are one body only because they are members of Christ.[143]

The Gnostic "Primal Man" Myth

Realizing the inadequacy of the Stoic metaphor to explain Paul's "body of Christ" concept, some scholars turn to the gnostic "Primal Man" myth.[144] The myth relates that the "Primal Man" had a gigantic body that once fell into the earth and was imprisoned in the physical world. Although a part of him was able to escape, fragments of his body remained in an earthly man. In order to redeem them, the "Primal Man" once again returned to earth and imparted to some individuals the special knowledge that enabled them to free themselves and to be reunited with the "Primal Man" in one body.[145]

This gnostic idea of the unity between the redeemed and the redeemer in one body has been employed to explain the origin of the body of Christ in

---

Ecclesiastical," *JBR* 31 (January 1963), 29-35, traces the idea behind the Menenius Agrippa story back to Aesop. She points out that it is told not only by Livy but also by Plutarch. See the discussions in Wikenhauser, *Kirche*, 130-43; Schweizer, "σῶμα," in *TDNT*, 7:1038-39; W. L. Knox, "Parallels to the N. T. Use of σῶμα," *JTS* 39 (July 1983), 243-46; Hanson, *Unity*, 52; and Best, *One Body*, 221-24.

[142]T. W. Manson, "Parallels to the N. T.Use of σῶμα," *JTS* 39 (July 1938): 385; also Best, *One Body*, 83.

[143]Ridderbos, *Paul*, 376.

[144]Based on the work of Reitzenstein and Bousset, numerous scholars attempt to explain both Adam and the body of Christ in Paul from the gnostic "Primal Man" myth. See Reitzenstein, *Hellenistic Mystery-Religions*, 426-96; Bousset, *Kyrios Christos*, 178, 188-200, 274-75; Brandenburger, *Adam und Christus*; Schlier, *Christus und die Kirche*; and Käsemann, *Leib und Leib Christi*, 59-94, 163-86.

[145]*Poimandres* 1:12-26. Cf. Reitzenstein, *Poimandres*, 81; idem, *Hellenistic Mystery-Religions*, passim; and Bousset, *Kyrios Christos*, 190-98.

Paul. H. Schlier, for example, employs this idea to explain Paul's conception of the head and the body found in Ephesians and Colossians. He, however, denies that it could have influenced the earlier letters because they lack the κεφαλή idea which is characteristic in Gnosticism.[146] Ernst Käsemann has made a more comprehensive attempt. He applies the gnostic explanation not only to Ephesians and Colossians but also to 1 Corinthians and Romans as well. According to him, Paul conceived the unity of believers with Christ in terms of the physical unity of the individual light/spirit fragments with the body of the giant "Primal Man" in the gnostic mythology. Noting the parallelism between "in one Spirit" and "into one body" in 1 Cor. 12:13, he concludes that by imparting his Spirit in the sacrament, Christ establishes his lordship over the church. He explains this lordship of Christ in the Spirit in terms of the gnostic myth of the aeon-anthropos in whom those who become a part of his body leave the evil aeon and enter the new aeon.[147]

Although this view seems appealing, it has critical problems: (1) The "Primal Man" is after all a modern composite figure.[148] There is no clear evidence for the existence of the "Primal Man" figure until a couple of centuries after Paul. Moreover, contrary to Käsemann's assumption, there is no clear evidence from the first century for the combination of the "Primal Man" and the giant aeon-anthropos whose body includes the redeemed. (2) In (later) Gnosticism the union is between the individual redeemed person and the redeemer; in Paul the body of Christ denotes the corporate union of believers with Christ. Moreover, the mutual relationship of believers with one another that is strongly emphasized in Paul is absent in Gnosticism. (3) There is also a fundamental difference between Paul and Gnosticism in the understanding of the term σῶμα. In Gnosticism σῶμα is the outer garment or prison of the soul; for Paul it is man in the outward aspect of his being. For Paul the body is the object of redemption; for Gnosticism it is the obstacle of redemption. Consequently, the unity between the redeemed and the redeemer in the one gigantic body in Gnosticism is, in a strict sense, non-physical, but in Paul the unity between believers and Christ, which the phrase "body of Christ" denotes, involves physicality.

---

[146]Schlier, *Christus und die Kirche*, 39-41; idem, "κεφαλή," in *TDNT*, 3:680-81.

[147]See Käsemann, *Leib und Leib Christi*, 59-74, 118-25.

[148]See Colpe, *Religionsgeschichtliche Schule*, 191; Scroggs, *Last Adam*, ix; and Black, "Second Adam," 177. Also, see p. 69-70 (ch. 2) above.

The Apocalyptic Conception of the Solidarity
of the Elect with the Messiah

A. Schweitzer argues that Paul's conception of the church as the body of Christ is derived from the apocalyptic conception of the pre-existent "Community of God in which the Elect are closely bound up with one another and with the Messiah."[149] He regards the participation of the Elect in the same corporeity with the Messiah as fundamental to this conception and believes that Paul derived his idea of the church as the body of Christ from this background.

Although Paul shares similar views with Jewish apocalyptic writings about the Messiah and his community, Schweitzer's attempt to derive the body of Christ from this conception involves too many assumptions.[150] It does not explain why Paul uses the term "body" to express the unity of believers with Christ and with one another nor why the apocalyptic writings provide no comparable usage of this term.[151] Moreover, as Käsemann points out, Paul is "not talking about the body of a collective (i.e., the body of the messianic community), but the body of an individual, namely, Christ."[152]

The Rabbinic Speculations on the Body of Adam

Recognizing the inadequacy of Schweitzer's view, W. D. Davies seeks to explain the origin of Paul's expression and conception in Rabbinic speculations about the body of Adam.[153] He points to certain Rabbinic writings where the physical body of Adam is described as made out of dust gathered from all the earth, as of enormous size extending from one end of the earth to the other, and as bisexual.[154] In Davies' view, this constitution of the

---

[149]Schweitzer, *Mysticism*, 116. For evidence for the conception, he cites Psalm 59:29, Dan. 7:27, 12:1, *1 Enoch* 38:1-5, 52:14-15, 103:2, 104:1, and 108:3. See pp. 39-41 above.

[150]See pp. 34-35 (ch. 1) above.

[151]Cf. Best, *One Body*, 208-14.

[152]Käsemann, "Theological Problem," 116.

[153]Davies, *Paul and Rabbinic Judaism*, 53-57.

[154]For example, see *m. San.* 4.5, *b. San.* 38a, *Pesiḳta R.* 115a, *Gen. R.* 8.1, *b. Ber.* 61a. For references, see Davies, *Paul and Rabbinic Judaism*, 45, 53-55 and Scroggs, *Last Adam*, 41-52. Cf. also W. A. Meeks, "The Image of the Androgyne: Some Uses of a Symbol in Earliest Christianity," *HR* 13 (Febuary 1974): 185-97, who surveys pagan, Jewish, and Gnostic sources of the androgyne myth.

physical body of Adam and the method of its formation symbolize the real oneness of mankind manifested in the body of Adam. Thus, he concludes that when Paul thought of the new humanity being incorporated "in Christ," he naturally conceived of it in Rabbinic fashion as the body of the eschatological· Adam in which there is neither Jew nor Greek, no male and female, neither slave nor free.[155]

Davies' view has at least two merits: (1) It links up the phrase "body of Christ" with Paul's Adam-Christ contrast of Romans 5 and 1 Corinthians 15. By doing so, (2) it provides a named individual's body, that is, the body of Christ, in whom the unity of believers exists.[156] The major problem with this view, however, is the absence of the vital phrase "the body of Adam" that connects Jewish speculations about Adam and the Pauline phrase "body of Christ." There is also no evidence that the phrase "body of Adam" was ever used to designate mankind. Paul certainly speaks of the existence of mankind "in Adam" and of the redeemed humanity "in Christ" and draws analogies between Adam/Eve and Christ/church (Eph. 5:31-32) and between the temptation of Eve and that of the church (2 Cor. 11:2-3). But does this fully explain Paul's concept of the body of Christ? In Paul's writings the Adam-Christ typology is nowhere directly related to the phrase "body of Christ."[157] Although Paul's rabbinic background may have some bearing on his conception of the body of Christ, one must look further for a full explanation of it.

The Eucharist

Led by A. E. J. Rawlinson, a number of scholars have derived the origin of Paul's phrase "body of Christ" from its use in the Eucharist.[158] They basically argue that in Paul's view believers become the body of Christ when

---

[155]Davies, *Paul and Rabbinic Judaism*, 57.

[156]See Ziesler, *Pauline Christianity*, 57.

[157]See Best, *One Body*, 82; Ridderbos, *Paul*, 385-87; and Shedd, *Man in Community*, 158.

[158]Jewett, *Anthropological Terms*, 246-48, attributes this view to A. E. J. Rawlinson. See A. E. J. Rawlinson, "Corpus Christi," in *Mysterium Christi*, ed. G. K. A. Bell and Adolf Deissmann (London:· Longmans, 1930), 227-30. This view is also supported by Cerfaux, *Church*, 262-82 and to certain extent by Conzelmann, *Theology*, 262 and J. A. T. Robinson, *Body*, 56-57.

they eat the bread which is the body of Christ. Conzelmann, for example, states:

> The origin of the expression 'body of Christ' probably lies here, in the eucharistic tradition. There is no other model either in the history of religion or in the history of the concept. Besides, Paul only uses the expression once outside the eucharistic tradition: 1 Cor. 12:27. Elsewhere, the formulation he uses is 'one body (in Christ)'.[159]

In view of the use of the "body" language in 1 Cor. 10:16-17 and 11:24-29, it can hardly be doubted that Paul saw a close connection between the broken bread representing Christ's individual body and the church that is his corporate body. Eucharistic practice probably reinforced the idea of participation of believers in the death and the resurrection of Christ and thus of their solidarity with him. There is, however, a logical gap between "feeding on" the body and "becoming" the body itself. J. A. T. Robinson who endorses Rawlinson's argument also recognizes this gap.[160] Thus, he concludes: "However significant the Eucharist may have been for Paul's theology of the Body, it is surely clear that it is not a complete explanation."[161]

The Old Testament and the Teachings of Jesus

Others trace the background of Paul's designation of the church as the body of Christ more broadly to the teachings of Jesus and further to Old Testament conceptions.[162] They do so by relating the "body of Christ" concept both to the "Adam-Christ" typology and to the "stone-temple" imagery.[163] The argument runs essentially as follows: First, Paul's designation of the church as the body of Christ occurs in analogy with the sexual union between husband and wife. The analogy involves basically two ideas: (1) The two participants in sexual intercourse become one body (flesh) and

---

[159]Conzelmann, *Theology*, 262.

[160]J. A. T. Robinson, *Body*, 56-57.

[161]Ibid., 57.

[162]Ellis, *Paul's Use*, 88-98; idem, *Pauline Theology*, 42-44; Shedd, *Man in Community*, 159-65.

[163]Ellis, *Pauline Theology*, 44; idem, *Paul's Use*, 91, 95, n. 7.

(2) the husband is the head of his wife.[164]   Paul, conceiving Christ as the second Adam and the church as the bride of Christ or possibly as the second Eve,[165] applies these ideas to explain the relationship between Christ and the church. Thus, he states (1) that Christ and the church become one body and (2) that Christ is the head of the church.[166]

Second, Paul's "body of Christ" concept is also closely connected with the "stone-temple" imagery.[167]   According to Ellis, "the 'stone-temple' imagery is a pre-Pauline *testimonium* current in the early Church" and is based on the idea of the "rejected stone" in Isa. 28:16, 8:14, and Psalm 118:22.[168] He argues that "in the Gospels it is primarily Christ's body that is the temple and the repeated reference to Jesus' claim to build the temple in three days evidences the significance of the idea for the Gospel writers."[169] The logical conclusion is that Paul may have derived his designation of the church as the body of Christ from this dominical tradition.

In this view it is further argued that the Old Testament conception of corporate personality underlies Paul's expression "body of Christ."[170] Shedd elaborates on this:

> In the historical Genesis account of the creation of Eve, the realism of the conception of the sharing of a common flesh and life was evidently appropriated by Paul to describe the realism of Christ living in His Body. Christ, as Adam did, exists in His Bride, yet apart from her. The Church exists literally only through the life which it derives from Christ; it is therefore identifiable with the Source of that life (1 Cor. 12:13) but distinct from it. The personality of Christ receives, so to speak, an extension in the life of the Body on earth, while He continues to be an Individual Personality. The doctrine of the Body of Christ is therefore an explicit

------

[164]Paul bases the former idea on Gen. 2:24 and the latter on the priority of Adam over Eve in creation. See 1 Cor. 6:16, Eph. 5:31, 1 Cor. 11:8-9; Ellis, *Pauline Theology*, 59-61; and Shedd, *Man in Community*, 161-64.

[165]Cf. 2 Cor. 11:2-3. Shedd, *Man in Community*, 164, argues that the idea of the church as the bride of Christ is rooted in the Old Testament conception that Israel is the wife of Yahweh and thus prior to Paul's postulation that the church is the body of Christ. See also Chavasse, *Bride of Christ*, 66-85.

[166]Cf. 1 Cor. 12:13, 27, 6:17, Eph. 5:23, Col. 1:18, 2:10, 19.

[167]1 Cor. 6:15-20, Eph. 2:19-22; cf. 1 Cor. 3:16.

[168]Ellis, *Paul's Use*, 89. Cf. Rom. 9:32-33, 10:11, Eph. 2:20, 2 Tim. 2:19.

[169]Ellis, *Paul's Use*, 91. Cf. John 2:19, 21, Matt. 26:61, 27:40, Mark 14:58, 15:29.

[170]Shedd, *Man in Community*, 165; Ellis, *Pauline Theology*, 10-13, 44; idem, "S ma," 138-40; idem, *Old Testament*, 110-12; Best, *One Body*, 99-100, 110-14.

application of the Hebraic conception of corporate personality.[171]

This explanation seems to do more justice to Paul's thought for the following reasons: (1) It seeks the background to which Paul himself appeals, namely the Old Testament and the teachings of Jesus. (2) It is more faithful to the text. Paul's designation of the church as the body of Christ is not an isolated expression. It occurs in a close connection with other similar Pauline concepts such as the "in Christ" formula, the analogy of the sexual union, and the church as the temple.[172] (3) By joining the "body of Christ" concept with the Adam-Christ typology, it provides a named individual's body, that is, the body of Christ, in which believers corporately exist. (4) Although Paul never uses the term "corporate personality," his designation of the church as the body of Christ well corresponds to the ideas pertaining to this concept.

This view, however, has the following problems: (1) The unity created in sexual intercourse may well explain the unity created between believers and Christ, but it does not explain why Paul designates the church not simply as one body, but as the body of Christ. He might have derived the expression from the analogy of Adam and Eve, but he does not explicitly state that Eve is the body of Adam or that the church is the eschatological Eve.[173] Moreover, Paul's designation of the church as the body of Christ is nowhere directly related to the Adam-Christ typology.[174] (2) It is possible that Paul utilized the Gospel writer's remark that Jesus referred to his own body when he spoke of the temple (John 2:19-20), but there is no clear evidence that Paul derived his "body of Christ" concept from "temple" imagery.[175] Christ is connected to the temple as the cornerstone, but Paul never identifies Christ as the temple

---

[171]Shedd, *Man in Community*, 164-65.

[172]For example, see Rom. 12:5, Eph. 3:6, 1 Cor. 6:15-19, and Eph. 5:23-33.

[173]Implicit reference to the wife (Eve) as the body of her husband (Adam) and to the church as the eschatological bride (Eve) of Christ occurs in Eph. 5:28-29 and 2 Cor. 11:2-3 respectively. See pp. 154-56, 161-62 (ch. 5) below.

[174]Cf. 1 Cor. 15:21-22, 35-49 where the "body" concept occurs in connection with the "Adam-Christ" typology.

[175]Shedd, *Man in Community*, 176, n. 208, also recognizes the uncertainty whether the conception of the church as the corporate temple is prior to the body-concept and whether Jesus' statement influenced Paul's choice and use of either the figure of the body or of the temple.

itself.[176]   Finally, (3) this view may have difficulty in explaining Paul's
reference to the church as the body of Christ in other passages where no
reference to sexual union or to "temple" imagery occurs.

As the diversity of opinion well demonstrates, it is extremely difficult to
know the exact source or sources from which Paul derived his expression and
conception.   The body analogy in Paul echoes to a certain extent the Stoic
metaphor, but there are fundamental conceptual differences between them.
The gnostic "Primal Man" myth also seems to share similar ideas with Paul,
but if so, the gnostic concept is chronologically later and more likely
dependent on Paul.   Moreover, its concept is basically incompatible with that
of Paul.   The rabbinic speculations about the body of Adam have several
advantages over the Stoic metaphor or the gnostic "Primal Man" myth, but
there is no direct, literary evidence that Paul derived his expression and
concept from them.   Since the expression "body of Christ" occurs in the
Eucharist in Pauline congregations (1 Cor. 10:16-17, 11:24), it is possible that
Paul utilized this eucharistic saying, but there is a logical gap between feeding
on the body and becoming the body itself.   The attempt to explain the body of
Christ by the analogy between Adam and Christ and the "stone-temple"
imagery is appealing, but this also does not satisfactorily explain where Paul
derived his conception.   Since it is extremely difficult to pinpoint the origin of
the conception, many regard it as basically Paul's own creation.[177]   Although
the specific origin of the concept is uncertain, the expression "body of Christ"
seems to share the basic ideas found in the Old Testament conception of
corporate personality.

------

[176]Eph. 2:20-21. Cf. John 2:21, Rev. 21:22. See Moule, *Origin*, 89-92; R. J. McKelvey,
The New Temple: The Church in the New Testament (London: Oxford University Press, 1969),
79, 106; and Robinson, *Body*, 64-65.
    [177]Wikenhauser, *Kirche*, 1; Best, *One Body*, 94; Schnackenburg, *Church*, 77; Conzel-
mann, *Theology*, 263.

CHAPTER 4

THE CHURCH AS THE TEMPLE, THE HOUSE, AND
THE BUILDING OF GOD.

Closely related to Paul's concept of the church as the body of Christ is his designation of the church as the temple (ναός), the house (οἰκιά or οἶκος), or the building (οἰκοδομή) of God.[1] The explicit references to the church as the temple occur in 1 Cor. 3:16-17, 2 Cor. 6:16, and Eph. 2:21. A reference to the temple also occurs in 1 Cor. 6:19, but here the temple denotes the body of individual believers rather than the church. The designation of the church as the building or the house occurs in 1 Cor. 3:9, Eph. 2:21, 1 Tim. 3:15, and possibly in 2 Cor. 5:1-2. Although Paul also uses the term οἰκοδομή in the figurative sense of edification,[2] the following analysis deals mainly with his specific use of the term in reference to the church.

---

[1]Although the concept of the church as God's temple, building, or house is important not only for Paul but also for other New Testament writers, not much work has been done on this subject. A few important books include A. Spatafora, *From the "Temple of God" to God as the Temple* (Rome: Gregorian University, 1997); McKelvey, *New Temple*; M.-J. Yves Congar, *The Mystery of the Temple or the Manner of God's Presence to His Creatures from Genesis to the Apocalypse*, trans. Reginald F. Trevett (Westminster, MD: Newman, 1962); Bertil Gärtner, *The Temple and the Community in Qumran and the New Testament: A Comparative Study in the Temple Symbolism of the Qumran Texts and the New Testament* (Cambridge: Cambridge University Press, 1965); Josef Pfammatter, *Die Kirche als Bau: Eine exegetisch-theologische Studie zur Ekklesiologie der Paulusbriefe* (Rome: Gregorian University, 1960); and Philipp Vielhauer, *Oikodome: Das Bild vom Bau in der christlichen Literatur vom Neuen Testament bis Clements Alexandrinus* (Karlsruhe-Durlach: Tron, 1940).

[2]For example, see Rom. 14:19, 15:2, 1 Cor. 3:10-15, 14:4, 12, 26, 2 Cor. 10:8, 12:19, 13:10, Eph. 2:20-22, 4:12-16, 29. The verb οἰκοδομεῖν is used in a similar sense in Rom. 15:20, 1 Cor. 8:1, 10; 14:2-5, 17, 26, Gal. 2:18, and 1 Thess. 5:11. For the discussion of Paul's use of the building metaphor, see Vielhauer, *Oikodome*; Pfammatter, *Kirche als Bau*; and Otto Michel, "οἰκοδομή," in *TDNT*, 5:119-59.

Analysis of Paul's Usage

1 Cor. 3:9, 16-17

In Corinthians 3 Paul refers to the church both as God's building and as God's temple in his response to the problem of division in the Corinthian church, a problem caused by those who claimed that they belonged either to Paul or to Apollos (v. 4).[3] He explains that he and Apollos are simply God's co-workers (v. 9) and that the Corinthian believers belong only to God (vv. 10, 23). His explanation involves a number of images: (1) the field (vv. 6-9a), (2) the building (vv. 9b-15), and (3) the temple (vv. 16-17). The transition from the image of the field to that of the building takes place in verse 9 where Paul describes the Corinthian believers as "God's field (γεώργιον) and God's building (οἰκοδομή)."[4] In the following verses (vv. 10-15), he expands the image of the building, laying more emphasis on the act of building than on the completed edifice. The image of the building, however, changes swiftly from the act of building (vv. 10-11)[5] to the building materials (vv. 12-13) and then to the judgment of the work (vv. 14-15). The transition from the image of the building to that of the temple seems rather sudden, but it is a logical shift because the temple is a building and in the Old Testament (e.g., Ezra 5:3-4) it is indeed referred to as a building. Such a transition takes places also in Eph. 2:20-22 where the building image merges into the temple image. The unspecified building (οἰκοδομή) in 1 Cor. 3:9 is now identified as the temple of God: "Do you not know that you are God's temple and that God's Spirit dwells in you? If anyone destroys God's temple, God will destroy him. For God's temple is holy, and that temple you are" (1 Cor. 3:16-17).[6]

This statement has a number of noteworthy features: (1) The introductory formula οὐκ οἴδατε ὅτι, which occurs frequently in 1

---

[3]Cf. 1 Cor. 1:12.

[4]The combination of "planting" and "building" frequently occurs in Jeremiah. See Jer. 1:9-10, 12:14-16, 18:7-10, 24:6, and 31:28. It also occurs in *1QS* 8.5. Gärtner, *Temple and the Community*, 28, traces the combination of temple and plantation in the Qumran texts to Jewish speculations on the subject of the rock of the temple and Paradise.

[5]Here Paul presents himself as an architect who lays the foundation, that is, Christ. Cf. Eph. 2:20 where he designates the apostles and the prophets as the foundation and Christ as the cornerstone.

[6]The plural relative pronoun οἵτινες in verse 17 does not have a proper antecedent. It can refer either to "temple" (ναός) or "holy" (ἅγιος). The context, however, strongly suggests the temple as its antecedent. See Fee, *1 Corinthians*, 149, n. 21.

Corinthians,[7] may signify that the concept of the church as the temple of God is not a new idea for the Corinthian believers. It probably refers either to Paul's earlier teaching or more likely to the early Christian tradition with which the Corinthian believers were familiar. (2) The corporate nuance of the temple image is apparent in the plural "you" (ὑμεῖς) as the unique temple of God. (3) The church is the dwelling place of God's Spirit. Paul's statement that "God's Spirit dwells in you (ὑμῖν)" probably means not that the Spirit dwells "in each of you," although such an idea appears elsewhere in Paul,[8] but that God's Spirit dwells "in the midst of you all."[9] Finally, (4) the presence of the Spirit makes the temple holy and "if anyone destroys the temple of God, God will destroy him" (3:17).

1 Cor. 6:19

In his argument against sexual immorality, Paul states: "Do you not know (οὐκ οἴδατε) that your body is a temple of the Holy Spirit in you, which you have from God?" The expression is similar to that of 1 Cor. 3:16-17 in that both passages begin with the formula οὐκ οἴδατε ὅτι and describe the temple as the dwelling place of the Holy Spirit. They differ, however, in that while the temple of God in 1 Cor. 3:16-17 refers to the community of believers, the temple in 1 Cor. 6:19 denotes the body of the individual believer.[10] Nevertheless, the corporate idea does not completely vanish from view. For example, Paul's reference to the temple occurs in the same context where he speaks of the corporate body of Christ of which believers are members. In addition, although Paul changes the plural σώματα (6:15) to the singular σῶμα (6:19), he retains the plural ὑμῶν and ἐν ὑμῖν. For this reason, Shedd concludes that it is difficult to know whether τὸ σῶμα in 1 Cor. 6:19 refers to the corporate body (i.e. of Christ) or to the individual bodies of

---

[7]1 Cor. 5:6, 6:2, 3, 9, 16, 19, 9:13, 24.

[8]Cf. 1 Cor. 6:19, Rom. 8:9-11.

[9]The underlying idea may correspond to Matt. 18:20 where Jesus states, "For where two or three are gathered in my name, there am I in the midst of them." For Paul's concept of "Christ in us," see pp. 19-21 (ch. 1) above.

[10]McKelvey, New Temple, 52; Fee, 1 Corinthians, 264; Bruce, 1 and 2 Corinthians, 65; Barrett, 1 Corinthians, 151. Cf. Shedd, Man in Community, 175.

believers.[11] This passage is probably a particular application of the general conception of the church as the temple to the individual believer[12] and, as such, it demonstrates that a certain oscillation exists in Paul's thought between the corporate and the individual. Barrett also implicitly recognizes this oscillation:

> When the unity and purity of the church are at stake Paul recalls that the church is the shrine in which the Spirit dwells; when the unity and purity of the moral life of the individual are threatened, he recalls that the Spirit dwells in each Christian, who ought not therefore to defile the Spirit's shrine.[13]

2 Cor. 5:1-10

Paul's reference to the house (οἰκία) and to the building (οἰκοδομή) in 2 Cor. 5:1-10 has been much debated in relation to his view of man (anthropology), of the future (eschatology), and more specifically of the intermediate state.[14] This passage raises a number of exegetical questions: (1) What is the "building (οἰκοδομή) that believers have from God, a house (οἰκία) not made with hands, eternal in the heavenlies" (5:1)? Is it identical with "our heavenly inhabitation" (τὸ οἰκητήριον ἡμῶν τὸ ἐξ οὐρανοῦ) that believers long to put on over (ἐπενδύσασθαι) (5:2)? The answers to these questions will determine the meaning of "our earthly tent-house" (ἡ ἐπίγειος ἡμῶν οἰκία τοῦ σκήνους) in which believers presently groan (5:1-2, 4). (2) What do the terms "naked" and "away from the body" imply (5:4, 8)? (3) When does Paul envision our heavenly inhabitation to be put on over (ἐπενδύσασθαι), at death or at the Parousia? (4) Does the passage indicate a change or a development in Paul's eschatology? Finally, (5) what is the

---

[11]Shedd, *Man in Community*, 175. See also Gärtner, *Temple and the Community*, 141, n. 2.   This difficulty may have prompted the textual variation "τὰ σώματα" in A^c L Ψ 33.81.104.365.1175.1505.1881.2464 *pm* sy^h bo.
    [12]So, McKelvey, *New Temple*, 52; Cerfaux, *Church*, 148; and Fee, *1 Corinthians*, 264. However, cf. Conzelmann, *1 Corinthians*, 112, n. 37.
    [13]Barrett, *1 Corinthians*, 151.
    [14]For a summary of the debate, see Pate, *Adam Christology*, 2-21; F. G. Lang, *2 Korinther 5, 1-10 in der neueren Forschung*, Beitrage zur Geschichte der biblische Exegese (Tübingen: J. C. B. Mohr, 1973); and Karel Hanhart, "Paul's Hope in the Face of Death," *JBL* 88 (December 1969): 445-9.

origin of Paul's thought here? Although all of these questions are important, the following analysis is primarily concerned with the first question. Other questions will be discussed later in the chapter.

Broadly speaking, there are two views of the "heavenly house": (1) One interprets it in an individualistic sense and (2) the other in a corporate sense. Those who support the first view usually equate the "heavenly house" in 2 Cor. 5:1 with σῶμα πνευματικόν in 1 Cor. 15:44 either in continuity or discontinuity[15] and regard the three terms, οἰκοδομή (5:1), οἰκία (5:1), and οἰκητήριον (5:2) basically as synonymous. The agreement among these scholars, however, ends here. They vary greatly as to the time of the reception and the nature of the resurrection body.[16] Some argue that Paul's view underwent a radical transformation from Jewish belief in the resurrection of the body to be received at the Parousia (1 Thess. 4:13-18, 1 Cor. 15:44-49) to hellenistic belief in the immortality of the soul to be received at death (2 Cor. 5:1-10, Phil. 1:20-26).[17] Others, however, reject such a theory of development and insist that the "heavenly house" is essentially the same as σῶμα πνευματικόν in 1 Cor. 15:44.[18]

Ellis offers an intriguing counterargument to the individualistic

---

[15]Cf. Albert Schweitzer, *Paul and His Interpreters: A Critical History*, trans. W. Montgomery (London: Black, 1912), 73-77; Knox, *Paul and the Church of the Gentiles*, 127-43; Vos, *Pauline Eschatology*, 176-200; C. F. D. Moule, "St. Paul and Dualism: The Pauline Conception of Resurrection," *NTS* 12 (January 1966): 106-23; R. Cassidy, "Paul's Attitude to Death in II Corinthians 5:1-10," *EvQ* 43 (April 1971): 210-17; Ridderbos, *Paul*, 487-562; and Ben Meyer, "Did Paul's View of the Resurrection of the Dead Undergo Development?," *TS* 47 (September 1986): 363-87.

[16]See Pate, *Adam Christology*, 1-21, who provides a helpful review of various opinions.

[17]This view was first suggested by Otto Pfleiderer, *Paulinism: A Contribution to the History of Primitive Christian Theology* (London: Williams and Norgate, 1877) and developed by E. Teichmann, *Die paulinischen Vorstellungen von Auferstehung und Gericht und ihre Beziehung zur jüdischen Apokalyptik* (1896); R. H. Charles, *A Critical History of the Doctrine of a Future Life* (London: Black, 1899); and Knox, *Paul and the Church of the Gentiles*. It is, however, vigorously criticized by Schweitzer, *Paul and His Interpreters*, 73-77 and by J. Jeremias, "Flesh and Blood Cannot Inherit the Kingdom of God," *NTS* 2 (Febuary 1956): 157-59.

[18]For example, see Kennedy, *Paul's Conception*; Vos, *Pauline Eschatology*, 172-214; Oscar Cullmann, *Immortality of the Soul or Resurrection of the Dead* (London: Epworth, 1958); John Lowe, "An Examination of Attempts to Detect Development in St. Paul's Theology," *JTS* 42 (1941): 129-42; Jeremias, "Flesh and Blood," 151-59; J. N. Sevenster, "Some Remarks on the Gumnos in II Cor. v. 3," in *Studia Paulina in honorem Johannis de Zwaan Septuagenarii*, ed. J. N. Sevenster and W. C. van Unnik (Bohn: Haarlem, 1953), 202-14; Moule, "Paul and Dualism," 106-23; and Ridderbos, *Paul*, 487-562.

interpretation of "our heavenly house."[19]   He argues that "our heavenly house" refers to the corporate temple that is used elsewhere in Paul to denote the present incorporation of the believer into the corporate body of Christ.[20] Paul's primary thought in the passage is, he continues, "not of individual bodies at all, but of corporate solidarities which inhere in Adam and in Christ, the old aeon and the new aeon."[21] To support this view, he points out the following evidence: (1) the three key words employed in 5:1, namely, καταλυθῇ, οἰκοδομήν, and ἀχειροποίητον, which are also used in Mark 14:58 with reference to the temple;[22] (2) the fact that whenever Paul uses the word οἰκοδομή, except in the purely figurative sense of edification, it means the body of Christ that is the church;[23] and (3) the word οἴδαμεν, which probably suggests that Paul calls attention to a well-known Christian concept.[24] He, therefore, concludes:

It is most probable then that in II Cor. v. 1ff. Paul has in mind the concept

---

[19]Ellis, "Structure," 35-57, develops the corporate meaning of the body image as set forth by Robinson. His view is accepted by A. Rupprecht, J. F. Collange, and R. G. Hamerton-Kelly, but criticized by scholars such as Philip Hughes, D. E. H. Whiteley, and R. O. Zorn. Others such as K. Hanhart, F. G. Lang, and V. Furnish agree to the temple reference of the building from heaven, but argue that the reality behind that reference is not so much the body of Christ. See A. Feuillet, "La demeure céleste et la destinée des chrétiens (II Cor. v. 1-10)," *RSR* 44 (1956), 161-92, 360-402; J. A. T. Robinson, *Body*, 75-76; Arthur A. Rupprecht, "Interpreting the Pauline Epistles," in *The Literature and Meaning of Scripture*, ed. Morris A. Inch and C. Hassell Bullock (Grand Rapids: Baker, 1981), 191-216; J. F. Collange, *Enigmes* (Cambridge: Cambridge University Press, 1972), 183-98; Hamerton-Kelly, *Pre-Existence*, 148-51; Philip Hughes, *Paul's Second Epistle to the Corinthians*, New International Commentary on the New Testament, ed. F. F. Bruce (Grand Rapids: Eerdmans, 1962), 184-85; Whiteley, *Theology*, 255-58; R. O. Zorn, "II Corinthians 5:1-10: Individual Eschatology or Corporate Solidarity, Which?" *RTR* 48 (September 1989): 93-104; K. Hanhart, "Paul's Hope," 445-57; Lang, *2 Korinther 5, 1-10*, 182-85; and V. Furnish, *II Corinthians*, Anchor Bible (New York: Doubleday, 1984), 291-95.

[20]Cf. 1 Cor. 3:16-17, 2 Cor. 6:16, Eph. 2:20-22, 4:12-16.

[21]Ellis, "Structure," 41.

[22]Cf. Acts 7:48, Heb. 8:2, 9:11, John 2:19, Acts 17:24. Ellis, "Structure," 41, states, "'Not made with hands' is a quasi-technical term in the New Testament pointing to the corporate realities of the new aeon. Used with 'house' or 'temple,' it refers to the corporate Body of Christ." See also A. Feuillet, *Destinee des Chretiens et Fondements de l'eschatologie paulinienne* (Institut Catholique de Paris, n. d.), 161-93, 360-402 and Michel, "οἰκοδομή," *TDNT*, 5:147.

[23]Cf. 1 Cor. 3:9, Eph. 2:21, 4:12, 16.

[24]Ellis, "Structure," 41; idem, *Paul's Use*, 30, n. 6. See also Michel, "οἰκοδομή," *TDNT*, 5:147.

of the New Temple which views the Messianic Community in terms of the "house of God." In an interchange of the two images, New Temple and Body of Christ, the house from heaven (οἰκητήριον, II Cor. v. 2) or building of God (κατοικητήριον, Eph. ii. 22) here refers to those ἐν Χριστῷ as they are incorporated into the Body of Christ in whom the new aeon has been fully actualized and who alone is individually present in the heavenlies. The corollary also follows: The "tent-house" (II Cor. v. 1) envisions primarily not the individual self (although this is included) but the whole ἐν 'Αδάμ corporeity which stands under death.[25]

To interpret the passage properly, one must view it in a broader literary context, particularly because it is an integral part of the discussion which Paul begins in the previous chapter (4:7-18), which speaks about believers' eschatological hope of glory in the midst of their present suffering.[26] Paul's discussion of the ministry of reconciliation in the following section (5:11-21) is also based on this eschatological hope. Within this expanded literary context (4:7-5:21), a series of antitheses occurs that can be displayed as follows:

earthen vessels	treasure (4:7)
death	life (4:10)
our outer man	our inner man (4:16)
momentary affliction	eternal glory (4:17)
visible	invisible (4:18a)
transient	eternal (4:18b)
our earthly tent-house	our house in the heavenlies (5:1)
naked	clothed (5:2-3)
mortal	life (5:4)
at home in the body	at home with the Lord (5:6a, 8b)
away from the Lord	away from the body (5:6b, 8a)
by faith	by sight (5:7)
in face	in heart (5:12)
old	new (5:17)
sin	righteousness (5:21)

---

[25]Ellis, "Structure," 42.

[26]Concerning the literary relationship of 2 Cor. 5:1-10 to the preceding passage, see Furnish, *II Corinthians*, 277-78; Pate, *Adam Christology*, 97, n. 4; Ellis, "Structure," 47; and Dunn, *Theology*, 489.

It is apparent in the display that the left-hand column is related in one way or another to the theme of present suffering and mortality while the right-hand column is related to that of future glory.

When viewed from this eschatological perspective, 2 Cor. 5:1-10 reveals a number of significant characteristics. First, several factors in the passage indicate that multiple images are at work: (1) The building image seems to merge with the temple image. For example, the house (οἰκία) that is identified as the building (οἰκοδομή) is described as "not made with hands, eternal in the heavenlies." The term "not made with hands" (ἀχειροποίητον) is often used elsewhere in the New Testament in reference to the eschatological temple.[27] Besides, Paul often uses the terms "building" and "house" in close connection with the temple to refer to the church.[28] (2) The building image also seems to imply the body of Christ concept as does the plural modifier in the phrases "our earthly house" and "our habitation from heaven" (5:1-2). Paul also combines "our heavenly habitation" with his concept of "putting on (the new man)" (5:2) which is closely related to the "body of Christ" elsewhere in Paul.[29] Moreover, whenever he uses the term οἰκοδομή, except in the purely figurative sense of edification, it refers to the body of Christ regarded as the church.[30] In this respect, Ellis' conclusion that when Paul speaks of the house or the building of God, he has in mind primarily the concept of the new temple and the body of Christ is essentially accurate.[31]

Second, there are two contrasting houses, namely, "our earthly tent-house" and the "heavenly house" (5:1). The "house not made with hands" is probably synonymous with the "building from God" (5:1) and also with "our heavenly inhabitation" that believers long to put on over (5:2). Within the expanded context, this "heavenly house" can be further equated with the "treasure" (4:7), "life of Jesus" (4:10-11), "inner man" (4:16), and the "new

---

[27]Cf. Mark 14:58, Acts 7:48, 17:24, Heb. 8:2, 9:11.

[28]Cf. 1 Cor. 3:9, 16-17, Eph. 2:20-22, 1 Tim. 3:15.

[29]Cf. Eph. 2:15, 4:24, Rom. 13:14. The combination of the "building" image and the "body of Christ" concept occurs in Eph. 4:12. However, see Bruce, *1 and 2 Corinthians*, 202, who states: "Some commentators see here the idea of integration into the body of Christ, but this is unsuitable to the context; moreover, the distinctively Pauline concept of the body of Christ (cf. 1 C. 12:12-27) is not elsewhere related to the life to come, but to the present existence of the church 'militant here in earth.'"

[30]Cf. 1 Cor. 3:9, Eph. 2:21, 4:12, 16.

[31]Ellis, "Structure," 42.

(creation)" (5:17). It is immortal, invisible, and eternal.[32] In contrast, the "earthly tent-house" can be equated with "earthen vessels" (4:7), "mortal flesh" (4:11), "outer man" (4:16), the "body" in which believers presently groan and from which Paul desires to be absent (5:6, 8), and the "old (creation)" (5:17). It is mortal, visible, and transient.[33] These descriptions of the two contrasting houses are very similar to those of the two contrasting bodies in 1 Cor. 15:42-49, namely, σῶμα ψυχικόν and σῶμα πνευματικόν.[34] Moreover, Paul's statements that believers will "put on over our heavenly inhabitation" and that "the mortal may be swallowed up by life" (2 Cor. 5:2-4) are basically the same as saying that at the Parousia believers will "put on immortality" and that "death is swallowed up in victory" (1 Cor. 15:53-54). These parallels between the two passages indicate that when Paul speaks of the "heavenly house," he has in mind the resurrection bodies (σώματα πνευματικά) of individual believers that are to be received at the Parousia.

Third, the present and the future elements are clearly juxtaposed. On the one hand believers already have the "heavenly house" (5:1).[35] The compound verb ἐπενδύσασθαι ("to be put on over") also indicates that in some sense believers have already put on the "heavenly inhabitation."[36] In fact, Paul states elsewhere that believers have put on the new man (Christ).[37] Consequently, they are already "a new creation" (5:17). They have received the Spirit as a guarantee (5:5) and thus the transcendent power is now at work (4:7). As a result, the life of Jesus is manifest in them and their inner man is being renewed every day (4:11, 16). On the other hand they presently groan

---

[32]Cf. 2 Cor. 4:11, 18, 19, 5:1, 4, 7.

[33]Cf. 2 Cor. 4:11, 5:4, 4:18, 5:7.

[34]See pp. 49-50 (ch. 2) above.

[35]Those who regard the Parousia as the time of the reception of the "heavenly inhabitation" interpret the present tense ἔχομεν as futuristic present while those who hold to the moment of death as the time of reception interpret it as real present referring to the time of death. For example, see H. E. Dana and Julius R. Mantey, *A Manual Grammar of the Greek New Testament* (Toronto: Macmillan, 1955), 185; Best, *One Body*, 161, n. 1; and A. Plummer, *A Critical and Exegetical Commentary on the Second Epistle of St. Paul to the Corinthians*, International Critical Commentary, ed. S. R. Driver and Others (Edinburgh: T. & T. Clark, 1914), 144. However, the verb ἔχομεν is also used in 4:7 and there it clearly refers to the present reality as of now. There is no reason that one should take the same verb in 5:1 otherwise. See J. A. T. Robinson, *Body*, 76-77 and Ellis, "Structure," 41.

[36]A textual variation appears in 5:3. The participle ἐνδυσάμενοι is supported by 𝔓[46] a C D[2] Ψ 0243. 33. 1739. 1881 𝔐 lat sy co while ἐκλυσάμενοι is supported only by D* a f^c; Mcion Tert Spec.

[37]Cf. Gal. 3:27, Col. 3:9-10.

in the "earthly tent-house," as does the whole creation,[38] longing to be put on over with the "heavenly habitation" (5:2-4).[39] Their mortal bodies must be swallowed up by life (5:4).[40] They want to be away from the body and to be at home with the Lord (5:8). They still await the glory that is yet unseen and eternal (4:17-18). And they must appear before the final judgment seat of Christ (5:10). Until then, they are encouraged to endeavor to please Christ so that they may receive good rewards from the Lord (5:9-10).[41]

In conclusion, 2 Cor. 5:1-10 is also a particular application of the general concept of the church as the building or the house to the individual believer[42] and, as such, it demonstrates the fluidity and the oscillation in Paul's thought between the corporate and the individual realities.[43] Hence, although "our heavenly house" in 2 Cor. 5:1 has strong implications for the resurrection bodies of individual believers, it must be understood in the framework of the corporate solidarity in Christ in whom the new aeon is already fully actualized, just as both σῶμα ψυχικόν and σῶμα πνευματικόν described in 1 Cor. 15:44-49 are to be understood in the framework of the Adam-Christ typology introduced in the preceding passage (15:21-22).

2 Cor. 6:14-7:1

Paul refers to the church as God's temple (ναός) in his admonition to the Corinthian believers not to be mismated with unbelievers. To demonstrate the incompatibility of such a relationship, he employs five antithetical questions (6:14b-16a):

---

[38]Cf. Rom. 8:19-23. See Ellis, "Structure," 36-37, who recognizes the parallel between 2 Corinthians 5 and Romans 8.

[39]The compound verb ἐπενδύσασθαι occurs only in this passage (vv. 2, 4) and means "to be put on over." See William F. Arndt and F. Wilbur Gingrich, *A Greek-English Lexicon of the New Testament and Other Early Christian Literature*, 2nd ed. (Chicago: University of Chicago Press, 1979), 284; Albrecht Oepke, "ἐπενδύω," in *TDNT*, 2:320-21; and Furnish, *II Corinthians*, 267.

[40]Cf. 1 Cor. 15:54.

[41]Cf. Phil. 1:20-26.

[42]See McKelvey, *New Temple*, 52; Cerfaux, *Church*, 148; and Fee, *1 Corinthians*, 264. Cf. Conzelmann, *1 Corinthians*, 112, n. 37.

[43]Cf. J. P. M. Sweet, "A House Not Made with Hands," in *Templum Amicitiae: Essays on the Second Temple Presented to Ernst Bammel*, ed. William Horbury (Sheffield: JSOT, 1991), 384.

What partnership (μετοχή) have righteousness and iniquity?
What fellowship (κοινωνία) has light with darkness?
What accord (συμφώνησις) has Christ with Belial?
What commonality (μερίς) has a believer with an unbeliever?
What agreement (συγκατάθεσις) has the temple of God with idols?

The last antithesis is clearly underpinned by the following statement, "We are the temple of the living God" (6:16b), a rationale immediately supported by a *catena* of Old Testament texts.[44]

Although the underlying concept is basically the same as that of 1 Cor. 3:16-17, this passage has several distinctive features: (1) Paul does not use the introductory phrase οὐκ οἴδατε ὅτι or οἴδαμεν ὅτι.[45] (2) By replacing the pronoun "you" with "we," he includes himself in the group that is designated as God's temple. (3) Most characteristically, however, he supports his argument with an extensive citation of Old Testament texts applied to the church as God's temple. This is significant because it may imply that Paul views the church as the fulfillment of the ancient biblical hope that God would one day dwell with his people in a new and more intimate way.[46] The messianic interpretation of the Old Testament texts in the sense of "prophecy and fulfillment" is also evident in the *pesher* form of the quotation. Ellis elaborates on this: "God's command to Israel regarding Babylon (αὐτῆς) is

---

[44]The Old Testament texts cited here include Lev. 26:12, Ezek. 37:27, Isa. 52:11, and 2 Sam. 7:14.

[45]McKelvey, *New Temple*, 100, argues that the absence of the phrase οὐκ οἴδατε ὅτι implies that 2 Cor. 6:16-17 is the earliest reference to the church as the temple of God in Paul and that 1 Cor. 3:16 refers to 2 Cor. 6:16-17. His argument relies on the assumption that 2 Cor. 6:16-17 is a part of what is generally regarded as Paul's "previous letter" to Corinth (2 Cor. 6:14-7:1). Those who view this passage as an interpolation include Heinz Dietrich Wendland, *Briefe an die Korinther*, Das Neue Testament Deutsch 7 (Göttingen: Vandenhoeck & Ruprecht, 1980), 212 and Schmithals, *Gnosticism*, 94-5. The authenticity and integrity of the passage, however, have been defended by Plummer, *Second Corinthians*, xxiii-xxvi, 208; Hughes, *Second Corinthians*, 241-4; Bruce, *1 and 2 Corinthians*, 214; Barrett, *Second Corinthians*, 194; and Gordon D. Fee, "II Corinthians VI.14-VII.1 and Food Offered to Idols," *NTS* 23 (January 1977): 140-3. Ellis, *Making of the New Testament Documents*, 99-100; Furnish, *II Corinthians*, 383; M. Carrez, *La deuxième épître de saint Paul aux Corinthiens* (Genève, 1986), 168-9; and R. P. Martin, *2 Corinthians*, Word Biblical Commentary, vol. 40, ed. Ralph P. Martin (Waco, TX: Word, 1986), 195, argue that it is a non-Pauline preformed *florilegium* that Paul incorporated when he composed the epistle.

[46]Cf. Ellis, *Paul's Use*, 144 and McKelvey, *New Temple*, 98. The combination of Lev. 26:12 and Ezek. 37:27 also occurs in a prediction of the new temple at *Jub.* 1:17.

now applied to the relation of Christians with unbelievers (αὐτῶν); the promise given to Israel 'personified' in Solomon (αὐτῷ . . . αὐτός) is fulfilled in true Israel, the members of Christ's body (ὑμῖν . . . ὑμεῖς)."[47] Since the church, like the tabernacle of the Old Testament, is God's dwelling, Paul argues, it should be set apart for its sacred purpose. With this in mind, he exhorts: "Let us cleanse ourselves from every defilement of body and spirit, and make holiness perfect in the fear of God" (7:1).

Eph. 2:19-22

Paul's reference to the church both as the building (οἰκοδομή) and as the temple (ναός) in Eph. 2:19-22 is an integral part of his discussion of the unity of Jews and Gentiles in Christ. In the preceding passage (2:11-18), he speaks of (1) the new status that the death of Christ has conferred upon the Gentiles, (2) the reconciliation of both Jews and Gentiles to God, and (3) their consequent union as a single entity. In verse 19, he summarizes what has been said thus far in such a way as to introduce his final thought about the nature of the church, namely, the church as the building and the temple (2:20-22). For a better view of the literary structure of the passage (2:20-22), the Greek text may be laid out as follows.

> 2:20a ἐποικοδομηθέντες ἐπὶ τῷ θεμελίῳ τῶν ἀποστόλων καὶ προφητῶν,
> 20b ὄντος ἀκρογωνιαίου αὐτοῦ Χριστοῦ Ἰησοῦ,
> 21 ἐν ᾧ πᾶσα οἰκοδομὴ συναρμολογουμένη αὔξει
>   εἰς ναὸν ἅγιον   ἐν κυρίῳ,
> 22 ἐν ᾧ καὶ ὑμεῖς συνοικοδομεῖσθε
>   εἰς κατοικητήριον τοῦ θεοῦ   ἐν πνεύματι

Interestingly, whereas in 1 Cor. 3:11 Paul designates Christ alone as the foundation (θεμέλιος), here he refers to the apostles and the prophets as the foundation and to Christ as the cornerstone (ἀκρογωνιαῖος). Some scholars argue that the term ἀκρογωνιαῖος refers not to the "cornerstone" at the foot of the building, but the "final stone" that goes at the top of the building as the keystone of the arch.[48] The term ἀκρογωνιαῖος is certainly used in this sense,

---

[47]Ellis, *Paul's Use*, 144.

[48]J. Jeremias, "κεφαλὴ γωνίας-ἀκρογωνιαῖος," *ZNW* 29 (1930): 264-80; idem, "γωνία, ἀκρογωνιαῖος, κεφαλὴ, γωνίας," in *TDNT*, 1:791-93; Best, *One Body*, 165-66; Hanson, *Unity*,

and the "final stone" may well suit the context of the Ephesian passage because it recognizes the unique position of Christ, distinguished from that of the apostles and the prophets, and also because it may well correspond to the concept of Christ as the head of the church. When Paul designates Christ as ἀκρογωνιαῖος, however, he probably has in mind the "cornerstone" in Isa. 28:19 that is christologically applied by the New Testament writers, sometimes in combination with the stumbling stone in Isa. 8:14.[49] If so, it is more likely that the term ἀκρογωνιαῖος denotes the cornerstone at the foot of the building. Paul's designation of the apostles and the prophets as the foundation probably denotes the foundational work that they have done for the building up of the church.[50]

The following verses (2:21-22) describe the relationship of believers with one another and with Christ the cornerstone. Christ is the cornerstone "in whom (ἐν ᾧ) the whole building, joined together, grows into the holy temple" (2:21) and "in whom (ἐν ᾧ) you (Jews and Gentiles) are built into the dwelling place of God" (2:22). A certain parallelism occurs between verse 21 and 22: (1) Πᾶσα οἰκοδομή is parallel to ὑμεῖς, implying that πᾶσα οἰκοδομή refers to believers. Although πᾶσα οἰκοδομή without the definite article can mean "every building," it should be translated as the "whole building" in this context because it denotes the corporate unity of believers, namely, the church.[51] (2) The phrase συναρμολογουμένη αὔξει in verse 21 corresponds to the verb συνοικοδομεῖσθε in the next verse, implying that believers are mutually related to one another as a unity. The building image merges here with the "body of Christ" concept, as in Eph. 4:15-16 and perhaps in Col. 2:19.[52] (3) The superstructure into which believers, joined together, grow and are built is now specifically defined as the "holy temple"

131-32; Cerfaux, *Church*, 346. For a critique of this view, see McKelvey, *New Temple*, 114-15, 195-204; idem, "Christ the Cornerstone," *NTS* 8 (July 1962): 352-59; Ernst Percy, *Die Probleme der Kolosser- und Epheserbriefe* (Lund: C. W. K. Gleerup, 1946), 328-32, 485-88; G. H. Whitaker, "The Chief Corner Stone," *Exp* 22 (December 1921): 470-72; and Congar, *Mystery of the Temple*, 164-65.

[49]Cf. Rom. 9:33, 1 Pet. 2:6-8, Matt. 21:42 par (=Ps. 118:22).

[50]Cf. Rom. 15:20.

[51]So, Hanson, *Unity*, 132. Otherwise, Best, *One Body*, 166. The Greek definite article stresses definiteness, but its absence does not necessarily mean lack of definiteness. Concerning the absence of the article, see Robertson, *Grammar*, 790-96.

[52]Hanson, *Unity*, 133-35; Ridderbos, *Paul*, 431; Congar, *Mystery of the Temple*, 160; G. H. Whitaker, "The Building and the Body (Eph. ii.21f.; iv. 16; Col. ii.19)," *Theo* 13 (1926): 335-36.

(2:21) and the "dwelling place of God" (2:22). The "holy temple" and the "dwelling place of God" are apparently descriptions of one and the same thing.[53]   Finally, (4) the phrases "in the Lord" and "in the Spirit" further qualify the "holy temple" and the "dwelling place of God" respectively.[54]

1 Tim. 3:15

In a short transitional passage (3:14-16), Paul identifies the house of God (οἶκος θεοῦ) as the church of the living God: "I am writing these instructions to you so that if I am delayed, you may know how one ought to behave in the house of God (οἶκος θεοῦ), which is the church of the living God, the pillar (στῦλος) and bulwark (ἑδραίωμα) of the truth" (3:14b-15).[55] Since the term οἶκος is used in the sense of household in the immediately preceding passage (3:4, 5, 12), οἶκος θεοῦ in verse 15 can also mean the household of God.[56]   However, the close connection of οἶκος θεοῦ with the architectural terms "pillar" (στῦλος) and "bulwark" (ἑδραίωμα) signifies that it more likely refers to the temple of God.[57]   The combination of the building image and the phrase "living God" also indicates that Paul's common concept of the church as God's temple is in view.[58]   A similar progression of the images from the household of God (οἰκεῖος τοῦ θεοῦ) to the building (οἰκοδομή) and then to the holy temple (ναὸς ἅγιος) has been already seen in Eph. 2:19-22.

The analysis of the passages in which Paul explicitly or implicitly designates the church as the temple, the building, or the house of God leads to

---

[53]See McKelvey, *New Temple*, 116.

[54]Hanson, *Unity*, 134, concludes that the phrase ἐν πνεύματι here is equivalent to πνευματικόν and expresses the uniqueness of the new dwelling of God in relation to the old temple. However, cf. Gärtner, *Temple and the Community*, 65 and McKelvey, *New Temple*, 117.

[55]Ellis, "Traditions in the Pastoral Epistles," 244-45, thinks that 1 Tim. 3:1b-13 is a preformed tradition. Cf. Kelly, *Pastoral Epistles*, 231.

[56]Cf. Otto Michel, "οἶκος," in *TDNT*, 5:121; Gordon Fee, *1 and 2 Timothy, Titus*, New International Biblical Commentary (Peabody, MA: Hendrickson, 1984), 92; and Arland J. Hultgren, *I-II Timothy, Titus*, Augsbury Commentary on the New Testament (Minneapolis, MN: Augsburg, 1984), 76. In the New Testament the phrase οἶκος θεοῦ can mean either the "house" or the "household" of God. For example, it means the "house of God" in 1 Pet. 2:5 while it denotes the "household of God" in 1 Pet. 4:17, Heb. 3:5-6, 2 Tim. 1:16, and Tit. 1:11.

[57]Cf. Rev. 3:12, Gal. 2:9.

[58]Cf. McKelvey, *New Temple*, 133 and Fee, *1 and 2 Timothy, Titus*, 92.

the following conclusions: (1) Paul uses the terms "temple" (ναός), "building" (οἰκοδομή), and "house" (οἰκιά or οἶκος) primarily in a corporate sense, denoting the church. (2) In a few specific cases, however, he uses them in an individual sense to refer to the present or future life of the individual believer (1 Cor. 3:16, 2 Cor. 5:1-2). (3) His frequent use of the introductory phrase οὐκ οἴδατε ὅτι or οἴδαμεν ὅτι indicates that the concept of the church as the temple was a well-known early Christian tradition. The occurrence of this concept in other New Testament writings also confirms this assumption.[59] (4) Interestingly, Paul always presents the temple as of God or of the Holy Spirit, but never as of Christ. He describes the relationship of Christ to the temple only in Ephesians as the cornerstone to the building. Finally, (5) he closely relates the concept of the church as God's temple to the presence of God or of the Spirit and thus to the idea of holiness.

Implications

The terms "temple," "building," and "house" are used in Paul's writings in a twofold sense: (1) the general use in the corporate sense and (2) the specific use in the individual sense. When used in the corporate sense, they denote the church in its totality. This is evident in Paul's statement that believers in plural are a single entity, either the building or the temple of God.[60] In 1 Tim. 3:15 the house of God is specifically identified as the church of the living God. The concept of the church as the temple of God strongly implies the oneness of the church and indicates that the principle of "one God one temple" must have been as central to the minds of the New Testament believers as it had been to their Jewish forbears.[61] Probably for this reason, Paul refers to the temple in his arguments against the disunity of the church (1 Cor. 3:16-17), for the unity of Jews and Gentiles in Christ (Eph. 2:19-22), and for the exclusive solidarity of believers (2 Cor. 6:16-17).

The unity of believers with one another is most clearly expressed in Eph. 2:21-22 where Paul says that believers, "joined together (συναρμο-λογουμένη), grow into the holy temple in the Lord" and that they "are built together (συνοικοδομεῖσθε) into the dwelling place of God in the Spirit."

---

[59]Cf. 1 Pet. 2:4-8, Heb. 3:6,

[60]1 Cor. 3:9, 16-17, 2 Cor. 6:16.

[61]Cf. Deuteronomy 12. The combination of one temple and one God occurs also in both Philo and Josephus. See Philo, *Spec. Leg.* 1:67 and Josephus, *Ap.* 2:193.

The basic underlying concept is the corporate solidarity that believers form together in Christ. As the various parts of the body make up the single whole body and as the various parts of the building create the single whole building,[62] so believers form a corporate solidarity. They are organically and structurally connected to one another.

This mutual unity of believers with one another is, however, not apart from their corporate unity with Christ. It is true that Paul's designation of the church as the temple, the building, or the house of God lays more emphasis on the church's relation to God than to Christ.[63] Nevertheless, the relationship of the church to Christ is clearly expressed in Eph. 2:20-22 as that of the whole building to the cornerstone:[64] "in whom (ἐν ᾧ) the whole building . . . grows into the holy temple in the Lord and in whom (ἐν ᾧ) you are built together into the dwelling place of God in the Spirit." The phrase ἐν ᾧ connects both "whole building" (πᾶσα οἰκοδομή) and "you" (ὑμεῖς) to Christ the cornerstone. This may indicate how the mutual unity of believers comes into existence: Believers are united with one another in Christ by their incorporation into Christ or into the body of Christ.[65] If so, the corporate entity referred to by the temple, the building, or the house is essentially the same as that referred to by the body of Christ.

Paul uses the term "temple," "building," or "house" also in the specific sense, denoting the individual believer. The most explicit example is 1 Cor. 6:19 where he calls the body of the individual believer a "temple of the Holy Spirit." Interestingly, his reference to the temple is closely connected with the term "body" that is also used in a twofold sense. When Paul states, for example, "He who joins himself to a prostitute becomes one body (literally, flesh) with her" (6:16) and "He who joins himself to the Lord becomes one spirit with him" (6:17), he clearly refers to the corporate body created by the union either with a prostitute or with Christ.[66] When he mentions "your bodies" (6:15), "outside the body" (6:18a), "against his own body" (6:18b), "your body" (6:19), and "in your bodies" (6:20), however, he clearly refers to

---

[62]Cf. Rom. 12:4-5, 1 Cor. 10:17, 12:12-27, Eph. 4:15-16, Col. 2:19, 1 Pet. 2:4-5.

[63]Cf. McKelvey, *New Temple*, 180-81.

[64]McKelvey, *New Temple*, 181, claims: "When the New Testament writers wish to describe Christ's place in the church and the relation of Christians to him, they either substitute the image of the building (οἰκοδομή) for the temple image or else fuse the two images and represent Christ as a part of the building."

[65]Hanson, *Unity*, 135; Congar, *Mystery of the Temple*, 165-66.

[66]See pp. 147-49, 167 (ch. 5) below.

the individual person. His use of the term "temple" is similar: Although he uses it primarily in the corporate sense, here he applies it to individual believers.

2 Cor. 5:1-2 may be another such example. The "our earthly tent-house" and the "house not made with hands" (5:1) strongly imply the corporate solidarities in Adam and in Christ.[67] This corporate sense, however, recedes into the background and the individual sense comes to the fore as his thought focuses on the subject of the eschatological hope of individual believers. Consequently, the "heavenly inhabitation" (τὸ οἰκητήριον τὸ ἐξ οὐρανοῦ) that believers long to be "put on over" clearly denotes the resurrection body that believers will individually receive at the Parousia. A similar pattern occurs in 1 Corinthians 15 where the nature of σῶμα ψυχικόν and σῶμα πνευματικόν (15:42-29) is set in the framework of Adam-Christ typology. While the typology signifies the two contrasting *corporate* solidarities in Adam and in Christ, σῶμα ψυχικόν and σῶμα πνευματικόν in the following verses (15:44-54) strongly imply the *individual* resurrection bodies of believers that are to be received at the Parousia.

An interrelationship between the corporate and the individual is also apparent in Paul's description of believers as growing into the holy temple and being built together into the dwelling place of God (Eph. 2:21-22). The underlying idea is basically the same as that of 1 Pet. 2:4-5 where it is said that believers, as "living stones" (λίθοι ζῶντες), are built into a "spiritual house" (οἶκος πνευματικός).

The result of the above discussion is significant for Paul's view of man. (1) It demonstrates that he understands the believer not only individually but also corporately, a being who exists in a corporate solidarity with Christ and with other believers. (2) It shows that there exists a certain oscillation in Paul's thought-pattern between the corporate and the individual. With this conclusion in hand, the following study now proceeds to investigate possible backgrounds of Paul's conception.

Possible Backgrounds

The phrase "temple of God" has a meaning in Paul significantly different from that in traditional Judaism. It refers no longer to the temple in

---

[67]See pp. 126-30 above.

Jerusalem, but denotes primarily the community of believers, namely, the church. What prompted such a radical change? This is a difficult question for several reasons. First, although the phrase "temple of God" strongly implies an Old Testament background, the concept of the community as the temple or the dwelling place of God is not immediately apparent in or from that background. Second, the concept includes not only the "temple of God" but also the "building" or the "house of God." Third, Paul does not provide any clue to the source of this concept but assumes that his readers are familiar with it. Nevertheless, possible backgrounds for the conception have been sought (1) in hellenistic writings, (2) in the Qumran texts, and (3) in the teachings of Jesus mediated by the leaders of the early church.

The Hellenistic Writings

Some scholars argue that Paul's conception of the church as the temple of God is a spiritualization of the temple that has its background in hellenistic literature.[68] They offer the following arguments: (1) Paul's designation of the individual believer as the temple of the Holy Spirit (1 Cor. 6:19) corresponds to the hellenistic (Stoic) notion of man as a temple.[69] (2) His reference to the "earthly tent-house" and to the "heavenly house" (2 Cor. 5:1) strongly implies the dualistic body/soul anthropology of Hellenism: The "earthly tent-house" refers to the transitory physical body that is subject to decay and the "heavenly house" or the "heavenly inhabitation" refers to the immortal soul.[70] Likewise, the terms "naked" and "away from the body" (2 Cor. 5:3, 8) imply the hellenistic concept of the disembodied state of the soul.[71] (3) The concept

---

[68]For example, see H. Wenschkewitz, "Die Spiritualisierung der Kultusbegriffe Tempel, Priester und Opfer im Neuen Testament," *Ang* 4 (1932): 77-230 and Schlier, *Christus und die Kirche*, 49-60. The hellenistic influence is also implied by Weiss, *Erste Korintherbrief*, 166, n. 1; Robertson and Plummer, *First Corinthians*, 128-29; Otto Michel, "ναός," in *TDNT*, 4:886; and Conzelmann, *2 Corinthians*, 77, n. 90.

[69]See Wenschkewitz, "Spiritualisierung," 178. McKelvey, *New Temple*, 122 also says: "The conception of the individual as the temple at 1 Cor. 6:19 and the view taken of the body at 2 Cor. 5:2ff owe some debt to Greek thought, either directly or indirectly."

[70]Cf. Bultmann, *Theology*, 1:202; Knox, *Paul and the Church of the Gentiles*, 128; R. F. Hettlinger, "2 Corinthians 5:1-10." *SJT* 10 (June 1957): 174-94; Käsemann, *Leib und Leib Christi*, 165; and Charles, *Critical History*, 441-61.

[71]Cf. Plummer, *Second Corinthians*, 147-48; Sevenster, "Gumnos in II Cor. v. 3," 211; and Schweitzer, *Mysticism*, 134.

of the building growing into the temple of God and being built into the dwelling place of God reflects the gnostic "Primal Man" myth that speaks of the absorption of the redeemed into the body of the "Primal Man."[72]

Although the Stoics do not actually call man a temple, they clearly imply it. Seneca, for example, declares that divine seeds are implanted in human bodies and that every human being houses a part of the divine spirit.[73] Epictetus expresses the same idea as follows: "Wherefore, when you close your doors and make darkness within, remember never to say that you are alone, for you are not alone; nay, God is within you, and your own genius (δαίμων) is within."[74] Philo also shares this idea when he states, "Be zealous, therefore, O soul, to become a house of God, a holy temple, a most beauteous abiding-place; for perchance, the Master of the whole world's household shall be thine too and keep thee under His care as His special house, to preserve thee evermore strongly guarded and unharmed."[75]

There are obviously some similarities between the Pauline conception and the Stoic and the Philonic notions of individual man as a temple. But they do not justify the conclusion that Paul derived his concept from these backgrounds because there are fundamental conceptual differences between them. For example, (1) whereas the Stoics think of the divine indwelling in terms of innate divine reason based on a pantheistic view of reality, Paul views it as a result of special blessing to particular individuals through the impartation of the Spirit.[76] (2) Paul's reference to the "earthly tent-house" or the "heavenly house" in 2 Cor. 5:1 probably reflects the corporate reality in Adam or in Christ and not the dualistic body/soul anthropology of Hellenism.[77] (3) The argument that the image of the building growing into the holy temple arises from the gnostic "Primal Man" myth is based on the

---

[72]On gnostic influence in relation to οἰκοδομή, see Vielhauer, *Oikodome*, 125, 141-43; Michel, "οἰκοδομή," *TDNT*, 5:145-46; Schlier, *Christus und die Kirche*, 49-60; and idem, *Epheser*, 143-45.

[73]Seneca, *Ep*. 63.16, 41.1-2.

[74]Epictetus, *Dis*. 1.14.13-14.

[75]Philo, *Som*. 1.149; also, cf. 1.21-34, 215, 251, *Cher*. 98, 100, 106, *Opif*. 145-46, and *Virt*. 188.

[76]Cf. Rom. 8:9-11, 1 Cor. 3:16, 12:13, Eph. 2:22. See Michel, "ναός," *TDNT*, 4:886, n. 25 and McKelvey, *New Temple*, 55.

[77]See pp. 142-49 above. Cf. Ellis, "Structure," 40-5; Sevenster, "Gumnos in II Cor. v. 3," 202-14; and Margaret Thrall, "'Putting On or Stripping Off' in 2 Cor. 5:3," in *New Testament Textual Criticism*, ed. Elden Jay Epp and Gordon D. Fee (Oxford: Clarendon, 1981), 221-39.

unwarranted assumption that Paul derived his body of Christ concept from the gnostic "Primal Man" myth.[78] (4) The Pauline notion of the body (σῶμα) as the dwelling place of deity is intolerable for the Stoics and also for Philo because for them the body is essentially evil and is destined to perish.[79] (5) Most significantly, the Stoic and the Philonic conception of man as a temple is individualistic but the Pauline conception is primarily corporate.[80]

The Qumran Texts

Because of the corporate nature of Paul's conception, a number of scholars contend that Paul's view of the church as the temple of God must have originated in the Qumran community, for it also speaks of the community as the temple or the house of God. It does so most explicitly in the *Rule of the Community (1QS)* 5.5-6:[81]

> They shall lay a foundation of truth for Israel, for the community of an eternal covenant. They shall atone for all those who devote themselves, for a sanctuary in Aaron and for a house of truth in Israel, and (for) those who join them for a community.[82]

---

[78]See pp. 113-14 (ch. 3) above.

[79]For example, see Seneca, *Ep.* 92.10, 120.14, *Marc.* 24.5, Philo, *Migr.* 9, *Leg. All.* 1.108, *Immut.* 150, and *Ebr.* 101. Philo suggests that only in the case of Adam, the perfect man, the body is the temple of God (*Opif.* 137). See Michel, "ναός," *TDNT*, 4:886; McKelvey, *New Temple*, 104; and J. N. Sevenster, *Paul and Seneca*, 75-76.

[80]So, Michel, "ναός," *TDNT*, 4:886, n. 25; McKelvey, *New Temple*, 104; and Cerfaux, *Church*, 148.

[81]*4QFlor.*, a midrash on 2 Sam. 7:10-14, may also contain a statement that can be interpreted as referring to the spiritual temple, depending how one translates the phrase אדם מקדש. Gärtner, *Temple and the Community*, 34, for example translates the statement, "And he proposed to build him a temple of (among) men (מקדש אדם), in which should be offered sacrifices before him, the works of the law" (1.6-7), thus implying the spiritual temple. J. Allegro, "Fragments of a Qumran Scroll of Eschatological Midrâsim," *JBL* 77 (December 1958), 352, however, translates the phrase as "to build for Him a man-made sanctuary," thus implying the physical temple to be built at the end-time. The latter interpretation is also adopted by A. Dupont-Sommer, *The Essene Writings from Qumran* (Oxford: Blackwell, 1961), 312 and by McKelvey, *New Temple*, 51.

[82]The translation of the Qumran texts here and in the following pages is from P. Wernberg-Møller, *The Manual of Discipline: Translated and Annotated with an Introduction* (Grand Rapids: Eerdmans, 1957), unless specified otherwise.

The members of the Qumran community are here designated as the two rooms of the temple, namely, a "sanctuary in Aaron" (the holy of holies) and a "house of truth in Israel" (the holy place). The Qumran community allocates special functions to the priests and always reserves the holy of holies for them.[83]

1QS 8.4-9 elaborates the concept:

> When these become in Israel--the council of the community being established in truth--an eternal plant, a holy house consisting of Israel, and a most holy congregation consisting of Aaron, true witnesses about uprightness, chosen by (divine) pleasure to atone for the earth and to punish the impious--then that is the tested wall, the costly cornerstone. Its foundations shall neither be shaken nor be dislodged from their place, a most holy dwelling consisting of Aaron, with [eternal] knowledge of [His] covenant of uprightness, offering up a sweet odour, and a house of integrity and truth made up of Israel.

The "council of the community" established in truth is described as the "holy house," a "most holy congregation," a "most holy dwelling," and a "house of integrity and truth."[84] Furthermore, it is the "tested wall" and the "costly cornerstone." The underlying idea of the passage is the immovability and the permanence of the eschatological community.

1QS 9.3-6 identifies the Qumran community not only with the temple but also with its cultus:

> When these become in Israel, according to all these norms, [a congregation] of the holy spirit of eternal truth, they shall atone for iniquitous guilt and for sinful faithlessness, and [pay off] (sin) for the earth by means of the flesh of burnt-offerings and from the fat pieces of the sacrifices of right offerings of lips as a proper sweetness, and a perfect way of life as a pleasing freewill offering. At that time the men of the community shall separate themselves

---

[83]Cf. Joachim Gnilka, "2 Cor. 6:14-7:1 in the Light of the Qumran Texts and the Testaments of the Twelve Patriarchs," in *Paul and Qumran: Studies in New Testament Exegesis*, ed. Jerome Murphy-O'Connor (Chicago, IL: Priory, 1968), 61.

[84]Since the section begins with a reference to twelve men and three priests, a question is raised as to whether the "council of the community" and what follows refer to a smaller group within the community. In view of other passages (3.2, 5.7, 6.13), however, it is more likely that the whole community is in view. See A. R. C. Leaney, *The Rule of Qumran and Its Meaning: Introduction, Translation and Commentary* (Philadelphia: Westminster, 1966), 211.

> as a sanctuary consisting of Aaron, of the community, as a Holiest of Holy
> and a house of community consisting of Israel who walk in integrity.

The acceptable, pleasing, and thus atoning sacrifice is no longer the flesh of burnt-offering or the fat of sacrifices, but the offering of the lips in accordance with the law and of the perfect way of life. The Qumran community, therefore, not only separates itself to become a "sanctuary consisting of Aaron" and a "house of the community consisting of Israel" but also transfers to itself all that the Jerusalem temple stood for, including its cultus.[85]

Those who find in the Qumran texts the origin of Paul's conception of the church as the temple often appeal to 2 Cor. 6:14-7:1 as the linking evidence. Fitzmyer, for example, argues that the passage is "a Christian reworking of an Essene paragraph which has been interpolated into the Pauline letter."[86] He adduces the following evidence: (1) the triple contrast of uprighteousness and iniquity, of light and darkness, and of Christ and Belial, (2) the opposition to idols, (3) the concept of the temple of God, (4) the separation from impurity, and (5) the concatenation of Old Testament texts.[87] Gärtner draws a similar conclusion, although more cautiously than Fitzmyer: "At this point the distance dividing Paul from the Qumran texts is minimal. . . ; the overall resemblance to the Qumran symbolism is so striking as to prompt the question whether the temple symbolism of the early Church . . . may not have originated in the Qumran tradition."[88] Having established 2 Cor. 6:14-7:1 as the linking evidence between Paul and Qumran, Gärtner traces Qumran parallels in other Pauline passages in which a reference to the church as God's temple occurs. He argues that 1 Cor. 3:16-17 reveals points of contact with the Qumran temple symbolism in the following resemblances with 2 Cor. 6:14-7:1: (1) the identification of the temple of God with the community, (2) the indwelling of God's Spirit in the congregation, (3) the idea of the holiness

---

[85]Cf. Gärtner, *Temple and the Community*, 18.

[86]Joseph A. Fitzmyer, "Qumrân and the Interpolated Paragraph in 2 Cor. 6.14-7.1," *CBQ* 23 (July 1961): 279-80. According to Fitzmyer, it was K. G. Kuhn who first noted the relationship between 2 Cor. 6:14-7:1 and the Qumran writings. See K. G. Kuhn, "Les rouleaux de cuivre de Qumrên," *RB* 61 (April 1954): 193-205, especially 203, n. 2 and Joachim Gnilka, "2 Cor. 6:14-7:1," 48-68.

[87]Fitzmyer, "Qumrân and the Interpolated Paragraph," 273-80; also Gärtner, *Temple and the Community*, 49-56. For an evaluation of Fitzmyer's argument, see Martin, *2 Corinthians*, 191-93 and McKelvey, *New Temple*, 97.

[88]Gärtner, *Temple and the Community*, 56.

of the temple, and (4) the demand for purity.[89] He argues that 1 Tim. 3:15 also reflects the Qumran influence because the expression "the church of the living God," which explains the term "house of God," resembles the phrase "the temple of the living God" in 2 Cor. 6:16 and also because the expression "the pillar and foundation of the truth" occurs in the Qumran texts as a part of the temple image.[90] In addition to these parallels, one may add the combination of the temple image with "planting" and "building" that occurs both in Eph. 2:19-22 and in Qumran texts (c.g., 1QS 8.4-9).

There are undeniable parallels between Paul's temple concept and that of the Qumran community, but they do not establish Paul's dependence upon the Qumran texts.[91] Pierre Benoit points out that "while this [parallelism] may be the result of an immediate dependence . . . , it may also be an example in the two communities of a way of thinking and speaking common throughout Palestine at the beginning of the Christian era."[92] The idea of a temple made up of a group of people is, as far as is known today, limited to Qumran and the New Testament writers. This may suggest a link between the two groups, but it is the only element, of the many cited above, that is so limited. Consequently, it is hardly sufficient to establish Paul's dependence on Qumran. Furthermore, if 2 Cor. 6:14-7:1 is a preformed non-Pauline tradition that the Apostle incorporated into his epistle,[93] the parallelism would indicate at most only a relationship between that particular tradition and Qumran. Even in the concept of the community as God's temple there are fundamental differences between Paul and Qumran: (1) While the Qumran sect applies the temple strictly to the community, Paul applies it both to the community (church) and to the individual believer. (2) He closely connects the church as God's temple with the person and the work of the Messiah,[94] a

---

[89]Ibid., 56-60.

[90]Ibid., 66-71. Cf. *1 QS* 5:5, 8:8, and 9:3.

[91]So, Congar, *Mystery of the Temple*, 159 and McKelvey, *New Temple*, 97.

[92]Pierre Benoit, "Qumran and the New Testament," in *Paul and Qumran: Studies in New Testament Exegesis*, ed. Jerome Murphy-O'Connor (Chicago, IL: Priory, 1968), 2.

[93]See p. 131, n. 45 above.

[94]McKelvey, *New Temple*, 122, correctly recognizes the different basis for Paul's concept of the church as God's temple: "The Stoics and Philo spiritualized the idea of the temple and cult because the thought of God dwelling in a temple made by men and accepting blood and other material offerings was intolerable to them, while the Jews of Qumran did so because they could not worship at the temple of Jerusalem. Paul's spiritualization rests upon a much more positive basis, the new and pneumatic order of worship that issues from the death

connection not made in Qumran documents published thus far. (3) Unlike Qumran he combines the temple image not only with the building but also with the body images.

The Teachings of Jesus

Paul's strong emphasis on the church's relationship to the person and the work of Christ and other New Testament writers' frequent use of the temple imagery[95] have prompted others to regard the temple concept as a pre-Pauline tradition that ultimately originated in particular teachings of Jesus in reference to the temple.[96] In the descriptions of the trial of Jesus Mark and Matthew refer to the allegations made by the false witnesses. Matthew (26:60-61) simply states that two witnesses testified, "This fellow (Jesus) said, 'I am able to destroy the temple of God, and to build it in three days.'" Mark, however, adds a couple of new elements: (1) He stresses that the accusers brought false witnesses against Jesus and that their testimony did not agree (14:57, 59), the implication being that the false witnesses either made up the story or misunderstood what Jesus really meant. (2) He qualifies the old temple to be destroyed as "made with hands" and the new temple to be built as "not made with hands." Mark refers to Jesus' saying again in 15:29 (par, Matt. 27:39-40) where he describes the mocking of Jesus by those who passed the cross. Luke does not include this saying in his Gospel, but alludes to it in Acts 6:14 where the false witnesses accuse Stephen of having said that Jesus would destroy the temple and the law.[97] John 2:19-22 refers to the

---

and resurrection of Jesus Christ and the gifts of the Spirit." See also Gartner, *Temple and the Community*, 101.

[95]Cf. 1 Pet. 2:4-10, Heb. 3:6, 9:1-12, 10:19-20.

[96]For example, see John 2:14-22, Mark 14:58, 15:29, Matt. 26:61, 21:42; cf. Matt. 12:1-8. See Ellis, *Paul's Use*, 91-92; idem, "Deity Christology in Mark 14:58," in *Jesus of Nazareth: Lord and Christ*, ed. Joel B. Green and Max Turner (Grand Rapids: Eerdmans, 1994), 195-202 (=*Christ and the Future*, 38-51); Congar, *Mystery of the Temple*, 138-72; Gärtner, *Temple and the Community*, 105-22; and C. F. D. Moule, "Sanctuary and Sacrifice, in the Church of the New Testament," *JTS* New Series 1 (April 1950): 29-41.

[97]For the discussion of the temple in Luke-Acts, see J. Bradley Chance, *Jerusalem, the Temple, and the New Age in Luke-Acts* (Macon, GA: Mercer University Press, 1988) and C. K. Barrett, "Attitudes to the Temple in the Acts of the Apostles," in *Templum Amicitiae: Essays on the Second Temple Presented to Ernst Bammel*, ed. William Horbury (Sheffield: JSOT, 1991), 345-67.

saying in the context of Jesus' ministry, specifically at his cleansing of the temple. Unlike the synoptic writers, he gives Jesus' own words and explains what he actually meant and how the disciples understood them.

The repeated reference in the Gospels to the saying evidences not only that Jesus actually said something about the destruction and the replacement of the temple but also that the Gospel writers attributed great significance to it.[98] What, then, did Jesus really mean by the saying and how did the people around him understand it? The accusers, the mockers, and the high priest evidently understood Jesus' teaching literally as referring to the destruction and the rebuilding of the temple in Jerusalem. The Jew's reaction described in John clearly affirms this: "The Jews then said, 'It has taken forty-six years to build this temple, and will you raise it up in three days?'" (John 2:20). Mark's description of the new temple as "not made with hands," however, shows that the new temple promised by Jesus does not refer to the temple in Jerusalem. If not the temple in Jerusalem, what is it? John says that it is the body of Christ and that the disciples understood it as such (2:21-22). It is, therefore, probable that Paul derived his concept of the church both as the body of Christ and as the temple of God from this and other dominical traditions.[99]

Some scholars argue that Paul's concept of the church as God's temple cannot have been derived from the teachings of Jesus because in the Gospels the temple refers to the individual body of Christ while in Paul it denotes primarily the community, namely, the church. This objection is based, however, on a sharp distinction between the individual and the corporate that Paul never makes. As argued above, his thought often flows from the individual to the corporate or vice versa.[100] As a result, he can identify the temple of God, without any conflict, both with individual believers and with the church.[101] Moreover, in Paul's thought the corporate body that is the church is implicated in the individual body of Christ that was crucified and raised. In other words, believers were corporately included in the death and

---

[98]Cf. McKelvey, *New Temple*, 138 and Ellis, *Paul's Use*, 91.

[99]Cf. Ellis, *Paul's Use*, 91 and A. Cole, *The New Temple: A Study in the Origins of the Catechetical 'Form' of the Church in the New Testament* (London: Tyndale, 1950), 31. Jesus' teaching at the Last Supper (Luke 22:19-20 par) also underlies Paul's understanding of the body of Christ. Cf. 1 Cor. 10:16, 11:23-26, 27-29.

[100]See pp. 123-24, 130, 136-37 above.

[101]Cf. 1 Cor. 6:19, 3:16, 2 Cor. 6:16, Eph. 2:21-22.

resurrection of Christ.[102] Consequently, the church is already implicated in the individual resurrection body of Christ, as the upcoming full harvest is involved in the first-fruits (ἀπαρχή).[103]

In conclusion, Paul's conception of the church as the temple, the building, or the house of God is far removed from the Stoic or the Philonic notion of man as a temple. Although the Qumran texts well demonstrate that the concept of the community as the temple existed prior to Paul, they do not provide evidence for Paul's direct dependence upon Qumran. Three factors-- (1) Paul's emphasis on the church's relationship to the person and the work of Christ, (2) other New Testament writers' use of the temple image, and (3) the Evangelists' repeated references to Jesus' temple sayings--indicate that both the concept of the church as the temple of God and the related "stone" imagery are pre-Pauline Christian traditions that most likely point to the "temple" teachings of Jesus.

---

[102]Rom. 6:3-11, Gal. 2:20, 1 Cor. 15:20.
[103]1 Cor. 15:20. See pp. 44, 46 (ch. 2) above.

CHAPTER 5

THE NATURE OF THE SEXUAL UNION

Paul's view of the nature of the sexual union underlies his teachings on sexual purity, marriage, and divorce. Closely related to his σῶμα concept, it has significant implications not only for his view of man but also for the relationship between Christ and the church. The reference to the sexual union occurs explicitly in 1 Cor. 6:12-20, Eph. 5:21-33, and implicitly in 1 Cor. 7:10-16. In addition, there are a number of other Pauline texts that have specific bearings on the interpretation of the key passages. They are 1 Cor. 11:2-16, 2 Cor. 11:2-3, and 1 Tim. 2:8-3:1a. These passages have been frequently employed in the discussion of the relationship of man and woman in general and of the role of women in ministry.[1] The following study is, however, primarily interested in their implications for Paul's view of the sexual union and subsequently for his view of man.

Analysis of Paul's Usage

1 Cor. 6:12-20

Paul's view of the nature of the sexual union underlies his argument against sexual immorality in 1 Cor. 6:12-20. The sexual union involves the

---

[1]See the discussion in Ellis, *Pauline Theology*, 57-86; Mary Hayter, *The New Eve in Christ: The Use and Abuse of the Bible in the Debate about Women in the Church* (Grand Rapids: Eerdmans, 1987): 118-45; Sharon H. M. Gritz, "A Study of 1 Timothy 2:9-15 in the Light of the Religious and Cultural Milieu of the First Century" (Ph.D. diss., Southwestern Baptist Theological Seminary, 1986), 127-48, 177-230; E. S. Fiorenza, *In Memory of Her: A Feminist Theological Reconstruction of Christian Origins* (New York: Crossroad, 1984), 226-33; M. D. Hooker, "Authority on Her Head: An Examination of 1 Corinthians XI.10," *NTS* 10 (April 1964): 410-16; James B. Hurley, *Man and Woman in Biblical Perspective* (Grand Rapids: Zondervan, 1981); and Paul K. Jewett, *Man as Male and Female: A Study in Sexual Relationships from a Theological Point of View* (Grand Rapids: Eerdmans, 1975), 112-49.

believer's body that is a member of Christ (v. 15a)[2] and the temple of the
Holy Spirit (v. 19)[3] and that belongs to Christ. Assuming that the Corinthian
believers are already familiar with this concept,[4] Paul argues that an immoral
sexual relationship with a prostitute makes a member of Christ a member of a
prostitute (6:16). He bases this argument upon his view that "he who is
united (ὁ κολλώμενος) to a prostitute becomes one body (ἓν σῶμα) with her"
(6:16), a concept that is derived from Gen. 2:24b, "The two shall become one
flesh." Paul applies this concept positively to the marriage union in Eph.
5:31. Although in 1 Cor. 6:16 he does not include the first part of Gen. 2:24,
"For this reason a man shall leave his father and mother and cleave to his
wife," he implies it with the term κολλᾶσθαι (6:16-17), a cognate of the
compound word προσκολλᾶσθαι used in Gen. 2:24.[5] The basic concept that
Paul advocates here is that the sexual relationship with a prostitute creates a
real and ontological union with her, a union that conflicts with the union that
the believer has with Christ.

In the following verse, therefore, Paul applies the "one body (flesh)"
concept to the union between Christ and believers: "But he who is united
(κολλώμενος) to the Lord becomes one spirit (ἓν πνῶμα) with him" (6:17).
Although the same word κολλᾶσθαι is used to describe the believer's union
with Christ, it does not necessarily mean that believers are united with Christ
by physical means.[6] The analogy does suggest, however, that Paul conceives
the union with Christ to be as real as the physical union created by sexual
intercourse.[7] Interestingly, he describes the union with Christ as "one spirit"

---

[2]See pp. 87-88 (ch. 3) above.

[3]See pp. 123-24 (ch. 4) above.

[4]The introductory phrase οὐκ οἴδατε ὅτι used three times in this passage alone (6:15,
17, 19) signifies that the Corinthian believers were familiar with the concept which Paul
advocates. See Ellis, "Traditions in 1 Corinthians," 487.

[5]Both terms are frequently employed to denote the sexual union. Matt. 19:5 (supported
by B D W Θ 078 087 f[13] and so forth) and 1 Cor. 6:16 use κολλᾶσθαι while Mark 10:7 and
Eph. 5:31 employ προσκολλᾶσθαι in their citation of Gen. 2:24. J. I. Miller, "A Fresh Look at
I Corinthians 6:16f.," NTS 27 (October 1980): 127, argues that by removing a prefix Paul takes
the directly sexual reference away from this passage (6:16-17). His argument is, however, not
convincing because the noncompound form is also used in Sir. 19:2 to denote sexual
relationship with a harlot. For further discussion, see K. L. Schmidt, "κολλάω, προσκολλάω,"
in TDNT, 3:822-23.

[6]The physical nature of the union with Christ via the sacraments is stressed to the
extreme by Schweitzer, Mysticism, 127-28 and J. A. T. Robinson, Body, 50-53 while it is
rejected completely by Gundry, Sōma, 68-69 and to certain extent by Best, One Body, 76.

[7]See further Ellis, Pauline Theology, 40-44.

rather than as "one body." This does not mean that the union with Christ is purely "spiritual" whereas the union with a prostitute is purely physical. It probably suggests that the believer's union with Christ is effected by the Holy Spirit. Although Paul does not explain here how believers were united to Christ, he writes elsewhere that they were united to Christ in baptism, that is, baptism in the Spirit, and as a result, they have become corporately the body of Christ and individually members of it.[8] The expression "one spirit," therefore, refers to the corporate body of Christ created by the Spirit-baptism into Christ.[9]

Paul draws a sharp contrast between believers' union with Christ and union with a prostitute. He thinks that both unions are so real and mutually exclusive that the sexual union with a prostitute inevitably negates one's union with Christ. It is, however, not the sexual relationship itself but an immoral kind of sexual relationship that breaks one's union with Christ.[10]

Eph. 5:21-33

Paul relates Gen. 2:24 to the sexual union also in Eph. 5:21-33, a passage that has been frequently employed in the discussion not only of the relationship between husband and wife in marriage but also of the relationship between Christ and the church. Ephesians 5 raises the following questions: (1) What is Paul's primary concern, the relationship between husband and wife or that between Christ and the church? (2) Which relationship is prior and normative? (3) What role does Gen. 2:24 play in Paul's argument? (4) What are the underlying traditions and concepts?

The literary structure of the whole household code (Eph. 5:21-6:9) and the movement of Paul's argument may help to answer these questions. It reveals two important keys: (1) Paul's specific designation of the target groups such as "wives" (5:22), "husbands" (5:25), "children" (6:1), "fathers" (6:4), "slaves" (6:5), and "masters" (6:9), and (2) his repeated use of the comparative particles ὡς, καθώς/ὡς . . . οὕτως. The first key divides the literary structure of the passage vertically while the second key divides it horizontally. Eph. 5:21 may well serve as an introduction to the entire

---

[8] 1 Cor. 12:13, 27, Rom. 6:3-5, Gal. 3:27, Eph. 5:30.

[9] See pp. 88, 109-10 (ch. 3) above.

[10] See Eph. 5:21-33 where Paul makes a positive comparison between the "one body" relationship of husband and wife and that of Christ and the church.

household code (5:22-6:9) and not only to the first section that deals with the relationship of husband and wife (5:22-33). Accordingly, the passage under investigation (5:22-33) can be divided as follows.[11] In the diagram below, column A represents the relationship between husband and wife while column B represents the relationship between Christ and the church.

Column A		Column B
5:21 *Introduction or Transition* (Submit to one another in the fear of the Lord)		

Exhortation To Wives (5:22-24)

Column A		Column B
5:22a *Appeal for submission* (Wives, [submit] to your own husbands)		
5:23a *Reason for submission* (For the husband as the head of the wife)	23b	*Model follows* (As Christ is the head of the church)
	24a	*Model precedes* (As the church submits to Christ)
5:24b *Re-appeal for submission* (So wives [submit] to their husbands)		

Exhortation To Husbands (5:25-33)

Column A		Column B
5:25a *Appeal for love* (Husbands, love your wives)	25b-27	*Model precedes* (As Christ loved the church . . .)
5:28-29a *Re-appeal for love* (So husbands should love their wives as [being]		

---

[11]Cf. J. Paul Sampley, *'And the Two Shall Become One Flesh': A Study of Traditions in Ephesians 5:21-33* (Cambridge: Cambridge University Press, 1971), 104, who makes a similar analysis.

their own bodies (σώματα)
. . . For no man ever hates
his own flesh (σάρκα), but
nourishes and cherishes it)

<table>
<tr><td></td><td>29b-30</td><td>Model follows
(as Christ [does] the church
because we are members of his
body)</td></tr>
</table>

5:31 *Appeal to Scripture* (Gen. 2:24)
      (For this reason . . .)

<table>
<tr><td></td><td>32</td><td>Implication for the
relationship of Christ and
the church
(This mystery is great, and I am
speaking of Christ and the
church)</td></tr>
</table>

5:33 *Concluding exhortation to
      husbands and wives*
      (Let each one of you love
      his wife as himself and let the
      wife reverence her husband)

Paul's instructions consist of two subsections: (1) instructions for wives (5:22-24) and (2) instructions for husbands (5:25-33). They are given in the format of the household code (*Haustafel*) common to first-century Judaism and to the hellenistic world,[12] but they are based on scripture[13] and christologically reshaped.[14]

------

[12]Concerning the origin of the New Testament household code, there are basically three different views: (1) It originated in hellenistic (Stoic) moral philosophy (M. Dibelius and Karl Weidinger); (2) It is a Christian tradition (D. Schroeder and L. Goppelt); (3) It is rooted in hellenistic Judaism (J. E. Crouch, E. Lohse, W. Schrage, and Eduard Schweizer). See M. Dibelius and H. Greeven, *An die Kolosser, Epheser, an Philemon* (Tübingen: Mohr, 1953), 48-50; Karl Weidinger, *Die Haustafeln: Ein Stück urchristlicher Paränese* (Leipzig: n.p., 1928); D. Schroeder, "Lists, Ethical," in Supplementary volume to *Interpreter's Dictionary of the Bible*, 546-47; L. Goppelt, "Jesus und die 'Haustafel'-Tradition," in *Orientierung an Jesus: Zur Theologie der Synoptiker*, ed. P. Hoffmann (Freiburg: Herder and Herder, 1973): 93-106; J. E. Crouch, *The Origin and Intention of the Colossian Haustafel* (Göttingen: Vandenhoeck &

Paul exhorts wives to submit to their husbands and husbands to love their wives as being their own bodies.[15] He finds the reason for the wife's submission in the headship of her husband and the reason for the husband's love of his wife in the concept of the "one body (flesh)" union between husband and wife in marriage, a concept that is rooted in the teaching of Gen. 2:24: "For this reason a man shall leave his father and mother and be joined to his wife, and the two shall become one flesh."

A question often arises as to the role of Gen. 2:24 in Paul's argument, whether it relates only to the section of his discussion that deals with the "one body" union between husband and wife (5:25-29) or also to the preceding section that speaks of the headship of the husband over his wife. Sampley argues that Gen. 2:24 relates to the whole passage which includes Paul's discussion of the headship of the husband over his wife (5:22-31). He points to the following evidence: (1) the presence of organic terminology, "one flesh" in the citation of Gen. 2:24 at verse 31 and "head" in verse 23, and (2) the widespread early Christian literary pattern that connects injunctions for

---

Ruprecht, 1972); Lohse, *Colossians*, 154-57; Wolfgang Schrage, "Zur Ethik der neutestamentlichen Haustafeln," *NTS* 21 (October 1974): 1-22; and Eduard Schweizer, "Traditional Ethical Patterns in the Pauline and Post-Pauline Letters and Their Development (Lists of Vices and House-tables)," in *Text and Interpretation: Studies in the New Testament Presented to Matthew Black*, ed. Ernest Best and R. McL. Wilson (Cambridge: Cambridge University Press, 1979), 195-209. For a more comprehensive list of literature, see Lincoln, *Ephesians*, 355-56.

[13]The scriptural citations in Ephesians include Gen. 2:24 at Eph. 5:31 and Ex. 20:12 (Deut. 5:16) at Eph. 6:2-3. Sampley, *One Flesh*, 30-34, argues that Lev. 19:18 also underlies Paul's statement in 5:28-29 and 33a. The combination of the instruction for wives' submission and a reference to Torah occurs also in 1 Cor. 11:3-4, 7-9, 14:34, and in 1 Tim. 2:11-14.

[14]The christological reshaping is evident in the qualifying phrases: Wives are instructed to submit to their husbands *as to the Lord* (5:22), children to obey their parents *in the Lord* (6:1), and slaves to obey their earthly masters *as to Christ (Lord) and as servants of Christ* (6:5-6). Likewise, husbands are instructed to love their wives *as Christ loved the church* (5:25), parents to bring up their children *in the discipline and instruction of the Lord* (6:4), and masters to treat their slaves with a good will, *knowing that they also have the master in heaven, that is, Christ* (6:9).

[15]The phrase ὡς τὰ ἑαυτῶν σώματα in 5:28 can also mean "as you love your own bodies," but this can hardly be the meaning here. In view of 5:23 where the wife is implied as the body of her husband and of Gen. 2:24 cited at 5:31 that declares the "one flesh" union of husband and wife, it seems more accurate to translate the phrase "as being your own bodies." So, Best, *One Body*, 177; Ellis, *Pauline Theology*, 41; T. K. Abbott, *A Critical and Exegetical Commentary on the Epistle to the Ephesians and to the Colossians*, International Critical Commentary (Edinburgh: T. & T. Clark, 1897), 170-71; Barth, *Ephesians*, 629-30; Franz Mussner, *Der Brief an die Epheser* (Gütersloh: Gütersloher, 1982), 159. Otherwise, see Lincoln, *Ephesians*, 378, who insists that the phrase must mean "as you love yourself."

subordination with texts from the Pentateuch.[16] Miletic accepts this view and further argues that since Paul's exhortations both for subordination (vv. 22-24) and for unity (vv. 25-29) are derived from his and Jewish forms of theological speculation about Adam,[17] they are theologically linked together and, consequently, Gen. 2:24 relates to the whole passage.

These arguments are, however, not fully convincing for several reasons. First, Paul's citation of Gen. 2:24 is directly related to the section where he exhorts husbands to love their wives as being their own bodies. The replacement of σώματα with σάρξ in verse 29 clearly prepares a way for the citation of Gen. 2:24 at verse 31 and thus connects the citation to the immediately preceding verses. Second, the basic concept underlying Gen. 2:24 is the "one flesh" union between husband and wife in marriage and not subordination. It is true that Paul's concept of the headship of the husband over his wife is grounded also in the Genesis accounts, but it is grounded in Gen. 1:27-28, 2:18-22, 3:6, 13 and not in Gen. 2:24.[18] In this respect, Lincoln's critique of both Sampley and Miletic seems accurate:

> I do not assume that subordination has nothing to do with mutuality, nor dispute that the two notions can be combined theologically, nor deny that the writer holds them both together in this passage. I simply dispute that the quotation from Gen. 2:24 performs this function in the writer's argument. Instead, it functions in a more limited way and is brought in to make his point about only one of these notions--the mutual 'one flesh' relationship.[19]

Third, although the image of the body and that of the head are closely related in the Ephesian letter, they are not one and the same imagery.[20] The passage implies that the wife is in a sense the body of her husband, but "there is no suggestion that the wife forms the rump or trunk of the body of which the husband is the head."[21] Ellis succinctly describes this in his comment on

---

[16]Sampley, *One Flesh*, 32-34, 113-16.

[17]Stephen Francis Miletic, *One Flesh: Eph. 5.22-24, 5.30: Marriage and the New Creation* (Roma: Editrice Pontificio Instituto Biblico, 1988), 25-98. Cf. also the references to "head" and "subordination" as they are applied to the relationship of God the Father and Christ in 1 Cor. 11:3 and 15:28.

[18]See 1 Cor. 11:7-9, 1 Tim. 2:13-14, and 2 Cor. 11:3.

[19]Lincoln, *Ephesians*, 361.

[20]For a discussion of the relationship of the body and the head in Ephesians, see pp. 93-98 (ch. 3) above.

[21]Best, *One Body*, 179.

Eph. 5:23: "The imagery is not 'head and torso,' but rather the leader or ruler and the 'body' that is distinct from him but that is nonetheless subject to his lordship and included under the umbrella of his corporate person."[22] In other words, "head" is not an organic term that is a part of Paul's "body" imagery. One may safely conclude, therefore, that Paul's citation of Gen. 2:24 qualifies only the second section which deals with the "one body" relationship of husband and wife.

Paul explains here the relationship between husband and wife in analogy with the relationship between Christ and the church, namely, the unity of Christ and the church and the headship of Christ over the church. His use of the comparative particles ὡς and καθώς/ὡς . . . οὕτως[23] indicates the shift from one relationship to the other. That is, wives are to submit to their husbands (5:21, 24b) as (ὡς) the church submits to Christ (5:24a) because the husband is the head of the wife as (ὡς) Christ is the head of the church (5:23).[24] Correspondingly, husbands are to love their wives sacrificially (5:25, 28) as (καθώς) Christ loved the church and gave himself up for her; they are to nourish and cherish them because their wives are their own bodies just as (καθώς) believers are members of Christ's body (5:29-30).[25]

As Paul constantly compares these two relationships, his thought often oscillates between them.[26] This is most evident in Eph. 5:31-32 where he cites Gen. 2:24 to support the unity between husband and wife and

---

[22]Ellis, *Pauline Theology*, 41.

[23]Eph. 5:23, 24, 25-28.

[24]A question arises as to the phrase αὐτὸς σωτὴρ τοῦ σώματος that comes at the end of verse 23, whether it refers only to the relationship between Christ and the church or also to that between husband and wife so that the husband may be understood as the savior of his wife as Christ is the savior of the body that is the church. The first view is accepted by Abbott, *Ephesians and Colossians*, 166; Dibelius and Greeven, *Kolosser, Epheser, Philemon*, 93; Barth, *Ephesians*, 614-17; Rudolf Schnackenburger, *Ephesians: A Commentary*, trans. Helen Heron (Edinburgh: T. & T. Clark, 1991), 247; and by Miletic, *One Flesh*, 40. The second view is advocated by Robinson, *One Body*, 124; W. Foerster, "σωτήρ," in *TDNT*, 7:1016; and by W. Hendriksen, *Exposition of Ephesians* (Grand Rapids: Baker, 1967), 248-49. Bruce, *Ephesians*, 385 and Lincoln, *Ephesians*, 370, argue that the phrase refers also to the relationship between husband and wife but the term "savior" should be taken in the sense of "protector" or "provider."

[25]The image of Christ nourishing his body (the church) is clearly seen in Eph. 4:11-16 and Col. 2:19.

[26]Barth, *Ephesians*, 659, states that "in this passage both topics are central, and both are ontologically and noetically so closely tied together that they cannot be unstrung--not even for the reconstruction of an original supposedly Jewish or Greek *Haustafel*."

immediately applies it to the unity between Christ and the church.[27] The inextricable interrelation and the oscillation of Paul's thought have caused many scholars to inquire as to which relationship is prior and normative and which is Paul's secondary concern. Chavasse suggests that Paul is less interested in the marriage relationship than he is in the union between Christ and the church and that he is more concerned about marriage as a symbol than he is about right relationships in marriage.[28] Similarly, Miletic states: "The citation from Gen. 2:24 applies first to Christ and the church, suggesting that Christ and the church--and not the wife and husband--are the primary referents of the σὰρξ μία ('one flesh') relationship."[29]

These assertions are, however, not entirely convincing. Since Paul employs the relationship between Christ and the church as a model to explain the relationship between husband and wife, he must regard the former as normative for the latter.[30] This does not mean, however, that Paul's primary concern in this passage is with the relationship of Christ and the church. As Lincoln correctly points out,[31] his thoughts about the two relationships have undoubtedly influenced each other, but the *paraenesis* is his primary concern, and in the end the christological and ecclesiological formulations serve that purpose. The phrase τὸ μυστήριον τοῦτο in Eph. 5:32 undoubtedly refers back to the concept underlying Gen. 2:24 cited at verse 31, thus implying some kind of connection between the two. But in contrast to Miletic's view, the primary referents of the "one flesh" relationship are husband and wife and not Christ and the church.

A certain typological comparison exists between the two relationships and Gen. 2:24, that is, the marriage relationship between Adam and Eve. As mathematical ratios it may be expressed as follows: Husband/wife (human marriage) = Christ/church (divine marriage) = Adam/Eve (original marriage). The human marriage relationship between husband and wife is explained in the framework of the divine union between Christ and the church, and both

---

[27]Cf. Lincoln, *Ephesians*, 352.

[28]Chavasse, *Bride of Christ*, 76-77.

[29]Miletic, *One Flesh*, 47.

[30]So, Barth, *Ephesians*, 652; Sampley, *One Flesh*, 103-08, 121-26; and Schnackenburger, *Ephesians*, 241-44.

[31]Lincoln, *Ephesians*, 353.

are grounded in the "one flesh" marriage union between Adam and Eve constituted in Gen. 2:24.[32]

A number of implications can be drawn from these equations: (1) The wife is the body of her husband not only as the church is the body of Christ but also as Eve was "one flesh" with Adam (Gen. 2:24).[33] (2) By the same analogy, Eve may be regarded as the body of Adam and (3) the church as the bride of Christ (2 Cor. 11:2-3). Indeed, the "cleansing," "washing," and "splendor of the church" in Eph. 5:25-27 may also correspond to the picture of Yahweh's marriage to Israel depicted in Ezek. 16:8-14 with its notions of cleansing, bathing with water, and the splendor of the bride.[34] (4) The concept underlying these equations is basically twofold, namely, (a) the ontological "one body" union created in marriage between Adam and Eve, between husband and wife, and between Christ and the church, and (b) the headship of Adam over Eve, of the husband over his wife, and of Christ over the church.

1 Cor. 7:10-16

Paul's view of the sexual union may also underlie his instructions on divorce in 1 Cor. 7:10-16. The instructions consist of two parts: (1) those for a marriage in which both partners are believers (vv. 10-11) and (2) those for a marriage in which only one partner is a believer (vv. 12-16). In the first case, Paul insists, they should not separate from each other. In the second case, however, divorce is conditional: If the unbelieving spouse consents to stay, the believer should not seek a divorce, but if the unbelieving spouse desires to separate, the believer is not bound to maintain the marriage (v. 15). Even in this case, however, Paul alludes that it is better for the believing partner to maintain the marriage in the hope of saving the unbelieving spouse (v. 16).

---

[32]See Sampley, *One Flesh*, 34-35, 113; Lincoln, *Ephesians*, 352, 362-63; Chavasse, *Bride of Christ*, 74-77; Batey, *NT Nuptial Imagery*, 20-31; and Best, *One Body*, 179.

[33]Cf. Lincoln, *Ephesians*, 354 and Ellis, *Pauline Theology*, 41-42.

[34]The phrase καθαρίσας τῷ λουτρῷ τοῦ ὕδατος (5:26) may refer to baptism. But many scholars recognize its resemblance to the bridal bath depicted in Ezek. 16:9. For example, see Sampley, *One Flesh*, 41-42; Abbott, *Ephesians and Colossians*, 168-69; Dunn, *Baptism*, 162-63; Bruce, *Ephesians*, 387; Lincoln, *Ephesians*, 375; Richardson, *Theology*, 257; and Barth, *Ephesians*, 669. However, cf. Jeremias, "νύμφη, νυμφίος," in *TDNT*, 4:1101-06; Schlier, *Epheser*, 275; and Richard A. Batey, "Jewish Gnosticism and the 'Hieros Gamos' of Eph. v. 21-33," *NTS* 10 (October 1963): 126.

Significantly, Paul attributes the first part of his instructions to the Lord (v. 10): "To the married I give charge, not I but the Lord." He probably refers to the teachings of Jesus that are recorded in Matt. 19:3-9 and Mark 10:2-9,[35] a *yelammedenu rabbenu* midrash on Gen. 2:24 and Deut. 24:1, 3.[36] The issue at stake is whether the Mosaic permission to divorce (Deut. 24:1-3) or, as Jesus argues, the divine (and Mosaic) injunction in the Genesis accounts (Gen. 2:24) is the normative and regulative passage for marriage.[37]

Although Paul does not cite Gen. 2:24 in 1 Cor. 7:10-16, he refers to it in the preceding chapter in reference to sexual union (1 Cor. 6:16).[38] Moreover, he attributes his instructions to Jesus' teaching on divorce that in Matthew 19 and Mark 10 is deeply rooted in Gen. 2:24. Paul's teaching on divorce is, therefore, basically the same as that of Jesus: Marriage creates an ontological "one body (flesh)" unity between the two participants, and this unity is real and intended to be permanent.

This conception continues in Paul's teaching on mixed marriages between the believer and the non-believer (1 Cor. 7:12-16). A strong sense of corporate solidarity underlies Paul's argument in verse 14 where he provides the reasons why the believing partner should not separate from the unbelieving spouse who is willing to stay in the marriage: "For the unbelieving husband is sanctified through (ἐν) his wife, and the unbelieving

---

[35]Cf. Matt. 5:31-32, Luke 16:18.

[36]On the literary form, see Ellis, *Old Testament*, 97-98. There are some discrepancies between the Matthean and the Marcan accounts. The most significant difference is Matthew's (19:9) inclusion of the exception clause for unchastity. A number of scholars argue that Mark depends on the original logion found in Q (Luke 16:18) and that Matthew abbreviates the Marcan account and inserts the clause on unchastity. See, for example, Rudolf Bultmann, *The History of the Synoptic Tradition*, trans. John Marsh (Oxford: Basil, 1968), 26, 136; T. W. Manson, *The Sayings of Jesus* (London: SCM, 1949), 136-38; and A. H. McNeile, *The Gospel according to St. Matthew* (London: Macmillan, 1915; reprint, Grand Rapids: Baker, 1980), 65. However, Ellis, *Prophecy and Hermeneutic*, 159 and idem, *Pauline Theology*, 81, n. 90, argues that on form-critical grounds the Matthean passage best represents the more original literary formulation. See also Abel Isaksson, *Marriage and Ministry in the New Temple: A Study with Special Reference to Mt. 19:3-12 and 1 Cor. 11:3-16* (Lund: Gleerup, 1965), 71-74, who contends that in view of Paul's reference to Jesus' teaching in 1 Cor. 7:11, the saying must have been a part of the widespread traditions that the early church had at its disposal and that the different Synoptic versions may be different formulations of a common original tradition and not deliberate changes made by an individual evangelist.

[37]Mark 10:6-9, Matt. 19:4-6; cf. Gen. 1:27, 2:24.

[38]See Ellis, *Pauline Theology*, 81.

wife is sanctified through (ἐν) her husband. Otherwise, your children would be unclean, but as it is they are holy."

This statement raises a number of exegetical questions that are difficult to answer: (1) What do the words "sanctified" and "holy" mean? (2) How and to what extent is the unbelieving spouse "sanctified" through (ἐν) the believing partner? (3) Who are "your children" and in what sense are they holy? In view of verse 16 where Paul considers the unbelieving spouse as still being outside the realm of salvation, the words "sanctified" and "holy" unlikely refer to the redeemed state of the believer as they normally do elsewhere in Paul's letters.[39] Whatever they may denote in this context, Paul seems to employ here the Old Testament principle of holiness by association: "Whatever touches it [the altar] becomes holy" (e.g., Exod. 29:37, 30:29).[40] The unbelieving spouse is "sanctified" because he or she is united to the believing spouse as "one flesh" in marriage. The familial corporate sphere is not limited to husband and wife; it also extends to their children. The fundamental conception that underlies Paul's teachings on divorce is,

---

[39]For example, see 1 Cor. 1:30, 6:11, Eph. 5:26, Col. 1:22, and 2 Thess. 2:13. So, Brian S. Rosner, *Paul, Scripture and Ethics: A Study of 1 Corinthians 5-7* (Leiden: E. J. Brill, 1994), 169-70. Cf. Schweitzer, *Mysticism*, 128, who interprets the statement in an extremely physical and realistic sense: "The unbelieving partner, through bodily connection with the believing, has a share in the latter's being-in-Christ and thereby becomes with him a member of the Community of the Sanctified. Because the married pair belong corporeally to one another, the unbelieving partner becomes, without his or her co-operation, attached to Christ and susceptible of receiving the powers of death and resurrection which go forth from Christ . . . . And similarly, children sprung from such a marriage belong to the Community of the Sanctified." Similarly, Robinson, *Body*, 54-55.

[40]So, Bruce, *1 and 2 Corinthians*, 69; Rosner, *Paul*, 169-70. Cf. D. Daube, "Pauline Contributions to a Pluralistic Culture: Re-Creation and Beyond," in *Jesus and Man's Hope* (Pittsburgh, PA: Pittsburgh Theological Seminary, 1971), 232-41, who interprets the passage in the light of certain rabbinic traditions. He argues that 1 Cor. 7:12-16 reflects the rabbinic teaching that in conversion a proselyte becomes as a newborn child and thus his/her former marriage relationship dissolves (223). Likewise, in conversion a believer becomes a new creation and consequently his/her former relationships including marriage dissolves (224). Since in the rabbinic materials the verb "to consecrate" sometimes means to consecrate a wife (e.g., a marriage) and since one of the means of such a consecration is through sexual intercourse (cf. *m. Kidd.* 1.1, *m. Nidd.* 5.4, *b. Kidd.* 10a, *b. Yeb.* 57b, *b. San.* 55b), Daube suggests that Paul teaches in 1 Cor. 7:14 that although the believer's former marriage relationship has been dissolved through conversion, he/she should live with the unbelieving spouse in the hope of his/her conversion and that by intercourse the believer consecrates the unbelieving spouse and thus the new marriage (235-36).

therefore, the ontological corporate solidarity that includes not only the husband and wife but also their children.[41]

Related Passages

1 Cor. 11:2-16, 1 Tim. 2:8-3:1a, and 2 Cor. 11:2-3 are also of interest for this study, although they are not directly related to Paul's view of the sexual union. They have specific bearings on the interpretation of Eph. 5:21-33, particularly on Paul's view of the husband as the head of his wife, of Christ as the head of the church, and of the church as the bride of Christ.

Paul refers to the headship of the male (ἀνήρ), of Christ, and of God in a passage where he deals with the practical issue of the head covering in worship (1 Cor. 11:3-16). He probably uses a preformed tradition that extends to a church situation the principle of the household code on the relationship between husband and wife.[42] If so, the teaching of the passage is intended primarily for husband and wife and not for man and woman in general.

The interpretation of the passage is difficult (1) because Paul's logic is not easy to follow, (2) because the precise meaning of certain terms (e.g., "veil," "authority on her head," and so forth) is uncertain, and (3) because the customs prevailing in the passage are little known to modern readers. Whether the veil refers to an external head covering or to long or loosed hair,[43] Paul insists that a woman but not a man should cover her head when

---

[41]So, Rosner, *Paul*, 169-70.

[42]Ellis, "Traditions in 1 Corinthians," 493-94, offers the following features in evidence: (1) It is prefaced by a reference to a tradition previously "delivered" to them and begins with an introductory formula θέλω δὲ ὑμᾶς εἰδέναι ὅτι (1 Cor. 11:1-2). (2) It concludes with an implicit identification of the teaching or the practices advocated in the pericope as a customary usage in "the churches of God" (v. 16). (3) The teaching is closely packed, with an oscillation in the meaning of "head" and of "man" and with allusions to an exegesis of Genesis 1-3 similar to that in 1 Cor. 14:34-35, Eph. 5:21-33, and 1 Tim. 2:11-3:1a. (4) It is a self-contained piece with a considerable number of Pauline hapax legomena. (5) It interrupts the immediate flow of thought. Cf. William O. Walker, "1 Corinthians 11:2-16 and Paul's Views regarding Women," *JBL* 94 (March 1975): 94-110, who rejects the passage as a non-Pauline interpolation; and Jerome Murphy-O'Connor, "The Non-Pauline Character of 1 Corinthians 11:2-16?" *JBL* 95 (December 1976): 615-21, who argues against Walker and defends its authenticity.

[43]Bruce K. Waltke, "1 Corinthians 11:2-16: An Interpretation," *BS* 135 (January-March 1978): 46-57, argues for external head covering while William J. Martin, "1 Corinthians 11:2-16: An Interpretation," in *Apostolic History and the Gospel: Biblical and Historical Essays*

she prays or prophesies. The reason is to be found in verse 3: "The head of every man is Christ, the head of a woman is the husband, and the head of Christ is God." The phrase κεφαλὴ δὲ γυναικὸς ὁ ἀνήρ is almost identical to that of Eph. 5:23a: ἀνήρ ἐστιν κεφαλὴ τῆς γυναικός. Two distinctions are, however, observable: (1) Christ is designated as the head of every man rather than of the church. (2) The headship of God over Christ is added.

The "head" here probably denotes "leadership" or "authority"[44] that requires the submission of the corresponding member. "Head" has this meaning in other Pauline texts: Because Christ is the head over all things (Eph. 1:22, Col. 2:10), all men shall bow to his name (Phil. 2:10, Rom. 14:11) and all things are subject to his authority and must be eventually put under his feet (1 Cor. 15:24-27). Because he is the head of the church (Eph. 4:15, 5:23, Col. 1:18, 2:19), the church must submit to him (Eph. 5:24). For God the Father to be Christ's "head" (1 Cor. 11:3) means that Christ subjects himself (ὑποτάσεσθαι) to God the Father (1 Cor. 15:28). Likewise, for the husband to be the head of his wife (1 Cor. 11:3, Eph. 5:23) means that wives are to submit themselves to their husbands (Eph. 5:22). Understood in the light of this pattern, the "authority" that woman, i.e., the wife, should put over her head (1 Cor. 11:10) probably refers to the "headship" or the "leadership" of her husband and may symbolize her submission to his leadership.[45]

In 1 Cor. 11:7-9 Paul appeals to the Genesis creation accounts for his conception of the headship of the husband over his wife.[46] He points out three reasons why a man should not cover his head: (1) Man is the image and the glory of God; but woman is the glory of man. (2) Man was not made from woman; but woman from man. (3) Neither was man created for woman, but woman for man. The phrase διὰ τοῦτο in verse 10 indicates that these are

---

Presented to F. F. Bruce on His 60th Birthday, ed. W. Ward Gasque and Ralph P. Martin (Grand Rapids: Eerdmans, 1970), 233, argues for long hair.

[44]So, Hurley, *Man and Woman*, 166-67; Grudem, "κεφαλή," 56-57; Ellis, *Pauline Theology*, 60. However, see Bedale, "Meaning of κεφαλή," 211-15; Barrett, *First Corinthians*, 248; Bruce, *1 and 2 Corinthians*, 103; Fee, *1 Corinthians*, 503; and Robin Scroggs, "Paul and the Eschatological Woman," *JAAR* 40 (September 1972): 300-01, who understand the "head" in a sense of "source."

[45]So, W. Foerster, "ἐξουσία," in *TDNT*, 2:573-74. However, cf. Hooker, "Authority," 414-16, who argues that the veil does not symbolize woman's subordination to the man, but it is demanded to hide the glory of man in the presence of God. This view is also accepted by Bruce, *1 and 2 Corinthians*, 106 and by Dunn, *Theology*, 590, but rejected by Waltke, "1 Corinthians 11:2-16," 52-53.

[46]Cf. Gen. 1:26-27, 2:21-22.

also reasons why woman should put the "authority over her head." The basis for Paul's conception of the headship of man over his wife is, therefore, the pre-eminence and the priority of the male in creation and the original purpose of the creation of woman.[47] Similarly, in Col. 1:18 headship is joined to the idea of pre-eminence and priority in Paul's description of Christ as the "head" (κεφαλή) of the church, the "beginning" (ἀρχή), and the "first-born (πρωτό-τοκος) from the dead."[48]

A corresponding pattern, combining the wife's submission with a reference to the Genesis accounts of Adam and Eve, occurs in 1 Tim. 2:8-15, which also may be a preformed tradition and an extension of the household code on the relationship between husband and wife to their appropriate conduct in the church.[49] A couple of distinctions are, however, noticeable: (1) No direct reference is made in 1 Timothy 2 to the headship of the husband over his wife, although the statement that woman should learn in silence with all submissiveness (ἐν πάσῃ ὑποταγῇ) suggests it. (2) The reason for the wife's submissiveness is not only the priority of Adam over Eve in creation but also that she, not Adam, was deceived (2:13-14).[50]

An allusion to the serpent's deception of Eve also occurs in 2 Cor. 11:2-3 where Paul discusses the relationship between Christ and the church in the image of a bridegroom and a bride. The bridal image is most evident in verse 2: "I betrothed you [the Corinthian church] to Christ to present you as a pure bride to her one husband" (11:2). The underlying image corresponds well to that of Eph. 5:26-27: ". . . that he [Christ] might sanctify her [the church], having cleansed her by the washing of water with the word, that he might present the church to himself in splendor, without spot or wrinkle or any such thing, that she might be holy and without blemish." The following distinctions are, however, observable in 2 Cor. 11:2-3 when compared to the

---

[47]So, Hurley, *Man and Woman*, 171-74; Ellis, *Pauline Theology*, 60. However, cf. Scroggs, "Eschatological Woman," 300-01, who argues that since 1 Cor. 11:7-9 speaks of man as the source of woman, no subordination of woman to man is intended in the passage. Fee, *1 Corinthians*, 515, also argues that "except for the allusion found in the further explanation in vv. 8-9 as to how woman is man's glory, nothing either in the language of this text or in its explicit statements directly refers back to v. 3."

[48]See p. 98-99 (ch. 3) above.

[49]Ellis, *Pauline Theology*, 72, offers the following evidence: (1) the relationship of the passage to 1 Cor. 14:34-35 and 1 Pet. 3:1-7, (2) the illustration used, namely, Adam and Eve, and (3) the promise·given to the observant woman, which is connected with childbirth. See also the discussion in Ellis, "Traditions in the Pastoral Epistles," 238-42.

[50]Cf. Gen. 1:27, 2:7, 22, 3:6, 13.

Ephesian passage: (1) The bride here refers to the local church rather than to the universal church. (2) The image in view is that of betrothal and not an actual marriage. The church is presented as the eschatological bride who will meet her husband at the Parousia. (3) It is Paul rather than Christ who presents the bride to the bridegroom.

In his description of the church as the bride of Christ, Paul would have been aware of the prophetic nuptial imagery in which God is depicted as the bridegroom and Israel as His bride.[51] He might also have been aware of the nuptial image in the Gospels where Christ is identified as the bridegroom.[52] Paul's allusion to the serpent's deception of Eve in verse 3, however, suggests that his conception of the church as the bride of Christ is rooted ultimately in the story of Adam and Eve.[53] Although Adam is not mentioned in the passage, the following ratios can be drawn by implication: Christ/the church = Adam/Eve = bridegroom/bride. These equations complement those drawn from the Ephesian passage.[54]

In conclusion, the analysis of the Pauline passages that reflect or allude to his view of the nature of the sexual union yields the following conclusions: (1) Paul thinks that sexual intercourse creates a real and ontological "one body" union between the two participants, whether it is between a believer and a prostitute or between a husband and a wife. He bases this understanding on the teaching of Gen. 2:24. (2) Likewise, he thinks that the believer's union with Christ creates an ontological corporate body that is as real as the physical union created by sexual intercourse. (3) He closely relates the "one body" concept to his view of the husband as the head of his wife and of Christ as the head of the church, a concept that is rooted in the Genesis accounts which also teach the priority and the pre-eminence of the male in creation (Gen. 1:27-28, 2:18-22). (4) Paul compares the relationship between husband and wife to that between Christ and the church, and he relates both of them to the Genesis accounts of Adam and Eve, interweaving the "body-head" image with that of "bride-bridegroom." As a result, the following ratios emerge: Christ/the church = husband/wife = Adam/Eve = bridegroom/bride = head/body. These ratios are significant because they show that Paul's view of the sexual union is conceptually interrelated to his Adam-Christ typology and to his conception of Christ as the head of the church and of the

---

[51]See Hos. 2:19, 20, Isa. 54:3, 6, and Jer. 3:1.
[52]See Mark 2:18-20 and Matt. 25:1-18.
[53]Chavasse, *Bride of Christ*, 66, 74.
[54]See p. 155 above.

church as his body. It is, however, difficult to determine from these equations which image or concept is prior. The study may now proceed to discuss what specific implications Paul's view of the sexual union has for his anthropology.

Implications

The implications of Paul's usage involve the following questions: (1) What does the "one body" union created by sexual intercourse denote? Does it simply refer to the temporary union of two individual bodies in sexual intercourse or to something more than that? (2) How is it that the "one body" union with a prostitute destroys one's union with Christ while that between husband and wife in marriage does not? (3) In what sense does the sexual union regarded as "one body" correspond to or contrast with the union with Christ that is described as "one spirit"? The answers to these questions heavily depend on how one understands Paul's use of the terms σῶμα, σάρξ, and πνεῦμα in reference to the "one body" union.

Most scholars rightly affirm that σῶμα and σάρξ are used synonymously in 1 Cor. 6:12-20 and in Eph. 5:21-33. Since ἓν πνεῦμα in 1 Cor. 6:17 stands in parallelism with ἓν σῶμα and μία σάρξ in the foregoing verse (1 Cor. 6:16), σῶμα and πνεῦμα are also somewhat equivalent.[55] Not every one, however, agrees as to what σῶμα denotes in these texts. Gundry, for example, insists that although σῶμα is essential to man's true and full being, it refers only to the physical frame of man.[56] Others, however, argue more convincingly that σῶμα both in 1 Cor. 6:12-20 and in Eph. 5:21-33 refers to the whole unified person.[57] They offer the following reasons: (1) In 1 Cor. 6:12-20 Paul substitutes σῶμα with the personal pronoun: "God . . . will raise *us* [=our bodies] up" (6:14); "*You* [=your bodies] are not your own" (6:19). (2) His statement, "*Your bodies* are members of Christ" (6:15) is basically the same as saying, "*We* are members of the body of Christ" (Eph. 5:30) or "*You* are the body of Christ and individually members of it" (1 Cor. 12:27). (3) His

---

[55]For example, see Bultmann, *Theology*, 1:194-95; Best, *One Body*, 74-75; J. A. T. Robinson, *Body*, 28-29; Conzelmann, *Theology*, 176-77; Ellis, "Sōma," 133; Barnabas Mary Ahern, "The Christian's Union with the Body of Christ in Cor, Ga, and Rom.," *CBQ* 23 (April, 1961): 202; and Stacy, *Pauline View of Man*, 183.

[56]Gundry, *Sōma*, 53.

[57]For example, see Best, *One Body*, 74-75; J. A. T. Robinson, *Body*, 27-28; Ellis, "Sōma," 133-34; and Stacy, *Pauline View of Man*, 183.

statement, "*Your body* is the temple of the Holy Spirit" (1 Cor. 6:19), is also similar to the saying, "*You* are the temple of God" (1 Cor. 3:16) or "*We* are the temple of the living God" (2 Cor. 6:16). (4) His exhortation, "Husbands should love their wives as *their own bodies* . . . ; for no one ever hated *his own flesh*" (Eph. 5:28-29), probably means that husbands should love their wives as *themselves*. Furthermore, (5) if σῶμα refers only to the physical frame of man as Gundry argues,[58] why does Paul regard fornication alone as sin against one's own body (εἰς τὸ ἴδιον σῶμα) (1 Cor. 6:18)? Other sins such as drunkenness, gluttony, and suicide also involve one's physical body.[59]

One's definition of σῶμα basically determines the meaning of the phrase "one body." For example, Gundry, who views σῶμα as referring only to the physical frame of man, argues that the somatic union between two human beings in 1 Cor. 6:12-20 is not comprehensive and thus "one body" primarily refers to the temporary union of two physical bodies in sexual intercourse.[60] To support this argument, he appeals to the physical connotation of "one flesh" in Gen. 2:24 upon which Paul's "one body" concept is dependent. He first points out the physical connotations of the verses before and after Gen. 2:24: (1) the creation of Eve out of the rib of Adam, (2) the closing up of the flesh of Adam's side (2:22), (3) Adam's response, "This [one] is now bone of my bones and flesh of my flesh" (Gen. 2:23), and (4) the statement, "And the man and his wife were both naked, and were not ashamed" (Gen. 2:25). He then argues that in the light of these surrounding verses, "one flesh" in Gen. 2:24 must be also referring to the physical union alone. The logical conclusion is that the "one body" union which is dependent on the "one flesh" concept of Gen. 2:24 must also denote only a temporary physical union in sexual intercourse.[61]

Best, who views the word σῶμα as referring to the whole person, offers an exegesis quite different from that of Gundry. He argues that "one body" basically refers to the "corporate personality" that two persons form together by sexual union. It, therefore, involves more than the momentary union of physical bodies in sexual intercourse.[62] J. A. T. Robinson, who shares a similar understanding of σῶμα, also thinks that "one body" refers to the single corporeity that the two unified persons form together, but his conception of

---

[58]Gundry, *Sōma*, 53.
[59]See Best, *One Body*, 75.
[60]Gundry, *Sōma*, 54.
[61]Ibid., 64.
[62]Best, *One Body*, 74-75.

the "one body" union is significantly different from that of Best: For Best it is something less physical, but for Robinson it is physical in a realistic sense.[63]

Although it may be debatable whether "corporate personality" is a proper term to describe the sexual union regarded as "one body,"[64] it is quite obvious that the "one body" union denotes something more than the temporary union of two physical bodies in sexual intercourse. It refers to a real and ontological corporate reality created by the sexual union between two unified persons.[65] Although it involves the union of physical bodies, it may not be only physical if one defines the term "physical" as visible, material, and outward substance of the individual man. The "one body," however, includes and is as real as the individual physical body. In fact, it is so real that becoming "one body" with a prostitute inevitably destroys the "one body" union with Christ. The realistic nature of the corporate union between husband and wife is also evident in Paul's assertion that the unbelieving spouse is sanctified through (ἐν) the believing partner in marriage.[66]

An individual person can form a corporate "one body" union not only with another individual sexually but also with Christ.[67] This is evident in Paul's statement, "He who is united to the Lord is one spirit with him" (1 Cor. 6:17). The corporate union with Christ is, however, not formed by sexual intercourse but by baptism "by one Spirit . . . into one body" (1 Cor. 12:13). This may be the reason why Paul designates the union with Christ as "one spirit" (1 Cor. 6:17) or "one body and one spirit" (Eph. 4:4) while describing the sexual union only as "one body" (1 Cor. 6:16).

The "one body" union created by sexual intercourse can either correspond to or contrast with the "one body (spirit)" union with Christ. Within the context of marriage, it provides a positive and compatible supplement to the "one body" union between believers and Christ, but in an immoral context (πορνεία) it contradicts the corporate union with Christ.[68] What makes this difference? Gundry explains the reason as follows:

---

[63]Cf. Best, *One Body*, 76 and J. A. T. Robinson, *Body*, 50-55.

[64]For the discussion of "corporate personality" and an evaluation, see pp. 75-79 (ch. 2) above.

[65]See Derrick S. Bailey, *The Mystery of Love and Marriage: A Study in the Theology of Sexual Relation* (London: SCM, 1952), 44, 51-52.

[66]See 1 Cor. 7:14.

[67]For the discussion of the church as the corporate body of Christ, see pp. 108-11 (ch. 3) above.

[68]Cf. Eph. 5:21-33, 1 Cor. 6:12-20.

Coitus with a prostitute is casual, occasional, momentary, and non-indicative of any larger union. On the other hand, union with Christ is fundamental, constant, and all-embracing--as is also marriage. Therein lies the reason that sexual union within marriage does not take away virtue and consequently does not contradict union with Christ. The very superficiality of fornication with a harlot makes that relationship spurious and interruptive of both Christian life and marriage.[69]

Based on this distinction between the two sexual unions, he concludes:

In Paul's thought, . . . the whole man, body and spirit, belongs to the Lord. Therefore, illicit union with a harlot, although it is "merely physical," . . . effects a oneness of physical relationship which contradicts the Lord's claim over the body and creates a disparity between the body (now given over to a harlot) and the spirit (still united to the Lord).[70]

This argument, however, faces the following criticism. First, the distinction between the union with a prostitute as momentary and superficial and that in marriage as constant and all-embracing seems arbitrary.[71] Paul does not make such a distinction either in his use of the phrase "one body" or in two citations of Gen. 2:24 (1 Cor. 6:12-20, Eph. 5:21-33). Moreover, in his conception of "one body" he places a strong emphasis on the realism of the corporate union, whether it is between a believer and a prostitute, between husband and wife, or between a believer and Christ.[72] The sexual union, no less than the union with Christ, is not merely what one does; it effects a qualitative change in who one is. Second, the argument that an illicit sexual relationship with a prostitute creates a disparity between the body and the spirit is based on the dualistic body/spirit view of man that is not grounded in the text. As pointed out above,[73] a body/spirit contrast simply does not exist in 1 Cor. 6:16-17. Moreover, Paul's primary concern in the passage is not about the disparity between the body and the spirit, but about immorality that involves one's body (σῶμα).

---

[69]Gundry, Sōma, 53.

[70]Ibid., 69.

[71]See Richard Batey, "The MIA ΣΑΡΞ Union of Christ and the Church," NTS 13 (April 1967), 279 and Best, One Body, 75.

[72]Cf. Mark 10:7-9, Matt. 19:5-6 where Jesus strongly emphasizes the permanence of the "one flesh" union in marriage in reference to Gen. 2:24.

[73]See pp. 163-64 above.

There are other scholars who, although they regard σῶμα as referring to the whole person, still find a certain contrast in Paul's expressions "one body" and "one spirit" in 1 Cor. 6:16-17. Best, for example, argues that the particle δέ which introduces verse 17 draws a contrast between σῶμα (6:16) and πνεῦμα (6:17) and thus between ἓν σῶμα (μία σάρξ) (6:16) and ἓν πνεῦμα (6:17).[74] Accordingly, he thinks that ἓν σῶμα, like μία σάρξ, highlights the physical side of man but that ἓν πνεῦμα goes in the opposite, non-corporeal direction. He denies, however, that ἓν πνεῦμα denotes the purely spiritual union between Christ and the believer.[75] Scholars such as Wikenhauser and Ahern also see a contrast between ἓν σῶμα and ἓν πνεῦμα in the sense of σῶμα ψυχικόν and σῶμα πνευματικόν described in 1 Cor. 15:44.[76] They think that in 1 Cor. 6:16-17 ἓν σῶμα is the natural, weak, earthly, and sinful, but ἓν πεῦμα is the supernatural, strong, holy, and heavenly. The terms σῶμα and πνεῦμα are equivalent comprehensive designations of the whole man, but they stand in contrast with reference to weakness versus strength, sinfulness versus holiness, and earthliness versus heavenliness.[77]

A certain kind of contrast between "one body" and "one Spirit" may be undeniable, but the distinction between "one body" as more physical or material and "one spirit" as less physical or non-material is unwarranted. As was argued above, the words σῶμα and σάρξ are used synonymously in reference to the sexual union and ἓν σῶμα and ἓν πνεῦμα stand in parallel and not in contrast to each other.[78] The phrases ἓν σῶμα and ἓν πνεῦμα simply denote two separate ontological corporate realities that are formed between a believer and a prostitute or between a husband and a wife, and between a believer and Christ, respectively. The only difference between them is the means by which they are created: The former is created by sexual intercourse; the latter, by the Spirit-baptism into Christ. The reason that the sexual union with a prostitute destroys one's union with Christ is, therefore, not because it is superficial but because it involves an immorality that is

---

[74]The particle δέ at the beginning of verse 17 signifies the contrast not between μία σάρξ and ἓν πνεῦμα, but between ὁ κολλώμενος τῇ πόρνῃ at verse 16 and ὁ κολλώμενος τῷ κυρίῳ at verse 17.

[75]Best, *One Body*, 76.

[76]Wikenhauser, *Kirche*, 102-08; Ahern, "Christian's Union," 202. See also A. R. G. Leaney, "The Doctrine of Man in 1 Corinthians," *SJT* 15 (December 1962): 394-99.

[77]Cf. Ahern, "Christian's Union," 202.

[78]1 Cor. 6:16, Eph. 5:28-31. The same is true of 1 Cor. 15:44-45 where "natural" (ψυχικόν) and "spiritual" (πνευματικόν) bodies do not refer to their substance but to their source and empowerment. See pp. 49-50 (ch. 2) above.

absolutely incompatible with the holy nature of the union with Christ. In fact, Paul emphasizes the holy nature of the union with Christ in the same passage by designating the body of the individual believer as the "temple of the Holy Spirit" (1 Cor. 6:19).

Participation in the "one body" corporeity does not mean the loss of the individuality of the participants. Husband and wife remain distinct individuals while they are, at the same time, one corporate body in marriage.[79] The "one body" union does not eliminate their individual distinctions. Otherwise, Paul's exhortations given to husbands and wives respectively would not make sense. In the same manner, believers maintain their individuality when they form a corporate body with others and with Christ. Paul's conception of Christ and the husband as the heads of their respective corporate bodies also draws a fine distinction between their individual and their corporate existence.[80]

The corporate union with Christ has sometimes been misunderstood as referring to the eradication of the individual's racial, social, and gender distinctives. Those who hold this view often appeal to Gal. 3:27-28:[81] "For as many of you as were baptized into Christ have put on Christ. There is neither Jew nor Greek, neither slave nor free, not male and female; for you are all one (εἷς) in Christ Jesus."[82] Paul, however, does not teach in this passage that incorporation into Christ abrogates one's racial, social, and gender distinctives. He is primarily concerned here with the corporate unity of all believers in Christ which in some respects transcends and transforms but does not eradicate their racial, social, and gender distinctions.[83]

---

[79]Eph. 5:21-33. See Ellis, *Pauline Theology*, 64; Barth, *Ephesians*, 641, 670; and Bailey, *Mystery*, 110.

[80]1 Cor. 11:3, Eph. 5:23; cf. Eph. 4:15, Col. 1:18, 2:10, 19.

[81]For example, Meeks, "Image of the Androgyne," 185. See also Krister Stendahl, *The Bible and the Role of Women: A Case Study in Hermeneutics*, trans. Emilie T. Sander (Philadelphia: Fortress, 1966), 32 and G. B. Caird, "Paul and Women's Liberty," *BJRL* 54 (Spring 1972): 268-81.

[82]A similar expression occurs also in Rom. 10:12, 1 Cor. 12:13, and Col. 3:9-11. Interestingly, however, the "male and female" pair appears only here and in Jesus' teaching on divorce (Matt. 19:3-9, Mark 10:2-12). For this reason, Ellis, *Pauline Theology*, 81, argues that "Paul probably has in mind Jesus' use of Genesis for understanding the marriage relationship and that he alters the wording apparently to conform it to Gen. 2:24."

[83]The phrases "baptized into Christ" and "put on Christ" in Gal. 3:27 clearly denote believers' incorporation into Christ, thus becoming corporately the body of Christ and individually members of it. See Rom. 6:3, 13:14, 1 Cor. 12:13, 27, Eph. 4:24, and Col. 3:10-11. See also pp. 85-86 (ch. 3) above and Ellis, *Pauline Theology*, 80-81.

He clarifies the teaching of Gal. 3:28, with respect to the Jew/Greek clause, in Eph. 2:11-3:6: "(Christ,) who made the two (groups) one (ἕν) and broke down the dividing wall of hostility . . . that he might create (κτίσῃ) the two (groups) into one new man in himself, thus making peace" (2:14-15). Paul's teaching in this passage is quite clear: In Christ Jesus the previously existing racial discrimination between Jew and Gentile (2:11-12), not their racial distinctives, has been completely removed as they are brought into one corporate body. Similarly in Rom. 10:12 he declares that with regard to salvation through faith in Jesus the Messiah, "there is no distinction between Jew and Greek." His exhortation to Philemon to receive Onesimus as a beloved brother in the Lord (Philem. 16) also indicates that in some sense one's being in Christ transcends one's social status, but he does not obliterate the social distinction between Philemon (the free) and Onesimus (the slave). In Eph. 5:21-33 he teaches that husband and wife become one body (flesh) in marriage and yet he emphasizes their distinctives as husband or as wife. The same principle probably underlies Gal. 3:28: As believers were baptized into Christ and have put on Christ, thus forming a corporate unity with other believers and with Christ, all the pre-existing discriminations based on their racial, social, and gender status have been completely removed. But their individual distinctives remain.

What has been discussed above has far-reaching implications for Paul's view of man. It implies that Paul understands man as a being whose existence is not limited to his individual person. He views man as extending himself beyond his individual boundaries to form a corporate unity (body) with others and with Christ, but without losing his own individuality. Accordingly, man can form an ontological corporate body with a prostitute or with his wife by having a sexual relationship with her. Within the context of marriage, this corporate body extends to their children. Likewise, by being joined to the Lord man forms one equally ontological corporate body with him. This means that in Paul's thought man exists not only individually but also corporately.

Possible Backgrounds

Two things are obvious about the origin of Paul's conception of the sexual union regarded as "one body (flesh)." First, Paul's citation of Gen.

2:24 in support of his conception[84] shows that he is dependent on that teaching. Second, his reference to Jesus' teaching that refers to Gen. 1:27 and 2:24[85] suggests that he draws upon and basically agrees with Jesus on the interpretation of these Old Testament texts. This means that one should seek the origin of Paul's conception primarily in the Old Testament and in the teachings of Jesus. Nevertheless, attempts have been made to find the origin in a broader context, namely, in the hellenistic and the gnostic androgyne myths and in Jewish androgynous interpretations of the Genesis accounts of the creation of man.[86] The following analysis, therefore, first investigates whether and to what extent Paul's conception was influenced by these backgrounds.

The ancient androgyne myth that speaks of the original oneness of man and woman was widespread in the hellenistic world.[87] Plato writes the myth told by Aristophanes as follows.[88] There were originally three kinds of human beings, namely, male, female, and bisexual (hermaphrodite). The form of each person was round all over, having four arms, four legs, and two faces. They were of surprising strength and vigor and so lofty in their notions that they even conspired against the gods. Fearful of their rebellion, Zeus proposed to other gods to slice every one of them in two, thus making them much weaker. When human beings had been cut in two, each half began to long for the other part and yearned to be grafted together again. The division caused them great sadness and distress. Seeing their deep sorrow, Zeus had pity on them and made a provision that they could be reunited again permanently by their mutual love.

The bisexual nature of the original man is more clearly expressed in the gnostic "Primal Man" myth.[89] *Poimandres* describes the creation of bisexual men (hermaphrodites) as follows.[90] The "Primal Man" who was created in

---

[84]1 Cor. 6:16, Eph. 5:31.

[85]1 Cor. 7:10; cf. Mark 10:6-9, Matt. 19:4-6.

[86]For example, see Meeks, "Image," 165-208; Richard A. Batey, "Hieros Gamos," 121-27; and idem, "ΜΙΑ ΣΑΡΞ Union," 270-81;

[87]For the survey of the hellenistic, Jewish, and gnostic evidence, see Meeks, "Image," 185; Ernst Ludwig Dietrich, "Der Urmensch als Androgyne," *ZKG* 58 (1939): 297-345; Batey, "ΜΙΑ ΣΑΡΞ Union," 271-77G; and Marie Delcourt, *Hermaphrodite: Mythes et rites de la bisexualité dans l'antiquité classique* (Paris: Presses Universiaires de France, 1958).

[88]Plato, *Sym.* 189-93.

[89]For the discussion of the gnostic "Primal Man" myth and a criticism, see pp. 66-70 (ch. 2) above.

[90]For a full reference to *Poimandres*, see p. 31, n. 132 (ch. 1) above.

the image of the mind (νοῦς) entered the created sphere. As he descended through the celestial spheres, he broke a hole in the celestial framework (ἁρμονία) and looked down through it. When nature beheld the beauty of his divine image, she loved him and reflected his image in the water. Observing his own reflection in the water, the "Primal Man" wanted to dwell there. So he took abode in matter devoid of reason. As the result, his nature became twofold, partly immortal and partly mortal. From this union between the "Primal Man" and nature sprang seven bisexual men (hermaphrodites) who were later separated by the god and became male and female. Immediately following the separation they began to increase and multiply. *Poimandres* implies that the division of the original bisexual men is the prime cause of human sufferings and the sign of the fall of the "Primal Man."[91]

Some (later) rabbis combined the hellenistic androgyne myth and the gnostic "Primal Man" myth with biblical conceptions of Adam. Meeks states that they employed the androgyne myth merely to solve an exegetical dilemma and to support monogamy.[92] This may be true because in rabbinic writings the hermaphrodite idea occurs in close relation to the exegesis of the Genesis accounts of the creation of man and to the discussion of their implications for marriage relationship. R. Abbahu recognizes an incongruity between the two statements in Gen. 1:27: "In the image of God created He him" and "Male and female created He them." He explains that at first God intended to create two human beings but ultimately He created only one.[93] R. Jeremiah states that the first man was hermaphrodite: "When the Holy One, blessed be He, created Adam, He created him hermaphrodite [bi-sexual], for it is said, *male and female created He them and called their name Adam.*"[94] Probably for the same reason, b. Megillah 9a changes the plural "them" to the singular "him" in his translation of Gen. 1:27: "Male and female He created him." R. Samuel b. Naḥman's description of the creation of the first man most clearly resembles Plato's description of the hellenistic androgyne myth: "When the Lord created Adam He created him double-faced, then He split him and made him of two backs, one back on this side and one back on the other side."[95] He thus interprets the Hebrew term צלע in Gen. 2:21-22 not as "rib" but as "side" and refers to Ex. 26:20 where the same word is used to

---

[91] *Poimandres* 1:12-19.
[92] Meeks, "Image," 186.
[93] *b. Erub.* 18a; see also *b. Ket.* 8a.
[94] *Gen. R.* 8.1; cf. Gen. 5:2.
[95] *Gen. R.* 8.1; cf. 17.6.

denote "the other side, the north side of the tabernacle." Since the rabbis believed that God took a rib (or side) of man and from it made woman, they thought that the union of the two would restore the wholeness of God's original creation and would bring joy, satisfaction, and peace to man.[96] For this reason, some rabbis considered unmarried man to be incomplete or not a proper man.[97] For them, the union of man and woman by which the two became one flesh was much more than a transient physical act and in some sense it lasted even after the two persons divorced from each other.[98]

Philo's interpretation of the Genesis accounts of the creation of man is quite different from those of rabbis. It more clearly reflects the Platonic dualistic view of reality and in certain respects the gnostic "Primal Man" myth[99] but, contrary to common belief, the influence of the androgyne myth is less apparent.[100] Philo sees in Genesis the creation of two types of man (ἄνθρωποι), the heavenly man in Gen. 1:26-27 and the earthly man in Gen. 2:7.[101] The heavenly man who is created in the image of God is, he states, "incorporeal, neither male nor female, by nature incorruptible."[102] This heavenly man is, therefore, "asexual, not hermaphrodite."[103] In contrast, God formed the earthly man by taking clay from the earth and breathed into his nostrils the breath of life. He is, according to Philo's description, "an object of sense-perception, partaking already of such or such quality, consisting of body and soul, man or woman, by nature mortal."[104] Since this man is formed from two different kinds of substance, namely, the clay and God's breath of life, his nature is twofold, mortal in respect of the body and immortal in respect of the soul. Philo's description of the heavenly man and the earthly

---

[96]*Gen. R.* 8.1, 17.2.

[97]Ibid., 17.2, *b. Yeb.* 63a.

[98]Cf. *b. Abod.* 39a, *Gen. R.* 17.3, 7.

[99]For the discussion of the "Primal Man," see pp. 66-67 (ch. 2) above.

[100]Allusions to the androgynous nature of the first man may occur in *Opif.* 76, 134, *Leg. All.* 2.13, 19-50, and *Quis Div.* 164. Interestingly, however, in *Vit. Cont.* 63 Philo scornfully ridicules Plato's myth of the androgynous man. Those who find close parallels between Philo and the androgyne myth include Jervell, *Imago Dei*, 56-58; C. H. Dodd, *Bible and the Greeks*, 151; Meeks, "Image," 186; and Batey, "ΜΙΑ ΣΑΡΞ Union," 273.

[101]*Leg. All.* 1.31, 2.4, *Opif.* 69, 134.

[102]*Opif.* 134.

[103]Richard A. Baer, *Philo's Use of the Categories Male and Female* (Leiden: E. J. Brill, 1970), 21, 34, 65, 68. However, see Jervell, *Imago Dei*, 64-66 and Dodd, *Bible and the Greeks*, 151.

[104]*Opif.* 134. It may be significant that Philo says here "man or woman." If he had understood the first earthly man as bisexual, he would have said "man and woman."

man resembles to a great extent Poimandres' description of the "Primal Man." A couple of discrepancies are, however, observable: (1) Whereas Poimandres speaks of the two stages of the single "Primal Man," Philo refers to the creation of two separate men, one heavenly and the other earthly. (2) The idea that the hermaphrodites sprang from the union between the "Primal Man" and nature is absent in Philo. His statements that God took one side (πλευρά) of man's body and from it created woman and that marriage "brings together and fits into one the divided halves, as it were of a single living creature" can be taken as implying the bisexual nature of the first (earthly) man;[105] but he never explicitly states that the first man was hermaphrodite. Moreover, Baer argues that his use of the categories "male" and "female" is "purely functional, never ontological."[106] He utilizes the "one flesh" concept only as a literary device to describe the ideal union of mind (νοῦς), the male quality, and sense perception (αἴσθησις), the female principle.[107] For Philo, therefore, Gen. 2:24 simply means that mind (νοῦς), deriving from God the Father, and wisdom, the mother of all things, cleaved to sense and became one flesh with her.[108]

Some second- and third-century gnostic-influenced Christian heretics embraced the androgyne myth in bizarre forms and affirmed the bisexual nature of the "Primal Man."[109] They thought (1) that man was originally hermaphrodite and was divided into male and female,[110] (2) that the division between male and female was the fundamental source of human plight, and (3) that the reunification of male and female was a prime symbol of salvation.[111] Consequently, they developed certain rituals by which the

---

[105]*Leg. All.* 2.19, 35, *Opif.* 53; cf. *Qu. Gen.* 1.26, 28.

[106]Baer, *Philo's Use*, 66.

[107]Batey, "ΜΙΑ ΣΑΡΞ Union,ς 273; Baer, *Philo's Use*, 38-44.

[108]*Leg. All.* 2.49.

[109]For example, the Marcosians, according to Irenaeus, *Adversus Haereses* 1.18.2 = Epiphanius, *Haereses* 34.16.4-5; Naassenes, Hippolytus, *Refutatio* 5.7.7-15. See Meeks, "Image," 188, n. 102.

[110]For example, Clement of Alexandria, *Excerpta ex Theodoto* 21.1-2, states: "The male remained in [Adam], but the entire female seed was taken from him and became Eve." Cf. Irenaeus, *Adversus Haereses* 1.18.2; Hippolytus, *Refutatio* 5.7.15 (=5.2); Clement of Alexandria, *Excerpta ex Theodoto*, 31.

[111]For example, *Gospel of Philip*, 71, says: "When Eve was in Adam, there was no death. But when she separated from him, death came into being. Again, if she enters into him and he takes her to himself, death will no longer exist" (cf. 78-79). Similarly, *Gospel of Thomas*, 22, states: "When you make the two one . . . , and when you make the male and the

original unity could be restored. They attributed special mystical merits to baptism and to the *hieros gamos* practiced in a bridal chamber.[112] They taught that in baptism the initiate bearing the female seed was united with the angelic or male counterpart and was elevated into the sphere of the *pleroma* and that the participants in the *hieros gamos* in a bridal chamber could come into *henosis* ("unity") with deity. They often regarded human marriage as a mystery that exemplified the *hieros gamos*.

A number of scholars argue that Paul's conception of the sexual union regarded as "one flesh" reflects these hellenistic and gnostic myths and that his interpretation of Gen. 1:27 and 2:24 corresponds to those of Philo and rabbis. They appeal to Gal. 3:28 and Eph. 5:21-33 for its evidence.[113] Meeks makes the following observations in reference to Gal. 3:28: (1) Gal. 3:28, 1 Cor. 12:13, and Col. 3:10-11 in which the unification language occurs is the early church's baptismal reunification formula. (2) The phrase "male and female" in Gal. 3:28 refers to Gen. 1:27 which speaks of the creation of man in God's image. (3) The new man whom believers put on is the man who is renewed according to the image of his creator (Col. 3:10). From these observations he draws the following conclusion:

> [Gal. 3:28] . . . suggests that somehow the act of Christian initiation reverses the fateful division of Genesis 2:21-22. Where the image of God is restored, there, it seems, man is no longer divided--not even by the most fundamental division of all, male and female. The baptismal reunification formula . . . presupposes an interpretation of the creation story in which the divine image after which Adam was modeled was masculofeminine.[114]

It is also argued that the nuptial image in Eph. 5:21-33 reflects the gnostic conception of the *hieros gamos* by which the union between the redeemer and

---

female into a single one, so that the male is not male and the female not female . . . then shall you enter (the kingdom)" (cf. 4, 11b, 106).

[112]Irenaeus tells of the mystic rite of the *hieros gamos*, *i.e.*, "holy wedding," practiced by some Marcosians in a bridal chamber. See *Adversus Haereses* 1.21.3 = Epiphanius, *Haereses* 34.20.1.

[113]Meeks, "Image," 166, 180-89; Batey, "Hieros Gamos," 121-27; idem, *NT Nuptial Imagery*, 33; Schlier, *Epheser*, 264-76.

[114]Meeks, "Image," 185. See also Scroggs, "Eschatological Woman," 288, who states: "There is, then, in the eschatological community of God no longer a person whose primary characteristic is woman nor any person whose primary status is man. But yet there are real distinctions that must be assessed in the light of the eschatological abolition of man/woman. There are still two different kinds of bodies."

his community takes place and that the "one flesh" union of husband and wife presupposes the division of the bisexual original man and implies the reunification of the divided halves.[115]

This "history of religions" approach to the Pauline texts has a number of problems both in method and in exegesis.[116]   First, it errs in method by reading back the statements of the later gnostic or rabbinic documents into the Pauline texts despite the fact that clearly contemporary parallels cannot be adduced. Allusions may occur in Philo, but he never explicitly states that the first man was bisexual. Although *Poimandres* makes explicit references to the hermaphrodite origin of man and to the subsequent division between male and female, the origin of the hermaphrodite "Primal Man" myth is uncertain.[117]   The androgynous notions of the first man may have existed earlier, but they first appear in Christianity only in the second- and third-century gnostic cults.

Second, Paul's interpretation of Genesis differs radically from those assumptions or conclusions that are represented by Philo, by rabbis, or by gnosticizing Christians. He neither speculates about Adam as did rabbis nor shows the same proclivity toward a strictly dualistic ontology which can be observed in Philo.[118] He refers to Genesis 1 and 2 basically for two reasons: (1) In 1 Cor. 6:16 and Eph. 5:31 he cites Gen. 2:24 to emphasize the realism and the permanency of the "one flesh" union created by the sexual relationship. (2) In 1 Cor. 11:7-9 and 1 Tim. 2:13 he refers to the Genesis accounts of the creation of Adam and Eve "to teach not androgyny but rather the priority of the male."[119]

Third, the argument that the nuptial idea present in Eph. 5:21-33 reflects the *hieros gamos* of the second- or third-century Gnosticism or gnostic-influenced Judaism is not convincing. The reasons are as follows: (1) Even though Paul explains the marriage relationship in the framework of the corresponding relationship of Christ and the church, he does not consider human marriage as a mystery that exemplifies the *hieros gamos* by which the

---

[115]Meeks, "Images," 205. The influence of the "Primal Man" and of the gnostic idea of the *hieros gamos* upon Eph. 5:21-33 has been pointed out by Schlier, *Epheser*, 275; Batey, "Hieros Gamos," 121-27; and idem, "ΜΙΑ ΣΑΡΞ Union," 276.

[116]See Ellis, *Pauline Theology*, 83.

[117]See p. 31, n. 132; p. 33, n. 138 (ch. 1), and pp. 66-70 (ch. 2) above.

[118]See Barth, *Ephesians*, 728-29.

[119]Ellis, *Pauline Theology*, 84; Ben Witherington, "Rite and Rights for Women--Gal. 3:28," *NTS* 27 (October 1981): 603, n. 22.

participants come into *henosis* with Christ. (2) Paul's conception of the church as the bride of Christ probably has its origin not in the gnostic *hieros gamos* but in the Old Testament texts where God is portrayed as the bridegroom and Israel as His bride and in the teachings of Jesus where the Messiah is identified as the bridegroom and the church as his eschatological bride.[120] Moreover, (3) Paul's conception of the "one flesh" relationship in marriage goes beyond the prophetic nuptial image because it is deeply rooted in the teaching of Gen. 2:24.[121]

Fourth, it is a mistake in exegesis to read hermaphrodite conceptions out of Gal. 3:28. (1) Ellis points out that "the second- and third-century Gnostics seldom if ever make an explicit reference to Gal. 3:28 to promote these notions, and on the very few occasions when they may allude to this passage, they give it a special twist."[122] (2) Although in Gal. 3:28 Paul closely relates the believers' corporate union with Christ to his conception of baptism,[123] he does not regard water baptism as a sacramental rite by which believers come to *henosis* with Christ. (3) The phrase "male and female" probably refers to Gen. 1:27 and the expression "putting on the new man (Christ)" may imply the restoration of true humanity, but Paul neither presupposes that the first man was androgynous nor implies that believers are united into a new

---

[120]Isa. 54:5-6, 62:4-5, Jer. 2:2, 3, 32, Ezek. 16:23, Hos. 2:19, 20, Mal. 2:14, Mark 2:18-22 par., John 3:23-30, Matt. 22:1-14 par., 25:1-13, Best, *One Body*, 172, n. 1, offers the following reasons why one should guard against a fully gnostic interpretation: (1) Paul uses ἀγάπη rather than ἔρως; (2) He refers to the sacrifice of Christ, a definite historical event of the immediate past, and not repeatable, as were gnostic conceptions with their basis in nature myths; (3) There is no absorption of the human by the divine, or vice versa, the church remaining distinct from Christ and subject to him. However, cf. J. Jeremias, "νύμφη, νυμφίος," in *TDNT*, 4:1101-06, who points out that nowhere in the Old Testament and in later Judaism is the Messiah presented as a bridegroom and thus concludes that "it may be conjectured, though it cannot be proved, that the mythologically derived and widespread hellenistic (esp. gnostic) reference of the νυμφίος image to the Soter exerted some influence on the NT Christ/νυμφίος allegory . . . (1105)."

[121]Chavasse, *Bride of Christ*, 71-82, argues that Paul's whole nuptial thought springs from the story of the first man and woman. He offers the following evidence: (1) the quotation of Gen. 2:24, (2) the mention of Eve in 2 Cor. 11:3, (3) the derivation of the metaphor of the body and head from that of the bride and bridegroom, (4) the church regarded not as "redeemed" from her fallen state but as a second wife, (5) Christians regarded not as children of the marriage but as members of the body, and (6) the fact that for the prophets the nuptial idea is only an allegory but for Paul it is a reality. However, see Best, *One Body*, 180-81, who criticizes Chavasse's view.

[122]Ellis, *Pauline Theology*, 82-83.

[123]Cf. Witherington, "Rite and Rights," 597 and Meeks, "Image," 180-82.

singular androgynous entity. On the contrary, he says that believers are all one ("εἷς" - masculine) in Christ Jesus (Gal. 3:28b). (4) As was argued above,[124] in Gal. 3:27-29 Paul speaks of the corporate inclusion in Christ, which in certain respects transcends but does not obliterate one's racial, social, and gender distinctions.[125] Nowhere in his letters does he imply that believers lose their individuality when incorporated into Christ. The incorporation into Christ does not mean the absorption of the individuality of the participants and much less the eradication of the male/female distinctions.

Therefore, regarding the origin of Paul's conception this study concludes as follows: (1) No matter how ancient the androgyne myth was and how widely it spread in the hellenistic world, there is no sufficient evidence in Paul's letters to support the argument that his conception of the sexual union regarded as "one body (flesh)" reflects this hellenistic or gnostic myth. The conception of androgyny contradicts Paul's teachings in 1 Cor. 11:7-9, Eph. 5:21-33, and 1 Tim. 2:13 where the Genesis accounts of the creation of man and woman are employed to teach the priority of the male in reference to the headship of the husband over his wife. (2) Paul cites Gen. 2:24 in support of his conception and refers to Jesus' teaching that is rooted in Gen. 1:27 and 2:24. These facts strongly suggest that his "one body (flesh)" conception is ultimately rooted in Gen. 2:24 and that it is to a certain extent indebted to Jesus' exposition of these Genesis passages.

---

[124]See pp. 168-69 above.

[125]Ellis, *Pauline Theology*, 80; Witherington, "Rite and Rights," 598; W. Grundmann, "χρίω," in *TDNT*, 9:552; Wilhelm Schneemelcher, "υἱός," in *TDNT*, 8:391.

CONCLUSION

The present study has investigated various corporate elements in Pauline anthropology in the light of his usage and background. Its primary purpose has been to determine whether and in what respect Paul understood man as a corporate being. It now draws the following conclusions as to his view of man and its possible background.

Pauline Corporate Anthropology

Corporate Dimension of Human Existence

Paul views man not as an isolated individual but as one who constantly interacts with others. Although the individual man is separated from others by the limits of his physical body, his existence is by no means limited to himself. In certain respects he extends beyond his individual being and exists in corporate relationships with others. Consequently, he exists not only individually but also corporately. Various Pauline terms, idioms, and concepts investigated above denote this corporate dimension of human existence.

Corporate Solidarity in Adam and in Christ

Paul expresses the most comprehensive human solidarity when he speaks of humanity as existing either in Adam or in Christ. He assumes a solidarity relationship between Adam and all men and also between Christ and all men when he repeatedly emphasizes the effect of one man, either Adam or Christ, upon the many, that is, upon all men (Rom. 5:15-19), and more specifically when he states, "As all in Adam (ἐν Ἀδάμ) die, so also all in Christ (ἐν Χριστῷ) shall be made alive" (1 Cor. 15:22). Paul regards Adam and Christ as distinct individuals in human history, but when he speaks of them as the ones who incorporate in themselves the rest of humanity and who determine the destiny of their respective followers, he presents them not merely as two individual persons whose existence is limited only to themselves but as two comprehensive corporate persons whose existence goes beyond their individual beings to include those who belong to them. The Adam-Christ typology that Paul employs to teach about redemption (Rom. 5:12-21) and resurrection (1 Cor. 15:20-22, 44-49) clearly depicts both the individual and the corporate dimensions of their existence.[1]

Perceiving the resurrection of Jesus as a new beginning (ἀρχή) in terms of a new creation,[2] Paul sets the new creation in Christ over against the old creation in Adam and consequently Christ over against Adam. He calls Adam "the first man" and Christ "the second man" or "the last (ἔσχατος) Adam" (1 Cor. 15:45, 47). In designating "two Adams," he basically identifies two ages or worlds, two spheres of existence, and two humanities. In contrast to the present age that is represented by Adam and characterized as evil and under the dominion of sin, death, and law, the coming age that has been inaugurated with the coming of Christ the Messiah and has been manifested in his resurrection is under the dominion of righteousness, life, and grace.[3]

In a spatial sense, Adam and Christ represent two spheres of human existence, spheres that divide humanity into two groups that exists either "in Adam" or "in Christ" (1 Cor. 15:22). Those who belong to Christ have been transferred from the sphere of existence in Adam to that in Christ.[4] Although their individual actualization of the resurrection reality of the coming age still awaits at the future Parousia of the Lord, they even now corporately participate in the Messianic age headed by Christ the last Adam. Paul's ἐν Χριστῷ formula demonstrates that all believers, dead or alive, of past, present, and future exist corporately in Christ in a genuinely locative sense[5] and that every aspect of their individual lives must be understood in the light

---

[1] For the discussion of Adam and Christ as distinct individuals and as corporate beings, see pp. 59-63 (ch. 2) above.

[2] Col. 1:18, 1 Cor. 15:20, 23, Rom. 8:29 ("the beginning," "the first fruits"), 2 Cor. 5:17, Gal. 6:15 ("the new creation"). See p. 61 (ch. 2) above.

[3] Gal. 1:4, Eph. 2:2, 6:12, Col. 1:13, 1 Cor. 15:20-23, Rom. 3:19, 5:12-21. For the antithetical comparisons between the Adamic age and the Messianic age, see pp. 50-51, 54 (ch. 2), and 127 (ch. 4) above.

[4] Gal. 1:4, Col. 1:13.

[5] The locative sense of the ἐν Χριστῷ formula is dominant in the following instances: Rom. 8:1, 16:7, 11, 1 Cor. 1:30, 15:22, 2 Cor. 5:17, 12:2, Gal. 1:22, Eph. 1:1, Phil. 1:1, 3:9, Col. 1:2, 1 Thess. 1:1, 4:16, 2 Thess. 1:1, 2:14. See pp. 13-14, 16 (ch. 1) above.

of their corporate being in Christ.[6] Since believers are in Christ, they exist corporately no longer in the flesh, that is, in the sphere of Adam, but in the Spirit, that is, in the sphere of the resurrected Christ. Consequently, they are empowered and directed not by the flesh but by the Spirit.[7]

Paul states that believers are incorporated into Christ by baptism in the Spirit.[8] They have been corporately united with Christ in his death and in certain respects also in his resurrection.[9] By dying and rising corporately with Christ, they have put off the old man Adam and have put on the new man Christ.[10] As a result, they now bear the image of the man of heaven as they once bore the image of the man of dust (1 Cor. 15:49). In other words, they have become a new or true humanity in Christ. In contrast to the old humanity in Adam, existing as the soulish body (σῶμα ψυχικόν) and destined for destruction, the new humanity in Christ exists as the spiritual body (σῶμα πνευματικόν) or more accurately the Spirit-animated body; it is destined to everlasting life in the image of the creator.[11]

As incorporated into Christ, believers not only find their existence in Christ but also form a corporate solidarity with Christ and with other believers. In Paul's designations, believers are "the body of Christ," "one body in Christ," "the body," or simply "one body," terms that describe the corporate solidarity of believers.[12] "In the Spirit we [believers] are all baptized into one body" (1 Cor. 12:13) that is, in view of 1 Cor. 12:12, nothing other than the body of Christ. As a result, they have become corporately "the body of Christ and individually members of it" (1 Cor. 12:27). Paul's designation of the church as the temple, the building, or the house of God also basically expresses this corporate solidarity of believers.[13]

---

[6]See pp. 14-17 (ch. 1) above.

[7]Cf. Rom. 8:9, 9:1, 14:17, 15:16, 1 Cor. 6:11, 12:3, 9, 13, 2 Cor. 6:6, Eph. 2:22, 3:5, 4:30, 5:18, 6:18, Col. 1:8, 1 Thess. 1:5, 1 Tim. 3:16. See pp. 49-50 (ch. 2) above.

[8]1 Cor. 12:13, Rom. 6:3, Gal. 3:27. See pp. 29-30 (ch. 1) and 109 (ch. 3) above.

[9]Rom. 6:3-11, 1 Cor. 15:20-23, Gal. 2:19-20, Eph. 2:5-6, Col. 2:12-13, 20, 3:1, 3, 9-10.

[10]Gal. 3:27, Eph. 4:22, 24, Col. 3:9-10, Rom. 13:14. See pp. 29-30 (ch. 1) above.

[11]Cf. 1 Cor. 15:42-49, 53-55, 2 Cor. 5:1-10, Eph. 4:24, Col. 3:10. See pp. 49-50 (ch. 2) above.

[12]1 Cor. 12:27, Eph. 1:22-23, 5:30, Col. 1:24 ("the body of Christ"), Rom. 12:5, Eph. 3:6 ("one body in Christ"), Eph. 5:23, Col. 1:18 ("the body"), 1 Cor. 10:17, Eph. 2:16, 4:4, Col. 3:15 ("one body"). See the discussion in ch. 3.

[13]1 Cor. 3:9, 16-17, 6:16, Eph. 2:21-22, 1 Tim. 3:15; cf. 2 Cor. 5:1-2. See the discussion in ch. 4.

As believers are corporately the body of Christ, they are also united to one another. They are, therefore, not only "the body of Christ and individually members of it" (1 Cor. 12:27), but also "one body in Christ and individually members one of another" (Rom. 12:5). The mutual unity of believers in Christ is also evident in Eph. 2:21-22 where Paul employs the building and the temple images to describe the growing aspect of the church: ". . . in whom [i.e., Christ the cornerstone] the whole structure, joined together, grows into a holy temple in the Lord; in whom you are built together into the dwelling place of God in the Spirit." As the various parts of the body, joined together, make up the single whole body and as the various parts of the building, connected together, create the single whole building, so believers, organically and structur-ally connected together, form a corporate solidarity in Christ.

Corporate Solidarity of the Family

Paul's view of the nature of the sexual union also demonstrates from a more anthropological perspective the corporate dimension of human existence. He teaches, on the basis of Gen. 2:24, that by uniting sexually with a prostitute or with his wife, the individual man becomes "one body (flesh)" with her.[14] The "one body" denotes a real and ontological corporate identity created between the two participants, whether it is between a believer and a prostitute or between husband and wife. Within the context of marriage, the familial corporeity extends to their children (1 Cor. 7:14).

Corporate Solidarity as an Ontological Reality

One of the most significant characteristics of Paul's conception of the corporate solidarity of man is its realistic nature. When he speaks of the solidarity of man either with Adam or with Christ (Rom. 5:12-21), he does not refer to a solidarity in a juridical or metaphorical sense. He refers to a human solidarity that, in a real sense, is incorporated into, identified with, and represented by its respective leader, Adam or Christ. He assumes a real and ontological solidarity between Adam and all men and also between Christ and

---

[14]1 Cor. 6:16, Eph. 5:31.

all believers when he states that all men sinned in Adam and that all believers died and rose again with Christ.[15] Similarly, when he confesses, "I have been crucified with Christ; nevertheless I live (ζῶ δὲ); yet not I, but Christ lives in me" (Gal. 2:19-20, KJV),[16] he does not simply refer to a psychological or existential change within himself; but he means that he actually died with Christ at the cross in A.D. 30, as also did all other believers corporately.[17]

The realistic nature of the corporate solidarity of man is also evident in his conception of the church as the body of Christ. As was argued above, the body of Christ regarded as the church is not a mere metaphor.[18] It denotes the real body of Christ, that is, his corporate body that includes all believers. Christ, therefore, exists in every part of his corporate body and believers as the members of his body reflect his character in their attitude and conduct.

Paul's view of the sexual union also reflects a realism at the most basic level. When he says that the sexual union with a prostitute or with his wife makes an individual man "one body (flesh)" with her (1 Cor. 6:16, Eph. 5:31), he regards the "one body" union as a real and ontological corporate reality. It is so real that when created by an immoral sexual union it destroys one's union with Christ. Within the context of marriage in which only one spouse is a believer, it sanctifies the unbelieving spouse and makes their children holy (1 Cor. 7:14). Whatever the words "sanctified" and "holy" may denote in this context, they clearly indicate that Paul conceives of the familial solidarity in a physical sense.

Relationship between the Individual and the Corporate Existence

Paul's understanding of the relationship between the individual and the corporate existence of man reveals the following characteristics. First, the corporate nature of man does not diminish the value of his individual existence. Believers are incorporated into Christ as his body without any loss of their individuality.[19] Paul never considers the incorporation of believers into Christ to be an absorption of their individuality. Although he identifies

---

[15]See pp. 62-65 (ch. 2) above.
[16]The KJV probably best catches Paul's understanding. The Apostle's individual and corporate personalities are not mutually exclusive alternatives; both co-exist together.
[17]See pp. 29-30 (ch. 1) above.
[18]See p. 101 (ch. 3) above.
[19]See pp. 30 (ch. 1), 109 (ch. 3), and 168-69 (ch. 5) above.

believers with Christ by calling them the body of Christ, he draws a distinction between them by designating believers as "one body in Christ" and Christ as the "head of the body."[20] Believers, therefore, remain distinct individuals while they become one corporate body of Christ. Similarly, Paul's conception of Adam and Christ as corporate persons does not weaken the significance of their individual existence. The same is also true for his view of the sexual union. Husband and wife become one corporate body in marriage; yet they remain distinct individuals. Paul's view of man, therefore, reflects a balanced appreciation of both his individual and corporate existence.

Second, Paul sees a continual, dynamic interaction rather than a sharp distinction between the individual and the corporate existences of man. This may be the reason that his thought often oscillates between the individual and the corporate realities. For example, he applies the term "body of Christ" to denote both the individual body of Jesus and also his corporate body, that is, the church. The two bodies are so closely related that it is sometimes extremely difficult, if not impossible, to determine which body he denotes.[21] The same is also true with his use of the term "temple of God." He uses it to designate sometimes the body of the individual believer (1 Cor. 6:19) and some other times the corporate solidarity of believers regarded elsewhere as the body of Christ (1 Cor. 3:16, 2 Cor. 6:16). His use of the terms "earthly house" and "heavenly house" (2 Cor. 5:1-2) also reveals such an oscillation. He uses them in such a way that although they basically denote the corporate solidarities in Adam and in Christ respectively, they have strong implications for the individual life of believers.

Third, Paul understands the value and the significance of the individual existence of believers in the light of their corporate reality in Christ. His ethical exhortations clearly demonstrate this. For example, (1) because believers who have been baptized into Christ were baptized into his death, they should consider themselves dead to sin and alive to God. Accordingly, they must avoid sin in their individual lives (Rom. 6:3-14). (2) Because they have put off the old man and have put on the new man (Christ), they should put away all kinds of falsehood and reflect the character of Christ in every aspect of their lives (Col. 3:9-17). (3) Because they are incorporate in Christ, they are expected to act individually in a certain way toward God and toward

---

[20]Rom. 12:5 ("one body in Christ"), Eph. 1:22, 4:15, 5:23, Col. 1:18, 2:10, 2:19 (Christ as the head of the church).

[21]For example, see 1 Cor. 10:16, 11:29, Eph. 2:16, 4:4, and Col. 3:15. See pp. 87-92 (ch. 3) above.

other people.[22]   (4) Because they are the body of Christ, they must avoid immorality that involves their bodies; and they must seek the unity in the church despite their individual differences.[23]   (5) Because they are the temple of God, they should be holy.[24]

Possible Background of Pauline Corporate Anthropology

The study has examined possible backgrounds of various Pauline conceptions in Hellenism, in Judaism, in the Old Testament, and in the teachings of Jesus. It reaches the following conclusions. First, Paul's repeated references and allusions to the teachings of Jesus and to the Old Testament indicate that he is heavily dependent on them for his conceptions. This means that one must seek the origin of Paul's thought primarily in these backgrounds. The evidence is as follows: (1) Paul derives his Adam-Christ typology from the Genesis creation accounts.[25]   (2) He bases his conception of the sexual union regarded as "one body (flesh)" on the teaching of Gen. 2:24.[26]   (3) He grounds his conception of the headship of the husband over his wife also on the Genesis accounts that teaches the priority of male in creation and the deception of Eve.[27]   (4) He cites a series of Old Testament texts with reference to his conception of the church as the temple of God.[28]   (5) He attributes his instructions on divorce to the teaching of Jesus that is rooted in Gen. 1:27 and 2:24.[29]   (6) When he designates the church as the body of Christ and as the temple of God, he is probably aware of dominical traditions that identified both the bread in the Lord's Supper and the eschatological new temple with the individual body of Jesus.[30]

---

[22]For example, see Rom. 16:2 (cf. Phil. 2:29), 16:22 (cf. 1 Cor. 16:19, Phil. 4:21), 1 Cor. 4:15a, 7:39, Eph. 4:17, 6:1, Phil. 4:2, 1 Thess. 4:2 (cf. 2 Thess. 3:12), and 5:12. See pp. 14-17 (ch. 1) above.

[23]1 Cor. 6:17-18, 10:16-22, 11:27-32, 12:12-31, Rom. 12:4-8.

[24]1 Cor. 6:19, 2 Cor. 6:16-7:1.

[25]1 Cor. 15:21-22, 45-49, Rom. 5:12-21. See pp. 81-82 (ch. 2) above.

[26]1 Cor. 6:16, Eph. 5:31. See pp. 148, 152-54, 175-76 (ch. 5) above.

[27]1 Cor. 11:7-9, 1 Tim. 2:13-14; cf. Gen. 1:26-27, 2:21-22, 3:6, 13.

[28]2 Cor. 6:16-18; cf. Lev. 26:12, Ezek. 37:27, Isa. 52:11, 2 Sam. 7:14.

[29]1 Cor. 7:10; cf. Matt. 19:3-9, Mark 10:2-9.

[30]1 Cor. 12:27, Eph. 1:22-23, Col. 1:24 ("the body of Christ"), 1 Cor. 3:16, 2 Cor. 6:16, Eph. 2:21-22 ("the temple of God"); cf. Mark 14:22, Matt. 26:26, Luke 22:19, Mark. 14:58, 15:29, Matt. 26:61, John 2:19.

Second, although Paul's view radically changed after his encounter with the risen Christ on the Damascus road, his thought still reflects to a certain extent that of first-century Judaism. For example, (1) his view of Adam's sin and its effect upon the humanity accords with the Jewish negative speculations about Adam.[31] (2) His conception of the two ages represented by Adam and Christ corresponds to the Jewish apocalyptic framework of the Primal Time (*Urzeit*) and the End Time (*Endzeit*). The difference is that while in Judaism the End Time (*Endzeit*) is still totally in the future, for Paul it has in certain respects already arrived with the coming of Christ the Messiah.[32] (3) His designation of the church as the temple of God resembles Qumran's view of the community as the temple of God.[33] This does not prove, however, that he was directly influenced by the Qumran community. It simply shows that he shared some ideas that were prevalent in various branches of first-century Judaism.

Third, certain similarities between Paul and Hellenism may be undeniable, but they are mostly at the verbal level and not at the conceptual level. Many of these similarities can be attributed to human thought-patterns common to all religions. Parallels or similarities between the two, therefore, do not necessarily mean that Paul was influenced by or dependent upon the hellenistic ideas. As an apostle to the hellenistic world, he might have been aware of the teachings of the hellenistic mystery religions when he spoke of the believer's dying and rising with Christ.[34] He might also have been aware of the widespread Stoic "body" metaphor and their notion of man as a temple when he designated the church as the body of Christ and as the temple of God.[35] He might also have heard about the gnostic "Primal Man" myth when he described Christ as the redeemer of fallen humanity, if the myth existed at that time.[36] It is, however, very unlikely that he borrowed ideas from these backgrounds, for there are irreconcilable conceptual differences between the two.

The most significant differences between Hellenism and Paul's teachings are as follows: (1) Deification through union with a god, that is, the ultimate goal of the mystery religions and of Gnosticism, is absolutely

---

[31]See pp. 70-72 (ch. 2) above.

[32]See pp. 72, 81-82 (ch. 2) above.

[33]1 Cor. 3:16, 2 Cor. 6:16, Eph. 2:21-22; cf. *1QS* 5.5-6, 8.4-9. 9.3-6.

[34]See pp. 32-34 (ch. 1) above.

[35]See pp. 112-13 (ch. 3) and 138-40 (ch. 4) above.

[36]See pp. 66-70 (ch. 2) and 113-14 (ch. 3) above.

unthinkable for Paul. Although he speaks of the believer's incorporation into Christ, he always maintains a distinction between Christ and the believer. (2) The hellenistic body/soul dualism which regards the human body basically as evil and subject to destruction contradicts Paul's view of the bodily resurrection. (3) While the gnostic "Primal Man" is an abstract, non-historical composite figure produced over a long period of time and space, Paul's conception of the redeemer is based on the concrete historical person of Jesus the Messiah. Most significantly for this study, (4) whereas the union with the deity in the hellenistic mystery religions and in Gnosticism is strictly individualistic, Paul's conception of believers' union with Christ has a corporate dimension.

Since anthropology is an underlying assumption for Paul, it is difficult to know for certain what shaped his view of man, particularly his corporate anthropology. The above conclusions, however, suggest that one must understand Paul's corporate anthropology primarily in the framework of the Old Testament-Jewish-Christian backgrounds rather than that of the hellenistic philosophy and religions. The Old Testament conception of man reveals the following characteristics:[37] (1) The group (e.g., family, tribe, and nation) is often identified with its leader (e.g., father, ancestor, and king) (*identification*). (2) The individual man is thought of as extending himself beyond his individual existence to include those who belong to him (*extension*). The father and the king, therefore, are understood as incorporating in themselves the household and the nation respectively. (3) The corporate personality that the individual man forms with a group is regarded as an ontological reality (*realism*). The act of the leader, therefore, often determines the destiny of the group that he represents. (4) An oscillation or fluidity exists between the individual and the group (*oscillation*). This Old Testament conception of the corporate solidarity of man continued even during the prophetic and the post-exile periods when a strong individualism emerged.[38] It also underlies various teachings of the New Testament. It may be seen best, however, in Paul's view of man that has been analyzed and summarized in the chapters of the present work.

---

[37]For the discussion of what follows, see pp. 75-79 (ch. 2) above.

[38]For example, see H. W. Robinson, *Doctrine of Man*, 30-60; De Fraine, *Family of Man*, 46-8; and Shedd, *Man in Community*, 42-89.

TABLE 1
OCCURRENCES OF THE ἐν Χριστῷ FORMULA
IN PAUL'S LETTERS

Book	Rom.	1 Cor.	2 Cor.	Gal.	Eph.
Occurrences	21	23	13	8	36
ἐν Χ. 'Ι.	3:24, 6:11 8:1, 8:2 16:3	1:2, 1:4 1:30, 4:15b 4:17b, 16:24		2:4, 3:14 3:26, 3:28 5:6	1:1, 2:6 2:7, 2:10 2:13, 3:6 3:21
ἐν Χ. 'Ι. Κ. Η.	6:23, 8:39	15:31			3:11
ἐν Χ.	9:1, 12:5 16:7, 16:9 16:10	3:1, 4:10 4:15a, 15:18 15:19, 15:22	2:14 2:17 3:14 5:17 5:19 12:2 12:19	1:22, 2:17	1:3, 1:10a 1:12, 1:20 4:32
ἐν Κ.	16:2, 16:8 16:11, 6:12a 16:12b, 16:13 16:22	1:31, 4:17a 7:22, 7:39 9:1, 9:2 11:11, 15:58 16:19	2:12 10:17	5:10	2:21b, 4:1 4:17, 5:8 6:1, 6:10 6:21
ἐν Κ. 'Ι.	14:14 15:17				1:15
ἐν Κ. 'Ι. Χ.					
ἐν 'Ι.					4:21b
ἐν αὐτῷ		1:15	1:19, 1:20 5:21 13:4		1:4, 1:9 1:10b 2:15 2:16, 4:21a
ἐν ᾧ					1:7, 1:11 1:13a 1:13b 2:21a 2:22 3:12
Other forms ἐν τῷ ἠγαπημένῳ					1:6

(continued)

Book	Phil	Col	1 Th	2 Th	1 Tim	2 Tim	Plm	Total
Occurrences	21	18	7	4	2	7	5	165
ἐν Χ. ᾽Ι.	1:1 1:26 2:5 3:3 3:14 4:7 4:19 4:21	1:4	2:14 5:18		1:14 3:13	1:1 1:9 1:13 2:1 2:10 3:12 3:15	23	44
ἐν Χ. ᾽Ι. Κ. Η.								4
ἐν Χ.	1:13 2:1	1:2 1:28	4:16				8 20b	32
ἐν Κ.	1:14 2:24 2:29 3:1 4:1 4:2 4:4 4:10	3:18 3:20 4:7 4:17	3:8 5:12	3:4			16 20a	43
ἐν Κ. ᾽Ι.	2:19		4:1	3:12				6
ἐν Κ. ᾽Ι. Χ.			1:1	1:1				2
ἐν ᾽Ι.								1
ἐν αὐτῷ	3:9	1:16 1:17 1:19 2:6 2:7 2:9 2:10		1:12				20
ἐν ᾧ		1:14 2:3 2:11 2:12						11
Other forms ἐν τῷ ἐνδυνα– μοῦντί	4:13							2

* Χ = Χριστῷ, ᾽Ι = ᾽Ιησοῦ, Κ = Κυρίῳ, Η = ῾Ημῶν

TABLE 2
CLASSIFICATION OF THE ἐν Χριστῷ FORMULA

A. Personal ("Someone")

Classification	Occurrences	Total #
(a) Being	Rom. 8:1, 16:7, 11 1 Cor. 1:30, 15:22 2 Cor. 5:17, 12:2 Gal. 1:22 Eph. 1:1 Phil. 1:1, 3:9 Col. 1:2 1 Thess. 1:1, 2:14, 4:16 2 Thess. 1:1	16
(b) Status/State	Rom. 6:11, 12:5, 16:3, 8, 9, 10, 13 1 Cor. 3:1, 4:10, 15b, 17a, 9:1, 2, 11:11 2 Cor. 5:21 Gal. 3:26, 28, 5:6 Eph. 2:21a, 3:6, 4:1, 5:8, 6:21 col. 1:28, 2:10, 4:7 Philem. 16, 23	28
(c) Activity	*(w/o object)* Rom. 14:14, 16:12a, 12b 1 Cor. 1:31, 15:18, 19 2 Cor. 10:17, 13:4 Gal. 5:10 Eph. 1:12, 2:21b, 6:10 Phil. 1:14, 2:19, 24, 3:1, 3, 4:1, 4, 10 Col. 2:6 1 Thess. 3:8 2 Thess. 3:4 Philem. 20a	24
	(non-personal object) Rom. 9:1 Eph. 1:13a, 3:12, 4:13 Philem. 8, 20b	6
	(personal object) Rom. 16:2, 22 1 Cor. 4:15a, 7:39, 16:19	

(continued)	2 Cor. 2:17, 12:19 Eph. 4:17, 6:1 Phil. 2:29, 4:2, 21 1 Thess. 4:1, 5:12 2 Thess. 3:12	15
	(God as subject) 2 Cor. 1:20, 2:14, 5:19 Eph. 1:3, 4, 6, 10, 11, 20, 2:6, 7, 15, 16, 4:32 Phil. 4:19 2 Tim. 1:9	16
	(action in passive form) 1 Cor. 1:2, 5, 7:22 Gal. 2:17 Eph. 1:11, 13b, 2:10, 13, 22, 4:21a Col. 2:7, 11, 12 2 Thess. 1:12	14

B. Non-personal ("Something")

Classification	Occurrences	Total #
(a) Being	Rom. 3:24, 8:39, 15:17 1 Cor. 4:17b, 15:31, 16:24 Gal. 2:4 Eph. 1:7, 9, 15, 3:11, 21, 4:21b Phil. 1:13, 2:1, 5, 3:14 Col. 1:4, 14, 2:3, 4:17 1 Tim. 1:14, 3:13 2 Tim. 1:1, 13, 2:1, 10, 3:12, 15.	29
(b) Status/State	Rom. 6:23 1 Cor. 15:58 2 Cor. 1:19 Col. 3:18, 20 1 Thess. 5:18	6
(c) Activity	Rom. 8:2 1 Cor. 1:4 2 Cor. 2:12, 3:14 Gal. 3:14 Phil. 1:26, 4:7 Col. 1:16, 17, 19, 2:9	11

BIBLIOGRAPHY

Books

Abbott, T. K. *A Critical and Exegetical Commentary on the Epistle to the Ephesians and to the Colossians*. International Critical Commentary. Edinburgh: T. & T. Clark, 1897.

Andrews, Elias. *The Meaning of Christ for Paul*. New York: Abingdon-Cokesbury, 1946.

Arndt, William F., and F. Wilbur Gingrich. *A Greek-English Lexicon of the New Testament and Other Early Christian Literature*, 2nd ed. Chicago: University of Chicago Press, 1979.

Arrington, French L. *Paul's Aeon Theology in 1 Corinthians*. Washington, D.C.: University Press of America, 1977.

Baer, Richard A. *Philo's Use of the Categories Male and Female*. Leiden: E. J. Brill, 1970.

Bailey, Derrick S. *The Mystery of Love and Marriage: A Study in the Theology of Sexual Relation*. London: SCM, 1952.

Baker, David L. *Two Testaments, One Bible: A Study of Some Modern Solutions to the Theological Problem of the Relationship between the Old and the New Testaments*, rev. ed. Downers Grove, IL: InterVarsity, 1977.

Barrett, C. K. *A Commentary on the First Epistle to the Corinthians*. Harper's New Testament Commentaries. New York: Harper & Row, 1968.

_____. *A Commentary on the Epistle to the Romans*. Harper's New Testament Commentaries. New York: Harper & Row, 1957.

_____. *A Commentary on the Second Epistle to the Corinthians*. Harper's New Testament Commentaries. New York: Harper & Row, 1973.

_____. *From First Adam to Last: A Study in Pauline Theology*. New York: Charles Scribner's Sons, 1962.

Barth, Karl. *Christ and Adam: Man and Humanity in Romans 5*. Translated by T. A. Smail. New York: Macmillan, 1968.

_____. *A Short Commentary on Romans*. Translated by D. H. van Daalen. London: SCM, 1959.

Barth, Markus. *Ephesians: Introduction, Translation, and Commentary on Chapters 1-3*. Anchor Bible. Garden City, NY: Doubleday, 1974.

Barth, Markus, and Helmut Blanke. *Colossians: A New Translation with Introduction and Commentary*. Anchor Bible Commentary. Garden City, NY: Doubleday, 1994.

Batey, Richard A. *New Testament Nuptial Imagery*. Leiden: E. J. Brill, 1971.

Baur, F. C. *Paul the Apostle of Jesus Christ, His Life and Work, His Epistles and His Doctrine: A Contribution to the Critical History of Primitive Christianity*, rev. ed. 2 vols. Edited and Translated by Eduard Zeller and A. Menzies. London: Williams and Norgate, 1875.

Beasley-Murray, G. R. *Baptism in the New Testament*. London: Macmillan, 1962.

Best, Ernest. *A Commentary on the First and Second Epistles to the Thessalonians*. New York: Harper & Row, 1972.

_____. *Ephesians*. International Critical Commentary. Edinburgh: T. & T. Clark, 1998.

_____. *One Body in Christ: A Study in the Relationship of the Church to Christ in the Epistles of the Apostle Paul*. London: S. P. C. K., 1955.

Betz, H. D. *The Greek Magical Papyri*. Chicago: University Press, 1986.

Billerbeck, Paul, and H. L. Strack. *Kommentar zum Neuen Testament aus Talmud und Midrasch III: Die Briefe des Neuen Testemanets und die Offenbarung Johannis Erläutert aus Talmud und Midrash*. München: C. H. Becksche Verlagsbuchhandlung, 1926.

Bornkamm, Günther. *Paul*. Translated by D. M. G. Stalker. New York: Harper & Row, 1971.

Borsch, F. H. *The Son of Man in Myth and History*. Philadelphia: Westminster, 1967.

Bousset, Wilhelm. *Kyrios Christos*, 5th ed. Translated by John Steely. Nashville, TN: Abingdon, 1970.

Bouttier, Michel. *En Christ: Etude d'Exegese et de Theologie Pauliniennes*. Paris: Presses Universitaires de France, 1962.

Brandenburger, Egon. *Adam und Christus: Exegetisch-religions-geschichtliche Untersuchung zu Röm. 5.12-21(I. Kor. 15)*. Neukirchen: Neukirchener, 1962.

_____. *Fleisch und Geist: Paulus und die dualistische Weisheit*. Neukirchen: Kreis Moers, 1968.

Brooks, James, and Carlton L. Winbery. *Syntax of New Testament Greek*. New York: University Press of America, 1979.

Brown, Raymond B. *Acts-1 Corinthians*. Broadman Bible Commentary. Nashville, TN: Broadman, 1970.

Bruce, F. F. *The Epistles to the Colossians, to Philemon, and to the Ephesians*. Grand Rapids: Eerdmans, 1984.

_____. *The Epistle to the Ephesians*. London: Fleming H. Revell, 1961.

_____. *The Epistle to the Hebrews*. International Commentary on the New Testament. Grand Rapids: Eerdmans, 1964.

_____. *1 and 2 Corinthians*. New Century Bible. London: Oliphants, 1971.

_____. *1 & 2 Thessalonians*. Word Biblical Commentary. Waco, TX: Words Books, 1982.

_____. *The Letter of Paul to the Romans: An Introduction and Commentary*, 2d ed. Tyndale New Testament Commentaries. Grand Rapids: Eerdmans, 1985.

Bultmann, Rudolf. *The History of the Synoptic Tradition*. Translated by John Marsh. Oxford: Basil, 1968.

_____. *Theology of the New Testament*. Translated by Kendrick Grobel. Vol. 1. New York: Charles Scribner's Sons, 1951.

Burkert, Walter. *Ancient Mystery Cults*. Cambridge, MA: Harvard University Press, 1987.

Cannon, G. E. *The Use of Traditional Materials in Colossians*. Macon, GA: Mercer University Press, 1983.

Capes, David B. *Old Testament Yahweh Texts in Paul's Christology*. Tübingen: J. C. B. Mohr, 1992.

Carrez, M. *La deuxième épôtre de saint Paul aux Corinthiens*. Genève: n.p., 1986.

Cerfaux, Lucien. *Christ in the Theology of St. Paul*. Translated by Geoffrey Wedd and Adrian Walker. New York: Herder and Herder, 1959.

_____. *The Church in the Theology of St. Paul*. Translated by Geoffrey Webb and Adrian Walker. New York: Herder and Herder, 1959.

Chance, J. Bradley. *Jerusalem, the Temple, and the New Age in Luke-Acts*. Macon, GA: Mercer University Press, 1988.

Charles, R. H. *The Apocrypha and Pseudepigrapha of the Old Testament*. 2 vols. Oxford: Clarendon, 1913. Reprint, Oxford: clarendon, 1963.

_____. *A Critical History of the Doctrine of a Future Life*. London: Black, 1899.

Charlesworth, James H., ed. *The Dead Sea Scrolls: Hebrew, Aramaic, and Greek Texts with English Translations*. Vol. 1, *Rule of the Community and Related Document*. Tübingen: J. C. B. Mohr, 1994.

Charlesworth, James H., and others, eds. *The Old Testament Pseudepigrapha*. 2 vols. Garden City, NY: Doubleday, 1983.

Chavasse, Claude. *The Bride of Christ: An Enquiry into the Nuptial Element in Early Church*. London: Faber and Faber, 1940.

Cole, A. *The New Temple: A Study in the Origins of the Catechetical 'Form' of the Church in the New Testament*. London: Tyndale, 1950.

Collange, J. F. *Enigmes*. Cambridge: Cambridge University Press, 1972.

Colpe, Carsten. *Die religionsgeschichtliche Schule: Darstellung und Kritik ihres Bildes vom gnostischen Erlösermythus*. Göttingen: Vandenhoeck & Ruprecht, 1961.

Congar, Yves M.-J. *The Mystery of the Temple or the Manner of God's Presence to His Creatures from Genesis to the Apocalypse*. Translated by Reginald F. Trevett. Westminster, MD: Newman, 1962.

Conzelmann, Hans. *A Commentary on the First Epistle to the Corinthians*. Edited by George W. MacRae. Translated by James W. Leitch. Philadelphia: Fortress, 1975.

_____. *An Outline of the Theology of the New Testament*. Translated by John Bowden. New York: Harper & Row, 1969.

Cooper, John W. *Body, Soul, and Life Everlasting: Biblical Anthropology and the Monism-Dualism Debate*. Grand Rapids: Eerdmans, 1989.

Craig, Claence Tucker. *The First Epistle to the Corinthians*. Interpreter's Bible. New York: Abingdon-Cokesbury, 1953.

Cranfield, C. E. B. *A Critical and Exegetical Commentary on the Epistle of Paul to the Romans*. International Critical Commentary. Edinburgh: T. & T. Clark, 1975.

Crouch, J. E. *The Origin and Intention of the Colossian Haustafel*. Göttingen: Vandenhoeck & Ruprecht, 1972.

Cullmann, Oscar. *Christ and Time: The Primitive Christian Conception of Time and History*, 3rd ed. Translated by Floyd Filson. London: SCM Press, 1962.

_____. *The Christology of the New Testament*, rev. ed. Translated by Shirley C. Guthrie and Charles A. M. Hall. Philadelphia: West-minster, 1963.

_____. *Immortality of the Soul or Resurrection of the Dead*. London: Epworth, 1958.

Dahl, M. E. *The Resurrection of the Body: A Study of I Corinthians 15*. Studies in Biblical Theology, vol. 36. London: SCM, 1962.

Dana, H. E., and Julius R. Mantey. *A Manual Grammar of the Greek New Testament*. Toronto: Macmillan, 1955.

Danby, Herbert, trans. *The Mishnah*. London: Oxford University Press, 1944.

Daube, D. *Studies in Biblical Law*. Cambridge: Cambridge University Press, 1947.

Davidson, Richard M. *Typology in Scripture: A Study of Hermeneutical ΤΥΠΟΣ Structures*. Berrien Springs, MI: Andrews University Press, 1981.

Davies, W. D. *Paul and Rabbinic Judaism: Some Rabbinic Elements in Pauline Theology*. New York: Harper & Row, 1967.

De Boer, Martinus C. *The Defeat of Death: Apocalyptic Eschatology in 1 Corinthians 15 and Romans 5*. Sheffield: Sheffield Academic, 1988.

De Fraine, Jean. *Adam and the Family of Man*. Translated by D. C. Raible. Staten Island, NY: Alba House, 1965.

Deissmann, G. Adolf. *Paul: A Study in Social and Religious History*, 2nd ed. Translated by William E. Wilson. New York: Harper & Brothers, 1957.

_____. *Die Neutestamentliche Formel "in Christo Jesu*. Marburg-Lahn: N. C. Elwert Verlag, 1892.

Delcourt, Marie. *Hermaphrodite: Mythes et rites de la bisexualité dans l'antiquité classique*. Paris: Presses Universitaires de France, 1958.

Deterding, Paul E. "The Role of the Corporate Personality in the Thought of Paul." Ph. D. diss., Concordia Seminary, 1981.

Dibelius, Martin and H. Greeven. *An die Kolosser, Epheser, an Philemon*. Tübingen: J. C. B. Mohr, 1953.

Dodd, C. H. *The Bible and the Greeks*. London: Hodder & Stoughton, 1954.

_____. *The Epistle to the Romans*. Moffatt New Testament Commentary. London: Collins, 1959.

_____. *The Meaning of Paul for Today*. New York: George H. Doran, 1922.

Dunn, James D. G. *Christology in the Making: A New Testament Inquiry into the Origins of the Doctrine of the Incarnation*. Philadelphia: Westminster, 1980.

_____. *Jesus and the Spirit: A Study of the Religious and Charismatic Experience of Jesus and the First Christians as Reflected in the New Testament*. Philadelphia: Westminster, 1975.

_____. *Romans 1-8*. Word Biblical Commentary. Waco, TX: Word Books, 1988.

_____. *The Theology of Paul the Apostle*. Grand Rapids: Eerdmans, 1998.

Dupont-Sommer, A. *The Essence Writings from Qumran*. Oxford: Blackwell, 1961.

Eichrodt, Walter. *Man in the Old Testament*. Translated by R. Gregor Smith. London: SCM, 1951.

_____. *Theology of the Old Testament*. Vol. 1. Translated by J. A. Baker. Philadelphia: Westminster, 1961.

Ellis, E. Earle. "The Biblical Concept of the Solidarity of the Human Race as Seen in Blessing and Punishment." B.D. thesis, Wheaton Graduate School, 1953.

_____. *Christ and the Future in New Testament History*. Leiden: E. J. Brill, 2000.

_____. *Eschatology in Luke*. Philadelphia: Fortress, 1972.

_____. *Making of the New Testament Documents*. Leiden: E. J. Brill, 1999.

_____. *The Old Testament in Early Christianity: Canon and Interpretation in the Light of Modern Research*. Grand Rapids: Baker, 1992.

_____. *Paul and His Recent Interpreters*. Grand Rapids: Eerdmans, 1961.

_____. *Paul's Use of the Old Testament*. Edinburgh: T. & T. Clark, 1957. Reprint, Grand Rapids: Baker, 1991.

_____. *Pauline Theology: Ministry and Society*. Grand Rapids: Eerdmans, 1989. Reprint, Lanham, MD: University Press of America, 1997.

_____. *Prophecy and Hermeneutic in Early Christianity: New Testament Essays*. Tübingen: J. C. B. Mohr, 1978.

Evans-Pritchard, E. E. *Nuer Religion*. New York: Oxford University Press, 1956.

Fee, Gordon D. *The First Epistle to the Corinthians*. New International Commentary on the New Testament. Grand Rapids: Eerdmans, 1987.

_____. *1 and 2 Timothy, Titus*. New International Biblical Commentary. Peabody, MA: Hendrickson, 1984.

_____. *The Pastoral Epistles*. Peabody, MA: Hendrickson, 1988.

Feuillet, A. *Destinee des Chretiens et Fondements de l'eschatolgie paulinienne*. Paris: Institut Catholique de Paris, n.d.

Fiorenza, E. S. *In Memory of Her: A Feminist Theological Recon-struction of Christian Origins*. New York: Crossroad, 1984.

Fitzmyer, Joseph A. *Romans*. Anchor Bible Commentary. New York: Doubleday, 1993.

Flew, R. N. *Jesus and His Church*, 2nd ed. London: Epworth, 1943.

Foulkes, Francis. *The Acts of God: A Study of the Basis of Typology in the Old Testament*. London: Tyndale, 1958.

France, Richard T. *Jesus and the Old Testament*. London: Tyndale, 1971.

Francis, Fred O., and J. Paul Sampley. *Pauline Parallels*, 2nd ed. Philadelphia: Fortress, 1984.

Fuller, R. H. *The Foundation of New Testament Christology*. New York: Charles Scribner's Sons, 1965.

Furnish, V. *II Corinthians*. Anchor Bible Commentary. New York: Doubleday, 1984.

Gaffin, Richard B. *Resurrection and Redemption*, 2nd ed. Phillipsburg, NJ: Presbyterian and Reformed, 1987.

Gärtner, Bertil. *The Temple and the Community in Qumran and the New Testament: A Comparative Study in the Temple Symbolism of the Qumran Texts and the New Testament*. Cambridge: Cambridge University Press, 1965.

Gnilka, Joachim. *Der Epheserbrief*. Herders Theologischer Kommentar zum Neuen Testament, vol. 10. Freiburg: Herder and Herder, 1990.

Goodspeed, Edgar J. *An Introduction to the New Testament*. Chicago: University of Chicago Press, 1937.

Goppelt, Leonhard. *Typos: The Typological Interpretation of the Old Testament in the New*. Translated by Donald H. Madvig. Grand Rapids: Eerdmans, 1982.

Grant, Robert. *Gnosticism and Early Christianity*, rev. ed. New York: Harper & Row, 1966.

Green, A. A., trans. and ed. *The Revised Hagada: Home Service for the First Two Nights of Passover*, 3rd ed. New York: Bloch, 1897.

Gritz, Sharon H. M. "A Study of 1 Timothy 2:9-15 in the Light of the Religious and Cultural Milieu of the First Century." Ph.D. diss., Southwestern Baptist Theological Seminary, 1986.

Gundry, Robert H. *Sōma in Biblical Theology with Emphasis on Pauline Anthropology*. Cambridge: Cambridge University Press, 1976.

Gutbrod, W. *Die Paulinische Anthropologie*. Stuttgart-Berlin: W. Kohlhammer, 1934.

Guthrie, Donald. *New Testament Introduction: The Pauline Epistles*. Downers Grove, IL: InterVarsity, 1970.

Hamerton-Kelly, R. G. *Pre-existence, Wisdom, and the Son of Man: A Study of the Idea of Pre-existence in the New Testament*. Cambridge: Cambridge University Press, 1973.

Hamilton, N. Q. *The Holy Spirit and Eschatology in Paul*. Edinburgh: Oliver and Boyd, 1957.

Hanson, S. *The Unity of the Church in the New Testament: Colossians and Ephesians*. Lexington, KY: American Theological Library Association, 1963.

Harris, Murray J. *Raised Immortal: Resurrection and Immortality in the New Testament*. Grand Rapids: Eerdmans, 1983.

Harrison, P. N. *The Problem of the Pastoral Epistles*. London: Oxford University Press, 1921.

Hawthorne, Gerald F. *Philippians*. Word Biblical Commentary. Waco, TX: Word Books, 1983.

Hayter, Mary. *The New Eve in Christ: The Use and Abuse of the Bible in the Debate about Women in the Church*. Grand Rapids: Eerdmans, 1987.

Hendriksen, W. *Exposition of Ephesians*. Grand Rapids: Baker, 1967.

Hengel, Martin. *Judaism and Hellenisim: Studies in Their Encounter in Palestine during the Early Hellenistic Period*. Translated by John Bowden. Minneapolis: Fortress, 1974.

Héring, J. *Le royaume de Dieu et sa venue: Étude sur l'espérance de Jésus et l'apôtre Paul*. Neuchatel: Delachaux & Niestlé, 1959.

Heyob, Sharon Kelly. *The Cult of Isis among Women in the Graeco-Roman World*. Leiden: E. J. Brill, 1975.

Hill, D. *Greek Words and Hebrew Meaning: Studies in the Semantics of Soteriological Terms*. London: Cambridge University Press, 1967.

Hirsch, W. *Rabbinic Psychology: Beliefs about the Soul in Rabbinic Literature of the Talmudic Period*. London: E. Goldston, 1947.

Hooker, Morna D. *From Adam to Christ: Essays on Paul*. Cambridge: Cambridge University Press, 1990.

_____. *The Son of Man: A Study of the Background of the Term 'Son of Man' and Its Use in St. Mark's Gospel*. Montreal: McGill University Press, 1967.

Hughes, Philip. *Paul's Second Epistle to the Corinthians*. New International Commentary on the New Testament. Grand Rapids: Eerdmans, 1962.

Hultgren, Arland J. *I-II Timothy, Titus*. Augsbury Commentary on the New Testament. Minneapolis, MN: Augsbury, 1984.

Hunter, A. M. *The Epistle to the Romans*. Torch Bible Commentaries. London: SCM, 1955.

_____. *Paul and His Predecessors*. London: Nicholson & Watson, 1940.

Hurley, James B. *Man and Woman in Biblical Perspective*. Grand Rapids: Zondervan, 1981.

Isaksson, Abel. *Marriage and Ministry in the New Temple: A Study with Special Reference to Mt. 19:3-12 and 1 Cor. 11:3-16*. Lund: Gleerup, 1965.

Jeremias, J. *The Eucharistic Words of Jesus*. London: SCM, 1966.

Jervell, Jacob. *Imago Dei: Gen 1,26f. im Spätjudentum, in der Gnosis und in der paulinischen Briefen*. Göttingen: Vandenhoeck & Ruprecht, 1960.

Jewett, Paul K. *Man as Male and Female: A Study in Sexual Relationships from a Theological Point of View.* Grand Rapids: Eerdmans, 1975.

Jewett, Robert. *Paul's Anthropological Terms: A Study of Their Use in Conflict Settings.* Leiden: E. J. Brill, 1971.

Johnson, Aubrey R. *The Cultic Prophet and Israel's Psalmody.* Cardiff: University of Wales Press, 1979.

_____. *The Cultic Prophet in Ancient Israel,* 2nd ed. Cardiff: University of Wales Press, 1962.

_____. *The One and the Many in the Israelite Conception of God,* 2nd ed. Cardiff: University of Wales Press, 1961.

_____. *Sacral Kingship in Ancient Israel.* Cardiff: University Of Wales Press, 1955.

_____. *The Vitality of the Individual in the Thought of Ancient Israel.* Cardiff: University of Wales Press, 1964.

Johnston, George. *The Doctrine of the Church in the New Testament.* Cambridge: University Press, 1943.

Judge, E. A. *The Social Pattern of the Christian Groups in the First Century: Some Prolegomena to the Study of New Testament Ideas of Social Obligation.* London: Tyndale, 1960.

Kabisch, R. *Die Eschatologie des Paulus.* Göttingen: Vandenhoeck & Ruprecht, 1893.

Kadushin, Max. *The Rabbinic Mind.* New York: The Jewish Theological Seminary of America, 1952.

Kaminsky, J. S. *Corporate Responsibility in the Hebrew Bible.* Sheffield: Sheffield Academic, 1995.

Käsemann, Ernst. *Commentary on Romans.* Translated and Edited by Geoffrey W. Bromiley. Grand Rapids: Eerdmans, 1980.

_____. *Leib und Leib Christi.* Tübingen: J. C. B. Mohr, 1933.

Kelly, J. N. D. *The Pastoral Epistles.* London: Black, 1963.

Kennedy, H. A. A. *St. Paul and the Mystery-Religions.* London: Hodder & Stoughton, 1913.

_____. *St. Paul's Conception of the Last Things.* London: Hodder & Stoughton, 1904.

_____. *The Theology of the Epistles.* London: Duckworth, 1919.

Kim, Seyoon. *The Origin of Paul's Gospel,* 2nd ed. Tübigen: J. C. B. Mohr, 1984.

Knight, G. W. III. *The Pastoral Epistles.* Grand Rapids: Eerdmans, 1992.

Knox, Wilfred L. *St. Paul and the Church of the Gentiles.* Cambridge: Cambridge University Press, 1939.

Kramer, Werner. *Christ, Lord, Son of God*. Translated by Brian Hardy. Naperville, IL: Alec R. Allenson, 1966.

Kraeling, C. H. *Anthropos and Son of Man: A Study in the Religious Syncretism of the Hellenistic Orient*. New York: AMS, 1966.

Kümmel, Werner Georg. *Introduction to the New Testament*, rev. ed. Translated by Howard Clark Kee. Nashville, TN: Abingdon, 1981.

_____. *Man in the New Testament*, rev. ed. Translated by John J. Vincent. Philadelphia: Westminster, 1963.

_____. *The Theology of the New Testament: According to Its Major Witnesses, Jesus-Paul-John*. Translated by John E. Steely. Nashville, TN: Abingdon, 1973.

Ladd, George Eldon. *A Theology of the New Testament*. Grand Rapids: Eerdmans, 1974.

Lang, F. G. *2 Korinther 5, 1-10 in der Neuren Forschung, Beitrage zur Geschichte der biblische Exegese*. Tübingen: J. C. B. Mohr, 1973.

Leaney, A. R. C. *The Rule of Qumran and Its Meaning: Introduction, Translation and Commentary*. Philadelphia: Westminster, 1966.

Leitzmann, Hans. *An die Korinther*. Tübingen: J. C. B. Mohr, 1940.

Levison, John Robert. *Portraits of Adam in Early Judaism: From Sirach to 2 Baruch*. Sheffield: JSOT, 1988.

Levy-Bruhl, Lucien. *How Natives Think*. Translated by Lilian A. Clare. Princeton, NJ: Princeton University Press, 1985.

_____. *Primitive Mentality*. Translated by Lilian A. Clare. Boston: Beacon, 1966.

_____. *The 'Soul' of the Primitive*. Translated by Lilian A. Clare. New York: Frederick A. Praeger, 1966.

Lincoln, Andrew T. *Ephesians*. Word Biblical Commentary. Dallas, TX: Word Books, 1990.

Lindblom, Johannes. *The Servant Songs in Deutro-Isaiah: A New Attempt to Solve an Old Problem*. Lund: C. W. K. Gleerup, 1951.

Lohse, Eduard. *A Commentary on the Epistles to the Colossians and to Philemon*. Translated by William R. Poehlmann and Robert J. Karris. Hermeneia. Philadelphia: Fortress, 1971.

Longenecker, Richard N. *Galatians*. Word Biblical Commentary. Dallas: Word Books, 1990.

_____. *Paul: Apostle of Liberty*. New York: Harper & Row, 1964.

Lüdemann, Hermann. *Die Anthropologie des Apostels Paulus und ihre Stellung innerhalb seiner Heilslehre nach den Vier Hauptbriefen*. Kiel: Universitäts-Buchhandlung, 1872.

Macquarrie, J. *An Existentialist Theology: A Comparison of Heidegger and Bultmann*. London: SCM, 1965.

Machen, J. Gresham. *The Origin of Paul's Religion*. New York: Macmillan, 1921. Reprint, Grand Rapids: Eerdmans, 1975.

MacDonald, Dennis. *There Is No Male and Female*. Philadelphia: Fortress, 1987.

Manson, T. W. *Jesus the Messiah*. London: Hodder & Stoughton, 1943.

_____. *The Sayings of Jesus*. London: SCM, 1949.

_____. *The Teaching of Jesus*. 2nd ed. Cambridge: Cambridge University Press, 1935.

Martin, R. P. *Carmen Christi: Phil. ii. 5-11 in Recent Interpretation and in the Setting of Early Christian Worship*. 2nd ed. Cambridge: Cambridge University Press, 1983.

_____. *2 Corinthians*. Word Biblical Commentary. Waco, TX: Word Books, 1986.

Martínez, Florentino García. *The Dead Sea Scrolls Translated: The Qumran Texts in English*. Translated by Wilfred G. E. Watson. Leiden: E. J. Brill, 1994.

Mascall, E. L. *Christ, the Christian and the Church: A Study of the Incarnation and Its Consequences*. London: Longmans, 1946.

McKelvey, R. J. *The New Temple: The Church in the New Testament*. London: Oxford University Press, 1969.

McNeile, A. H. *The Gospel according to St. Matthew*. London: MacMillan, 1915. Reprint, Grand Rapids: Baker, 1980.

Meeks, Wayne A. *The First Urban Christians: The Social World of the Apostle Paul*. New Haven, CT: Yale University Press, 1983.

Mehl-Koehnlein, H. *L'homme selon l'apôtre Paul*. Neuchatel: Delachaux Niestlé, 1951.

Menoud, P. H. *Le sort des trépassés d'aprßes le Nouveau Testament*. Neuchatel: Delachaux Niestlé, 1945.

Mersch, E. *The Theology of the Mystical Body*. London: Herder and Herder, 1952.

_____. *The Whole Christ: The Historical Development of the Doctrine of the Mystical Body in Scripture and Tradition*. Translated by John R. Kelly. Milwaukee, WI: Bruce, 1938.

Metzger, Bruce M., ed. *The Apocrypha of the Old Testament*. New York: Oxford University Press, 1977.

Meuzelaar, J. J. ·*Der Leib des Messias: Eine exegetische Studie über den Gedanken vom Leib Christi in den Paulusbriefen*. Kampen: Kok, 1979.

Meyer, Marvin W., ed. and trans. *The "Mithras Liturgy."* Missoula, MT: Scholars, 1976.

Miletic, Stephen Francis. *One Flesh: Eph. 5.22-24, 5.30: Marriage and the New Creation*. Roma: Editrice Pontificio Instituto Biblico, 1988.

Minear, P. S. *Images of the Church in the New Testament*. Philadelphia: Westminster, 1960.

Mitton, C. L. *Ephesians: Its Authorship, Origin, and Purpose*. Oxford: Clarendon, 1951.

Morris, Leon. *The First Epistle of Paul to the Corinthians*. Tyndale New Testament Commentaries. Grand Rapids: Eerdmans, 1958.

Moule, C. F. D. *The Origin of Christology*. Cambridge: Cambridge University Press, 1977.

Moulton, James H., and Wilbert F. Howard. *A Grammar of New Testament Greek*. Vol. 2, *Accidence and Word-Formation*. Edinburgh: T. & T. Clark, 1908.

Mowinckel, S. *The Psalms in Israel's Worship*. 2 vols. Translated by D. R. Ap-Thomas. Nashville, TN: Abingdon, 1962.

Müller, Peter. *Der Soma-Begriff bei Paulus: Studien zum paulinischen Menschenbild und seine Bedeutung für unsere Zeit*. Stuutgart: Urachhaus, 1988.

Munck, Johannes. *Paul and the Salvation of Mankind*. Translated by Frank Clarke. Richmond: John Knox, 1959.

Murphy-O'Connor, Jerome, ed. *Paul and Qumran: Studies in New Testament Exegesis*. Chicago: Priory, 1968.

Murray, John. *The Epistle to the Romans*. New International Commentary on the New Testament. Grand Rapids: Eerdmans, 1959.

_____. *The Imputation of Adam's Sin*. Grand Rapdis: Eerdmans, 1959.

Müssner, Franz. *Der Brief an die Epheser*. Gütersloh: Gütersloher, 1982.

Neugebauer, Fritz. *In Christus*. Göttingen: Vandenhoeck & Ruprecht, 1961.

Nock, Arthur Darby, ed. *Corpus Hermeticum*. Société d'édition "Les Belles Letteres." 4 vols. Paris: n. p., 1945.

_____. *Early Gentile Christianity and Its Hellenistic Background*. New York: Harper & Row, 1964.

_____. *Essays on Religion and the Ancient World*. 2 vols. Edited by Zeph Stewart. Oxford: Clarendon, 1986.

North, C. R. *The Suffering Servant in Deutero-Isaiah: An Historical and Critical Study*. London: Oxford University Press, 1956.

Nygren, Anders. *Commentary on Romans*. Translated by Carl C. Rasmussen. Philadelphia: Muhlenberg, 1979.

O'Brien, Peter T. *Colossians, Philemon*. Word Biblical Commentary. Waco, TX: Word Books, 1982.

Owen, D. R. G. *Body and Soul: A Study on the Christian View of Man*. Philadelphia: Westminster, 1956.

Pate, C. Marvin. *Adam Christology as the Exegetical & Theological Substructure of 2 Corinthians 4:7-5:21*. Lanham, MD: University Press of America, 1991.

Pearson, Birger A. *The Pneumatikos-Psychikos Terminology in 1 Corinthians: A Study in the Theology of the Corinthian Opponents of Paul and Its Relation to Gnosticism*. Missoula, MT: University of Montana for the Society of Biblical Literature, 1973.

Pedersen, J. *Israel: Its Life and Culture*. 2 vols. Translated by A. Müller and A. I. Fausbell. Oxford: University Press, 1959.

Percy, Ernst. *Der Leib Christi (soma Christou) in den paulinischen Homologoumena und Antilegomena*. Lunds Universities Arsskrift. Lund: Harrassowitz, 1942.

_____. *Die Probleme der Kolosser- und Epheserbriefe*. Lund: C. W. K. Gleerup, 1946.

Pfammatter, Josef. *Die Kirche als Bau: Eine exegetisch-theologische Studie zur Ekklesiologie der Paulusbriefe*. Rome: Gregorian University, 1960.

Pfleiderer, Otto. *Paulinism: A Contribution to the History of Primitive Christian Theology*. London: Williams and Norgate, 1877.

Plummer, A. *A Critical and Exegetical Commentary on the Second Epistle of St. Paul to the Corinthians*. International Critical Commentary. Edinburgh: T. & T. Clark, 1914.

Prat, Ferdinand. *The Theology of St. Paul*. 2 vols. Translated by John L. Stoddard. London: Burns, Oats and Washbourne, 1945.

Rad, Gerhard von. *Old Testament Theology*. Vol. 2, *The Theology of Israel's Prophetic Traditions*. Translated by D. M. G. Stalker. New York: Harper & Row, 1965.

Rawlinson, A. E. J. *The New Testament Doctrine of the Christ*. London: Longmans, 1926.

Reitzenstein, Richard. *Hellenistic Mystery-Religions: Their Basic Ideas and Significance*. 3rd ed. Translated by John E. Steely. Pittsburgh, PA: Pickwick, 1978.

_____. *Poimandres: Studien zur Griechisch-Ägyptischen und Frühchristlichen Literatur*. Leipzig: Druck, 1904.

Richards, E. Randolph. *The Secretary in the Letters of Paul*. Tübingen: J. C. B. Mohr, 1991.

Richardson, Alan. *An Introduction to the Theology of the New Testament.* New York: Harper & Row, 1958.

Ridderbos, Herman. *Paul: An Outline of His Theology.* Translated by John Richard de Witt. Grand Rapids: Eerdmans, 1975.

Robertson, A. T. *A Grammar of Greek New Testament in the Light of Historical Research.* Nashville, TN: Broadman, 1934.

Robertson, A. T., and Alfred Plummer. *A Critical and Exegetical Commentary on the First Epistle of St. Paul to the Corinthians.* International Critical Commentary. Edinburgh: T. & T. Clark, 1914.

Robinson, H. Wheeler. *The Christian Doctrine of Man*, 3rd ed. Edinburgh: T. & T. Clark, 1947.

_____. *Corporate Personality in Ancient Israel*, rev. ed. Edinburgh: T. & T. Clark, 1981.

Robinson, John A. T. *The Body: A Study in Pauline Theology.* Chicago: Henry Regnery, 1952.

Rogerson, J. W. *Anthropology and the Old Testament.* Atlanta, GA: John Knox, 1978.

Roller, Otto. *Das Formular der paulinischen Briefe.* Stuttgart: W. Kohlhammer, 1933.

Rosner, Brian S. *Paul, Scripture and Ethics: A Study of 1 Corinthians 5-7.* Leiden: E. J. Brill, 1994.

Sampley, J. P. *"And the Two Shall Become One Flesh": A Study of Tradition in Ephesians 5:21-33.* Cambridge: Cambridge University Press, 1971.

Sanday, William, and Arthur C. Headlam. *A Criticial and Exegetical Commentary on the Epistle to the Romans.* International Critical Commentary. Edinburgh: T. & T. Clark, 1902.

Sanders, E. P. *Paul and Palestinian Judaism: A Comparison of Patterns of Religion.* Minneapolis, MN: Fortress, 1977.

Sapp, David A. "An Introduction to Adam Christology in Paul: A History of Interpretation, the Jewish Background, and an Exegesis of Romans 5:12-21." Ph.D. diss., Southwestern Baptist Theological Seminary, 1990.

Schlier, H. *Der Brief an die Epheser: Ein Kommentar.* Düsseldorf: Patmos, 1962.

_____. *Christus und die Kirche im Epheserbrief.* Tübingen: J. C. B. Mohr, 1930.

Schmauch, Werner. *In Christus: Eine Untersuchung zur Sprache und Theologie des Paulus.* Gütersloh: Bertelsmann, 1935.

Schmithals, W. *Gnosticism in Corinth: An Investigation of the Letters to the Corinthians*. Translated by John E. Steely. Nashville, TN: Abingdon, 1971.

Schnackenburg, Rudolf. *Baptism in the Thought of St. Paul*. Translated by G. R. Beasley-Murray. New York: Herder and Herder, 1964.

_____. *The Church in the New Testament*. New York: Herder and Herder, 1965.

_____. *Ephesians*. Translated by Helen Heron. Edinburgh: T & T Clark, 1991.

Schneemelcher, Wilhelm, ed. *New Testament Apocrypha*, rev. ed. 2 vols. Translated by R. McL. Wilson. Louisville, KY: Westminster, 1992.

Schnelle, Udo. *Neutestamentliche Anthropologie: Jesus-Paulus-Johannes*. Neukirchen-Vluyn: Neukirchener, 1991.

Schoeps, Hans J. *Paul: The Theology of the Apostle in the Light of Jewish Religious History*. Translated by Harold Knight. Philadelphia: Westminster, 1961.

Schweitzer, Albert. *Geschichte der pauline Forschung von der Reformation bis auf die Gegenwart*. Tübingen: J. C. B. Mohr, 1911.

_____. *The Mysticism of Paul the Apostle*. Translated by William Montgomery. London: A. & C. Black, 1931.

_____. *Paul and His Interpreters: A Critical History*. Translated by W. Montgomery. London: Black, 1912.

Schweizer, Eduard. *The Church as the Body of Christ*. Richmond, VA: John Knox, 1964.

_____. *Jesus*. Translated by David E. Green. Richmond, VA: John Knox, 1971.

_____. *The Letter to the Colossians: A Commentary*. Minneapolis, MN: Augsburg, 1982.

_____. *The Lord's Supper according to the New Testament*. Translated by J. M. Davies. Philadelphia: Fortress, 1967.

Scott, C. A. A. *Christianity according to St. Paul*. Cambridge: Cambridge University Press, 1966.

Scott, Walter, ed. and trans. *Hermetica: The Ancient Greek and Latin Writings Which Contain Religious or Philosophic Teachings Ascribed to Hermes Trismegistus*. 3 vols. Oxford: Clarendon, 1924.

Scroggs, Robin. *The Last Adam: A Study in Pauline Anthropology*. Philadelphia: Fortress, 1966.

Sevenster, J. N. *Paul and Seneca*. Leiden: E. J. Brill, 1961.

Shedd, Russell Philip. *Man in Community: A Study of St. Paul's Application of Old Testament and Early Jewish Conceptions of Human Solidarity.* Grand Rapids: Eerdmans, 1964.

Smith, Z. *Map Is Not Territory: Studies in the History of Religions.* Leiden: E. J. Brill, 1978.

Soiron, T. *Die Kirche als Leib Christi.* Düsseldorf, 1951.

Solmsen, Friedrich. *Isis among the Greeks and Romans.* Cambridge, MA: Harvard University Press, 1979.

Spatafora, A. *From the "Temple of God" to God as the Temple.* Rome: Gregorian University, 1997.

Stacey, W. David. *The Pauline View of Man: In Relation to Its Judaic and Hellenistic Background.* London: MacMillan, 1956.

Stendahl, Krister. *The Bible and the Role of Women: A Case Study in Hermeneutics.* Translated by Emilie T. Sander. Philadelphia: Fortress, 1966.

Steward, James S. *A Man in Christ: The Vital Elements of St. Paul's Religion.* New York: Harper and Brothers, 1935.

Synge, F. C. *St. Paul's Epistle to the Ephesians: A Theological Commentary.* London: S. P. C. K., 1959.

Takács, Sarolta A. *Isis and Sarapis in the Roman World.* Leiden: E. J. Brill, 1995.

Tannehill, Robert C. *Dying and Rising with Christ: A Study in Pauline Theology.* Berlin: Alfred Töpelmann, 1966.

Taylor, Vicent. *The Person of Christ.* London: Macmillan, 1958.

Tennant, F. R. *The Sources of the Doctrine of the Fall and Original Sin.* N.p., 1903. Reprint, New York: Schoken Books, 1968.

Thornton, L. S. *The Common Life in the Body of Christ,* 4th ed. London: Dacre, 1963.

Thrall, Margaret E. *A Critical and Exegetical Commentary on the Second Epistle to the Corinthians.* International Critical Commentary. Edinburgh: T. & T. Clark, 1994.

Turner, David L. "Adam, Christ, and Us: The Pauline Teaching of Solidarity in Romans 5:12-21." Th.D. diss., Grace Theological Seminary, 1982.

Turner, Nigel. *A Grammar of New Testament Greek.* Vol. 3, *Syntax.* Edinburgh: T. & T. Clark, 1963.

Tyler, Ronald L. "The Pauline Doctrine of Jesus Christ as the Last Adam." Ph.D. diss., Baylor University, 1973.

Vermaseren, M. J. *Mithras: the Secret God.* Translated by Therese and Vincent Megaw. New York: Barnes & Noble, 1963.

Versteeg, J. P. *Is Adam a "Teaching Model" in the New Testament?: An Examination of One of the Central Points in the Views of H. M. Kuitert and Others*. Translated by Richard B. Gaffin. Nutley, NJ: Presbyterian and Reformed, 1977.

Vielhauer, Philipp. *Oikodome: Das Bild vom Bau in der christlichen Literatur vom Neuen Testament bis Clements Alexandrinus*. Karlsruhe-Durlach: Tron, 1940.

Vögtle, Anton. *'Der Menschensohn' und die paulinische Christologie*. Rome: Pontifical Bible Institute, 1963.

Vos, Geerhardus. *The Pauline Eschatology*. Grand Rapids: Eerdmans, 1952.

Warne, G. J. *Hebrew Perspectives on the Human Person in the Hellenistic Era: Philo and Paul*. Lewiston, NY: Edwin Mellen, 1995.

Wedderburn, A. J. M. "Adam and Christ: An Investigation into the Background of 1 Corinthians 15 and Romans 5:12-21." Ph.D. diss., University of Cambridge, 1970.

_____. *Baptism and Resurrection*. Tübingen: J. C. B. Mohr, 1987.

Weidinger, Karl. *Die Haustafeln: Ein Stück urchristlicher Paränese*. Leipzig: N.p., 1928.

Weiss, Johannes. *Der erste Korintherbrief*, rev. ed. Göttingen: Vandenhoeck & Ruprecht, 1977.

_____. *The History of Primitive Christianity*. 2 vols. Translated and Edited by Frederick C. Grant. New York: Wilson-Erickson, 1937.

Wendland, Heine Dietrich. *Briefe an die Korinther*. Das Neue Testament Deutch 7. Göttingen: Vandenhoeck & Ruprecht, 1980.

Wernberg-Møller, P. *The Manual of Discipline: Translated and Annotated with an Introduction*. Grand Rapids: Eerdmans, 1957.

Whiteley, D. E. H. *The Theology of St. Paul*, 2nd ed. Philadelphia: Fortress, 1964.

Wikenhauser, Alfred. *New Testament Introduction*. Translated by Joseph Cunningham. New York: Herder and Herder, 1958.

_____. *Die Kirche als der mystische Leib Christi nach dem Apostel Paulus*. Münster: Aschendorf, 1940.

_____. *Pauline Mysticism: Christ in the Mystical Teaching of St. Paul*. Translated by Joseph Cunningham. New York: Herder and Herder, 1960.

Williams, Norman Powell. *The Ideas of the Fall and of Original Sin: A Historical and Critical Study*. London: Longmans, 1927.

Willis, W. L. *Idol Meat in Corinth: The Pauline Argument in 1 Corinthians 8 and 10*. Chico, CA: Scholars, 1985.

Wright, G. E. *The Biblical Doctrine of Man in Society*. London: SCM, 1954.

Wright, N. T. *The Climax of the Covenant: Christ and the Law in Pauline Theology*. Minneapolis, MN: Fortress, 1992.

Yamauchi, E. M. *Pre-Christian Gnosticism*. Grand Rapids: Eerdmans, 1973.

Zahn, Theodor. *Introduction to the New Testament*. Translated by John Moore Trout and others. 3 vols. Edinburgh: T. & T. Clark, 1909.

Ziegler, Josef Georg, ed. *In Christ*. St. Ottilien: EOS, 1987.

Ziesler, J. A. *Pauline Christianity*, rev. ed. Oxford: Oxford University Press, 1990.

_____. *Paul's Letter to the Romans*. Philadelphia: Trinity, 1989.

Articles

Ahern, Barnabas Mary. "The Christian's Union with the Body of Christ in Cor, Ga, and Rom." *Catholic Biblical Quarterly* 23 (April 1961): 199-209.

Allan, John A. "The 'In Christ' Formula in Ephesians." *New Testament Studies* 5 (October 1958): 54-62.

_____. "The 'In Christ' Formula in the Pastoral Epistles." *New Testament Studies* 10 (October 1963): 115-21.

Allegro, J. M. "Fragments of a Qumran Scroll of Eschatological Midrâsim." *Journal of Biblical Literature* 77 (December 1958): 35-60.

Barrett, C. K. "Attitudes to the Temple in the Acts of the Apostles." In *Templum Amicitiae: Essays on the Second Temple Presented to Ernst Bammel*. Edited by William Horbury, 345-67. Sheffield: JSOT, 1991.

_____. "The Significance of the Adam-Christ Typology for the Resurrection of the Dead: 1 Co 15, 20-22. 45-49." In *Résurrection du Christ et des Chrétiens (1 Co 15)*, 99-126. Rome: Abbaye de S. Paul, 1985.

Barth, Markus. "Traditions in Ephesians." *New Testament Studies* 30 (January 1984): 3-25.

Batey, Richard A. "Jewish Gnosticism and the 'Hieros Gamos' of Eph. v. 21-33." *New Testament Studies* 10 (October 1963): 121-27.

_____. "The ΜΙΑ ΣΑΡΞ Union of Christ and the Church." *New Testament Studies* 13 (April 1967): 270-81.

Bedale, S. "The Meaning of κεφαλή in the Pauline Epistles." *Journal of Theological Studies* 5 (October 1954): 211-15.

BeDuhn, Jason David. "'Because of the Angels': Unveiling Paul's Anthropology in 1 Corinthians." *Journal of Biblical Literature* 118 (Summer 1999): 275-320.

Benoitt, Pierre. "Qumran and the New Testament." In *Paul and Qumran: Studies in New Testament Exegesis.* Edited by Jerome Murphy-O'Connor, 1-30. Chicago, IL: Priory, 1968.

Black, Matthew. "The Pauline Doctrine of the Second Adam." *Scottish Journal of Theology* 7 (June 1954): 170-79.

_____. "Servant of the Lord and Son of Man." *Scottish Journal of Theology* 6 (1953): 1-11.

Brandenburger, Egon. "Alter und neuer Mensch, erster und letzter Adam-Anthropos." In *Vom alten zum neuen Adam: Urzeitmythos und Heilsgeschichte.* Edited by W. Strolz, 182-223. Freiburg: Herder and Herder, 1986.

Breed, James L. "The Church as the 'Body of Christ': A Pauline Analogy." *Theological Review* 6 (November 1985): 9-32.

Brockington, L. H. "The Hebrew Conception of Personality in Relation to the Knowledge of God." *Journal of Theological Studies* 47 (January-April 1946): 1-11.

Bruce, F. F. "Paul on Immortality." *Scottish Journal of Theology* 24 (November 1971): 457-72.

Büchsel, Friedrich. "'In Christus' by Paulus." *Zeitschrift für die Neutestamentliche Wissenschaft und die Kunde der Ältern Kirche* 42 (1949): 141-58.

Bultmann, Rudolf. "Adam and Christ According to Romans 5." In *Current Issues in New Testament Interpretation: Essays in Honor of Otto A. Pipe.* Edited by Willaim Klassen and Gaydon F. Snyder, 143-65. New York: Harper & Row, 1962.

_____. "Gnosis." *Journal of Theological Studies* 3 (April 1952): 10-26.

Burkill, T. A. "Two into One: The Notion of Carnal Union in Mark 10:8; 1 Cor. 6:16; Eph. 5:31." *Zeitschrift für die Neutestamentlich Wissenschaft und die Kunde der Älteren Kirche* 62 (1971): 115-20.

Caird, G. B. "Paul and Women's Liberty." *Bulletin of the John Rylands Library* 54 (Spring 1972): 268-81.

Cassidy, R. "Paul's Attitude to Death in II Corinthians 5:1-10." *Evangelical Quarterly* 43 (April 1971): 210-17.

Cervin, Richard S. "Does κεφαλή Mean 'Source' or 'Authority" in Greek Literature? A Rebuttal." *Trinity Journal* 10 NS (1989): 85-112.

Charles, Gary W. "1 Corinthians 12:1-13." *Interpretation* 44 (January 1990): 65-68.

Colijn, Brenda B. "Paul's Use of the 'in Christ' Formula." *Ashland Theological Journal* 23 (1991): 9-26.

Colpe, Carsten. "New Testament and Gnostic Christology." In *Religions in Antiquity, Essays in Memory of E. R. Goodenough*. Edited by Jacob Neusner, 227-43. Leiden: E. J. Brill, 1968.

Craig, William Lane. "The Bodily Resurrection of Jesus." In *Gospel Perspectives*. Vol. 1. Edited by R. T. France and D. Wenham, 47-74. Sheffield: JSOT, 1980.

Cranfield, C. E. B. "On Some of the Problems in the Interpretation of Romans 5:12." *Scottish Journal of Theology* 22 (September 1969): 324-41.

Creed, J. M. "The Heavenly Man." *Journal of Theological Studies* 26 (January 1925): 113-36.

Crockett, W. V. "Ultimate Restoration of All Mankind: 1 Corinthians 15:22." In *Studia Biblica 1978 III. Papers on Paul and Other New Testament Authors*. Edited by E. A. Livingston, 83-87. Sheffield: JSOT, 1980.

Cullmann, Oscar. "The Meaning of the Lord's Supper in Primitive Christianity." In *Essays on the Lord's Supper*. Edited by F. J. Leenhardt. Translated by J. G. Davies, 5-23. Richmond, VA: John Knox, 1958.

Dahl, N. A. "Christ, Creation and the Church." In *The Background of the New Testament and Its Eschatology*. Edited by W. D. Davies and D. Daube, 422-43. Cambridge: Cambridge University Press, 1964.

Daines, Brian. "Paul's Use of the Analogy of Body of Christ--with Special Reference to 1 Corinthians 12." *Evangelical Quarterly* 50 (April-June 1978): 71-78.

Danker, F. W. "Romans V.12. Sin under Law." *New Testament Studies* 14 (April 1968): 124-39.

Daube, D. "Pauline Contributions to a Pluralistic Culture: Re-Creation and Beyond." In *Jesus and Man's Hope*, 232-41. Pittsburgh, PA: Pittsburgh Theological Seminary, 1971.

De Fraine, Jean. "Adam and Christ as Corporate Personalities." *Theology Digest* 10 (Spring 1962): 99-102.

Dietrich, Ernst Ludwig. "Der Urmensch als Androgyne." *Zeitschrift für Kirchengeschichte* 58 (1939): 297-345.

Dillistone, F. W. "How is the Church Christ's Body?" *Theology Today* 2 (April 1945): 56-58.

Dodd, C. H. "Matthew and Paul." *Expository Times* 58 (1947): 293-98.

Eichrodt, W. "Is Typological Exegesis an Appropriate Method?" In *Essays in Old Testament Hermeneutics*. Edited by C. Westermann, 224-45. Richmond, VA: John Knox, 1963.

Ellis, E. Earle. "The Authorship of the Pastorals." In *Paul and His Interpreters*, 49-57. Grand Rapids: Eerdmans, 1979.

_____. "Biblical Interpretation in the New Testament Church." In *Mikra: Text, Translation, Reading and Interpretation of the Hebrew Bible in Ancient Judaism and Early Christianity*. Edited by Martin Jan Mulder, 703-37. Philadelphia: Fortress, 1988.

_____. "Deity Christology in Mark 14:58." In *Jesus of Nazareth: Lord and Christ*. Edited by Joel B. Green and Max Turner, 195-202. Grand Rapids: Eerdmans, 1994.

_____. "Jesus' Use of the Old Testament and the Genesis of of New Testament Theology." *Bulletin for Biblical Research* 3 (1993): 59-75.

_____. "New Directions in the History of Early Christianity." In *Ancient History in a Modern University*. Vol. 2. Edited by T. W. Hillard and others, 71-92. Grand Rapids: Eerdmans, 1998.

_____. "New Testament Teaching on Hell." In *The Reader Must Understand: Eschatology in Bible and Theology*. Edited by K. E. Brower and M. W. Elliot, 199-219. Leicester, UK: Apollos, 1997.

_____. "Pastoral Letters." In *Paul and His Letters*. Edited by G. F. Hawthorne and Ralph P. Martin, 658-66. Downers Grove, IL: InterVarsity, 1993.

_____. "Sōma in First Corinthians." *Interpretation* 44 (April 1990): 132-44.

_____. "The Structure of Pauline Eschatology (II Corinthians v. 1-10)." In *Paul and His Recent Interpreters*, 35-48. Grand Rapids: Eerdmans, 1979.

_____. "Toward a History of Early Christianit." In *Christ and Future in the New Testament Histroy*, 212-241. Leiden: E. J. Brill, 2000.

_____. "Traditions in 1 Corinthians." *New Testament Studies* 32 (October 1986): 481-502.

_____. "Traditions in the Pastoral Epistles." In *Early Jewish and Christian Exegesis: Studies in Memory of William Hugh Brownlee*. Edited by Craig A. Evans and William F. Stinespring, 237-53. Atlanta, GA: Scholars, 1987.

Emerton, J. A. "The Origin of the Son of Man Imagery." *Journal of Theological Studies* 9 (October 1958): 225-42.

Fatum, Lone. "Image of God and Glory of Man." In *Image of God and Gender Models*. Edited by K. Børresen. Oslo: Solum Forlay, 1991.

Fee, Gordon D. "II Corinthians VI.14-VII.1 and Food Offered to Idols." *New Testament Studies* 23 (January 1977): 140-61.

Fennema, D. "Unity in Marriage: Ephesians 5,21-33." *Reformed Review* 25 (Autumn 1971): 62-71.

Feuillet, A. "La demeure céleste et la destinée des chréstiens (II Cor. v.1-10)." *Recherches de Science Religieuse* 44 (1956): 161-92, 360-402.

Field, Barbara. "The Discourse behind the Metaphor 'the Church is the Body of Christ' as Used by Paul and the 'Post-Paulines.'" *The Asia Journal of Theology* 6 (April 1992): 88-107.

Fischer, Karl Martin. "Adam und Christus." In *Altes Testament-Frühjudentum-Gnosis: Neue Studien zu 'Gnosis und Bibel'*. Edited by Karl-Wolfgang Tröger, 283-98. Gütersloh: Mohn, 1980.

Fitzmyer, Josephy A. "Qumrân and the Interpolated Paragraph in 2 Cor. 6.14-7.1." *Catholic Biblical Quarterly* 23 (July 1961): 279-80.

Glasson, T. Francis. "2 Corinthians 5.1-10 versus Platonism (Paul's Opponents) in Corinth." *Scottish Journal of Theology* 43 (1990): 45-55.

Gnilka, Joachim. "2 Cor. 6:14-7:1 in the Light of the Qumran Texts and the Testaments of the Twelve Patriarchs." In *Paul and Qumran: Studies in New Testament Exegesis*. Edited by Jerome-Murphy-O'Connor, 48-68. Chicago, IL: Priory, 1968.

Goppelt, L. "Jesus und die 'Haustafel'-Tradition." In *Orientierung an Jesus für Theologie der Synoptiker*. Edited by P. Hoffmann, 93-106. Freiburg: Herder and Herder, 1973.

Grayston, K., and G. Herdan. "The Authorship of the Pastorals in the Light of Statistical Linguistics." *New Testament Studies* 6 (October 1959): 1-15.

Griffiths, J. G. "A Note on the Anarthous Predicate in Hellenistic Greek." *Expository Times* 62 (July 1951): 314-16.

Grudem, Wayne. "Does κεφαλή ('Head') Mean 'Source' or 'Authority Over' in Greek Literature? A Survey of 2,336 Examples." *Trinity Journal* 6 NS (Spring 1985): 38-59.

_____. "The Meaning of κεφαλή ('Head'): A Response to Recent Studies." *Trinity Journal* 11 NS (Spring, 1990): 3-72.

Guénel, Victor. "Tableau des emplois de Sèma dans la Ire Lettre aux Corinthiens." In *Le Corps et le Corps du Christ dans la Première Épître aux Corinthiens*. Edited by Victor Guénel. Paris: Les Éditions du Cerf, 1983.

Hanhart, Karel. "Paul's Hope in the Face of Death." *Journal of Biblical Literature* 88 (December 1969): 445-49.

Harris, Murray J. "2 Corinthians 5:1-10: Watershed in Paul's Eschatology?" *Tyndale Bulletin* 22 (1971): 32-57.

_____. "Paul's View of Death in 2 Corinthians 5:1-10." In *New Dimensions in New Testament Study*. Edited by R. N. Longenecker and Merrill C. Tenney, 317-28. Grand Rapids: Zondervan, 1974.

Harrison, P. N. "The Authorship of the Pastoral Epistles." *Expository Times* 67 (December 1955): 77-81.

Hettlinger, R. F. "2 Corinthians 5:1-10." *Scottish Journal of Theology* 10 (June 1957): 174-94.

Hicks, R. I. "The Body Political and the Body Ecclesiastical." *Journal of Bible and Religion* 31 (January 1963): 29-35.

Hill, C. E. "Paul's Understanding of Christ's Kingdom in I Corinthians 15:20-28." *Novum Testamentum* 30 (October 1988): 297-320.

Hooker, Morna D. "Adam in Romans I." In *From Adam to Christ: Essays on Paul*, 73-85. Cambridge: Cambridge University Press, 1990.

_____. "Authority on Her Head: An Examination of I Cor. XI.10." *New Testament Studies* 10 (April 1964): 410-16.

_____. "A Further Note on Romans I." In *From Adam to Christ: Essays on Paul*, 86-87. Cambridge: Cambridge University Press, 1990.

_____. "Philippians 2.6-11." In *From Adam to Christ: Essays on Paul*, 96-110. Cambridge: Cambridge University Press, 1990.

Howard, G. "The Head/Body Metaphors of Ephesians." *New Testament Studies* 20 (April 1974): 350-56.

_____. "Phil. 2:6-11 and the Human Christ." *Catholic Biblical Quarterly* 40 (July 1978): 368-87.

Jeremias, J. "Flesh and Blood Cannot Inherit the Kingdom of God." *New Testament Studies* 2 (Febuary 1956): 151-59.

_____. "κεφαλὴ γωνίας-ἀκρογωνιαῖος," *Zeitschrift für die neutestamentliche Wissenschaft* 29 (1930): 264-80.

Käsemann, Ernst. "A Critical Analysis of Philippians 2:5-11." *Journal for Theology and Church* 5 (1968): 45-88.

_____. "Eine urchristliche Taufliturgie." In *Festschrift Rudolf Bultmann*, 133-48. Stutgart and Cologne: n.p., 1949.

_____. "Pauline Doctrine of the Lord's Supper." In *Essays on New Testament Themes*. Translated by W. J. Montague, 113-19. Philadelphia: Fortress, 1982.

_____. "The Theological Problem Presented by the Motif of the Body of Christ." In *Perspectives on Paul*. Translated by Margaret Kohl, 102-21. Philadelphia: Fortress, 1971.

Kearns, Conleth. "The Church the Body of Christ according to St. Paul." *Irish Ecclesiastical Record* 90 (July 1958): 1-11; (September 1958): 145-57; 91 (January 1959): 1-15; (May 1959): 313-27.

Kertelge, Karl. "The Sin of Adam in the Light of Christ's Redemptive Act according to Romans 5:12-21." *Communio (US)* 18 (Winter 1991): 502-13.

Kirby, John T. "The Syntax of Romans 5:12: A Rhetorical Approach." *New Testament Studies* 33 (April 1987): 283-86.

Knox, W. L. "Parallels to the N. T. Use of σῶμα." *Journal of Theological Studies* 39 (July 1983): 243-46.

Kostenberger, Andreas. "The Mystery of Christ and the Church: Head and Body, 'One Flesh' (Eph 5:22-33)." *Trinity Journal* 12 (Spring 1991): 79-94.

Kreitzer, Larry. "Christ and Second Adam in Paul." *Communio Viatorum* 32 (Spring-Summer 1989): 55-101.

Kuhn, K. G. "Les rouleaux de cuivre de Qumrên." *Revue biblique* 61 (1954): 193-202.

Laeuchli, S. "Monism and Dualism in the Pauline Anthropology." *Biblical Research* 3 (1958): 15-27.

Leaney, A. R. G. "The Doctrine of Man in 1 Corinthians." *Scottish Journal of Theology* 15 (December 1962): 394-99.

Lindars, B. "Re-Enter the Apocalyptic Son of Man." *New Testament Studies* 22 (October 1976): 52-72.

Longenecker, Richard. "The Nature of Paul's Early Eschatology." *New Testament Studies* 31 (January 1985): 85-95.

Lowe, John. "An Examination of Attempts to Detect Development in St. Paul's Theology." *Journal of Theological Studies* 42 (1941): 129-42.

Malina, B. J. "Some Observations on the Origin of Sin in Judaism and St. Paul." *Catholic Biblical Quarterly* 31 (1969): 18-34.

Manson, T. W. "Parallels to the N.T. Use of σῶμα." *Journal of Theological Studies* 39 (July 1938): 243-46.

Marchant, G. J. C. "The Body of Christ." *Evangelical Quarterly* 30 (January-March, 1958): 3-17.

Martin, William J. "I Corinthians 11:2-16: An Interpretation." In *Apostolic History and the Gospel: Biblical and Historical Essays Presented to F. F. Bruce on His 60th Birthday.* Edited by W. W. Gasque and R. P. Martin, 231-41. Grand Rapids: Eerdmans, 1970.

McKelvey, R. J. "Christ the Cornerstone." *New Testament Studies* 8 (July 1962): 352-59.

Meeks, Wayne A. "The Image of the Androgyne: Some Uses of a Symbol in Earliest Christianity." *History of Religions* 13 (February 1974): 165-208.

Mendenhalls, G. E. "The Relation of the Individual to Political Society in Ancient Israel." In *Biblical Studies in Memory of H. C. Alleman*. Edited by J. M. Meyers, O. Reimherr, and H. N. Bream, 89-108. Locust Valley, NY: Augustin, 1960.

Meyer, Ben. "Did Paul's View of the Resurrection of the Dead Undergo Development?" *Theological Studies* 47 (September 1986): 363-87.

Miller, J. I. "A Fresh Look at I Corinthians 6:16f." *New Testament Studies* 27 (October 1980): 125-27.

Milne, D. J. W. "Genesis 3 in the Letter to the Romans." *Reformed Theological Review* 39 (January-April 1980): 10-18.

Moule, C. F. D. "'Fullness' and 'Fill' in the New Testament." *Scottish Journal of Theology* (March 1951): 79-86.

_____. "Sanctuary and Sacrifice in the Church of the New Testament." *Journal of Theological Studies* NS 1 (April 1950): 29-41.

_____. "St Paul and Dualism: The Pauline Conception of Resurrection." *New Testament Studies* 12 (January 1966): 106-23.

Muddiman, John. "Adam, the Type of the One to Come (Rom 5:14)." *Theology* 87 (1984): 101-10.

Muirhead, I. A. "The Bride of Christ." *Scottish Journal of Theology* 5 (1952): 175-87.

Murphy-O'Connor, Jerome. "The Non-Pauline Character of 1 Corinthians 11:2-16?" *Journal of Biblical Literature* 95 (December 1976): 615-21.

Murray, Robert. "New Wine in Old Wineskins XII First Fruits." *Expository Times* 86 (March 1975): 164-68.

Nelson, W. R. "Pauline Anthropology: Its Relation to Christ and His Church." *Interpretation* 14 (January 1960): 14-27.

Neugebauer, F. "Das Paulinische 'In Christo'." *New Testament Studies* 4 (January 1958): 124-38.

Nock, A. D. "Early Gentile Christianity." In *Essays on the Trinity and the Incarnation*. Edited by A. E. J. Rawlinson, 124-26. London: Longmans, 1928.

_____. "Hellenistic Mysteries and Christian Sacraments." In *Essays on Religion and the Ancient World*. Vol. 2, 791-820. Oxford: Clarendon, 1972.

Oudersluys, Richard C. "Paul's Use of the Adam Typology." *Reformed Review* 13 (May 1960): 1-10.

Pagels, E. "Adam and Eve: Christ and the Church." In *The New Testament and Gnosis*. Edited by A. H. B. Logan and A. J. M. Wedderburn, 146-75. Edinburgh: T. & T. Clark, 1983.

Perriman, Andrew. "'His Body, which is the Church. . .': Coming to Terms with Metaphor." *Evangelical Quarterly* 62 (April 1990): 123-42.

Plank, K. A. "Resurrection Theology: The Corinthian Controversy Re-examined." *Perspectives in Religious Studies* 8 (Spring 1981): 41-54.

Porter, J. R. "The Pauline Concept of Original Sin in Light of Rabbinic Background." *Tyndale Bulletin* 41 (May 1990): 3-30.

_____. "The Legal Aspects of the Concept of 'Corporate Personality' in the Old Testament." *Vetus Testamentum* 15 (July 1965): 361-80.

Porter, Stanley E. "Two Myths: Corporate Personality and Language/Mentality Determinism." *Scottish Journal of Theology* 43 (1990): 289-307.

Quek, Swee-Hwa. "Adam and Christ according to Paul." In *Pauline Studies: Essays Presented to F. F. Bruce on His 70th Birthday*. Edited by D. A. Hagner and M. J. Harris, 67-79. Grand Rapids: Eerdmans, 1980.

Rawlinson, A. E. J. "Corpus Christi." In *Mysterium Christi*. Edited by G. K. A. Bell and Adolf Deissmann, 225-44. London: Longmans, 1930.

Rodd, Cyril S. "Introduction to *Corporate Personality in Ancient Israel*, rev. ed. by H. W. Robinson, 7-14. Edinburgh: T. & T. Clark, 1981.

Rogerson, J. W. "The Hebrew Conception of Corporate Personality: A Re-examination." *Journal of Theological Studies* 21 (April 1970): 1-16.

Rupprecht, Arthur A. "Interpreting the Pauline Epistles." In *The Literature and Meaning of Scripture*. Edited by Morris A. Inch and C. Hassell Bullock, 191-216. Grand Rapids: Baker, 1981.

Schrage, Walfgang. "Zur Ethik der neutestamentlichen Haustafeln." *New Testament Studies* 21 (October 1974): 1-22.

Schweizer, Eduard. "Dying and Rising with Christ." In *New Testament Issues*. Edited by Richard Batey, 173-90. New York: Harper & Row, 1970.

_____. "Traditional Ethical Patterns in the Pauline and Post-Pauline Letters and Their Development (lists of vices and house-tables)." In *Text and Interpretation: Studies in the New Testament Presented to Matthew Black*. Edited by Ernest Best and R. McL. Wilson, 195-209. Cambridge: Cambridge University Press, 1979.

Scroggs, Robin. "Paul and the Eschatological Woman." *Journal of the American Academy of Religion* 40 (September 1972): 283-303.

Sevenster, J. N. "Some Remarks on the Gumnos in II Cor. v. 3." In *Studia Paulina in honorem Johannis de Zwaan Septuagenaii*. Edited by J. N. Sevenster and W. C. van Unnik, 202-14. Bohn: Haarlem, 1953.

Snaith, N. H. Review of *The One and the Many* by A. R. Johnson. *Journal of Theological Studies* 44 (January-April 1943): 81-84.

Sweet, J. P. M. "A House Not Made with Hands." In *Templum Amicitiae: Essays on the Second Temple Presented to Ernst Bammel*. Edited by William Horbury, 368-90. Sheffield: JSOT, 1991.

Thrall, Margaret E. "The Origin of Pauline Christology." In *Apostolic History and the Gospel: Biblical and Historical Essays Presented to F. F. Bruce on His 60th Birthday*. Edited by W. Ward Gasque and Ralph P. Martin, 304-16. Grand Rapids: Eerdmans, 1970.

_____. "Putting On or Stripping Off in 2 Cor. 5:3." In *New Testament Textual Criticism*. Edited by Elden Jay Epp and Gordon D. Fee, 221-39. Oxford: Clarendon, 1981.

Walker, William O. "1 Corinthians 11:2-16 and Paul's Views regarding Women." *Journal of Biblical Literature* 94 (March 1975): 94-110.

Waltke, Bruce K. "1 Corinthians 11:2-16: An Interpretation." *Bibliotheca Sacra* 135 (January-March 1978): 46-57.

Wallis, Wilber B. "The Problem of an Intermediate Kingdom in 1 Corinthians 15:20-28." *Journal of the Evengelical Theological Society* 18 (Fall 1975): 229-42.

Watson, N. M. "2 Cor 5:1-10 in Recent Research." *Australian Biblical Review* 23 (October 1975): 33-36.

Wedderburn, A. J. M. "Adam in Paul's Letter to the Romans." In *Studia Biblica 1978 III. Papers on Paul and Other New Testament Authors*. Journal for the Study of the New Testament Supplement Series 3. Edited by E. A. Livingstone, 413-30. Sheffield: JSOT, 1980.

_____. "The Body of Christ and Related Concepts in 1 Corinthians." *Scottish Journal of Theology* 24 (February 1971): 74-96.

_____. "Some Observations on Paul's Use of the Phrases 'in Christ' and 'with Christ.'" *Journal for the Study of the New Testament* 25 (October 1985): 83-97.

Wenschkewitz, H. "Die Spiritualisierung der Kultusbegriffe Tempel, Priester und Opfer im Neuen Testament." *Angelos* 4 (1932): 77-230.

Whitaker, G. H. "The Building and the Body (Eph. ii.21f.; iv. 16; Col. ii.19)." *Theology* 13 (1926): 335-36.

_____. "The Chief Corner Stone." *Expositor* 22 (December 1921): 430-32.

Wilson, J. H. "The Corinthians Who Say There Is No Resurrection of the Dead." *Zeitschrift für die Neutestamentliche Wissenschaft und die Kunde der Älteren Kirche* 59 (1968): 90-107.

Witherington, Ben III. "Rite and Rights for Women--Galatians 3.28." *New Testament Studies* 27 (October 1981): 593-604.

Worgul, George S. "People of God, Body of Christ: Pauline Ecclesiological Contrasts." *Biblical Theology Bulletin* 12 (January 1982): 24-28.

Yates, R. "A Note on Colossians 1:24." *Evangelical Quarterly* 42 (April-June 1970): 88-92.

_____. "A Re-examination of Ephesians 1:23." *Expository Times* 83 (Feburary 1972): 146-51.

Zorn, R. O. "II Corinthians 5:1-10: Individual Eschatology or Corporate Solidarity, Which?" *Reformed Theological Review* 48 (September 1989): 93-104.

INDEX OF PASSAGES

I. Old Testament

II. New Testament

III. Apocrypha and Pseudepigraphy

IV. Qumran Literature

V. Josephus and Philo

VI. Rabbinic Literature

INDEX OF MODERN AUTHORS

Finito di stampare
nel mese di Dicembre 2001

presso la tipografia
"Giovanni Olivieri" di E. Montefoschi
00187 Roma - Via dell'Archetto, 10,11,12